The New SocialLearning

Connect. Collaborate. Work.   **2nd** EDITION

TONY BINGHAM AND MARCIA CONNER

FOREWORD BY DANIEL H. PINK

PRESS

Back Cover: "Social learning thrives in a culture of service and wonder. It is inspired by leaders, enabled by technology, and ignited by opportunities that have only recently unfolded."–from "Where Social Learning Thrives," Marcia Conner, *Fast Company*, February 11, 2010.

ATD Press is an internationally renowned source of insightful and practical information on talent development, workplace learning, and professional development.

ATD Press
1640 King Street
Alexandria, VA 22314 USA

Ordering information: Books published by ATD Press can be purchased by visiting ATD's website at www.td.org/books or by calling 800.628.2783 or 703.683.8100.

Library of Congress Control Number: 2015939475

ISBN-10: 1-56286-996-5
ISBN-13: 978-1-56286-996-0
e-ISBN: 978-1-60728-287-7

ATD Press Editorial Staff
Director: Kristine Luecker
Manager: Christian Green
Community of Practice Manager, Learning Technologies: Justin Brusino
Editor: Kathryn Stafford
Text Design: Maggie Hyde
Cover Design: Anthony Julien
Printed by Versa Press, East Peoria, IL, www.versapress.com
Photograph of Marcia Conner on page 321 by April Bennett Photography

Contents

Foreword

ONE AFTERNOON IN THE EARLY 1990s, I found myself at a meeting in my boss's office when a computer-support guy showed up to demonstrate a new-fangled technology called instant messaging. I'd never seen IM before, but I was intrigued—so I volunteered for the demo.

My boss sat down in front of his computer. I stationed myself at another computer just outside the office. And away we went—typing and tapping a silent conversation in real time.

"Wow," I shouted to the others back in the room. "Very cool." And when I returned to the meeting, I offered—unsolicited, of course—my thoughts on what we'd just witnessed.

"This could be big," I said. "Instant messaging is going to be incredibly useful for the hearing impaired, who can't just pick up the phone and talk to someone. It's not something most people will use much, but for that slice of the population it's amazing."

Today, more than two decades after instant messaging has become a part of everyday communication around the world—when literally tens of millions of people with perfectly good hearing are IM-ing right now—there's a moral to this tale: Sometimes we miss the point.

That's especially true of social technology. In business terms, most people—myself included—think of Twitter, Facebook, LinkedIn, and other social media as tools for marketing. But now that I've read this smart and incisive book and its update, I realize that I was as wrong about that as I was about IM technology back in the early 1990s.

As authors Tony Bingham and Marcia Conner show, social media have already had an enduring impact on learning.

There's a certain intuitive, forehead-slapping logic to that insight. Of course! In so many ways, learning is a fundamentally social act. From circle time in kindergarten, to study groups in college, to team projects in the workforce, sociability has always greased the gears of learning.

As this book shows, smart devices and software applications brought social technology into the workplace much faster than most people expected and made continual, far-reaching interactions part of everyday work. Employees now routinely use social tools to work and learn in tandem, to innovate, and to measure the impact of their work on customers.

The New Social Learning is a terrific guide to that emerging ecosystem. It will give you a set of core principles to help you navigate it. And with examples that range from firms such as LAZ Parking to Boston Children's Hospital, National Australian Bank to pharmaceutical giant Sanofi Pasteur, and CENTURY 21 to Cigna, it will show you how social media can improve the way you recruit talent, engage employees, and build workforce capability.

Social learning isn't a replacement for training and other forms of talent development. But it can accomplish what traditional approaches often cannot. For instance, it can supplement instruction with collaboration and co-creation and, in so doing, blur the boundary between the instructor and the instructed and enhance the experience of all. It can leave a "digital audit trail" that reveals the path of a learning journey and allows others to retrace it. It can re-energize your conferences and classes by providing a backchannel of feedback and questions.

It's exciting when two of the most respected names in this arena come together again to update *The New Social Learning*. When you read this book and the impressive examples of organizations all over the world that have embraced social tools for better and more meaningful collaboration, you'll understand how social learning has begun to transform the pursuit of knowledge and how it promises even greater things in the future.

But what you might realize most of all is that Twitter, Facebook, LinkedIn, and their newer social media kin that have come on to the scene in recent years aren't all about marketing. They're equally, if not more so, about how to get work done through better connection and collaboration with each other. This book helped me understand that and avoid missing the point of a new social tool once again. It can do the same for you.

Daniel H. Pink

Washington, D.C.

April 2015

Acknowledgments

WE WROTE THIS BOOK TO ENCOURAGE senior leaders to embrace the power of mobile social media to augment the timeless power of learning. While developing this content, we took our own counsel by using various social tools to connect with several hundred people teeming with stories of adventure and "aha" moments.

By describing their challenges and successes, the people introduced in this book demonstrate the tremendous impact social tools can have in companies, on communities, and for those who engage with them. We hope their examples inspire you as much as they have inspired us.

We deeply appreciate the extra time given by Traci Wolbrink, Jeffrey Burns, Geoff Fowler, Rob Cross, Dan Pontefract, Simon Terry, Andi Campbell, and Kevin Jones, who shared their organizations' progress.

Alvaro Caballero, Dany DeGrave, Sheila Babnis, Ayelet Baron, Ben Brooks, Jamie Pappas, Kevin Prentiss, Janhavi Kirtane, Natalie Burke, Graham Brown-Martin, Rachel Happe, Trisha Liu, Laurie Ledford, Wendy Lamin, Monty Flinsch, Will Deyamport, David Birnbaum, and Karen Kocher contributed their firsthand experiences so that we could share them with you.

Rick Ladd, who served as developmental editor, wrangled big ideas into carefully worded passages. Steve LeBlanc brought courage to challenging subjects. Paula Thornton surfaced the design assumptions below the message. Nicole Radziwill found the pattern under thorny data streams. Lucian Tarnowski unknowingly catalyzed the updating of this book. Joel Getzendanner and Salima Nathoo infused global sensibilities into local know-how.

Sandra Kogan, Heidi Forbes Öste, Nancy White, Rafiq Phillips, Terri Griffith, Sadat Shami, Susan Scrupski, Aaron Silvers, Gina Minks, Ed Brill, Master Burnett, Tim Collins, Chris Boyce, Megan Bowe, Tony Loyd, Rawn Shah, Karen Watson, Stewart Sarkozy-Banoczy, Heather Cole, Charlie Brown, Brent Schlenker, Harold Jarche, Jon Husband, Doug Newburg, and Trisha Martinez took the time to broaden our perspective.

Marie Kenerson, Nicole Lazzaro, Jane Bozarth, Jane Hart, Clark Quinn, Mark Bonchek, Meredith Singer, Valdis Krebs, Allison Anderson, Patricia Romeo, Eugene Kim, Luis Suarez, Jay Cross, Jerry Michalski, Megan Murray, Estee Solomon Gray, Mark Oehlert, Michael Idinopulos, Judee Humburg, Dion Hinchcliffe, Deb Schultz, Rich Persaud, Ginger Sall, Alec Couros, John Seely Brown, Don Burke, Kalimah Priforce, Wayne Hodgins, Kellee Sikes, John Stepper, Ellen Wagner, Mark Frazier, and the Change Agents Worldwide community illuminated our path. Dan Pink has generously supported our effort.

Marcia also wants to thank Karl, Clarke, and JoAnn Conner, who provided compassion, patience, and understanding in a way that proved diplomacy could exist amid last-minute meals, late-night conversations, and laptop-laden family time.

The team at ATD exemplified how people can come together for the greater good. Jennifer Homer managed the process with uncommon grace. Kathryn Stafford smoothed out our words, Justin Brusino looped in community voices, and Kristen Fyfe-Mills, Pat Galagan, Christian Green, and Kris Luecker provided terrific support on many aspects of the book.

Together these extraordinary educators made quick work of a daunting task, and we will be appreciative forever.

Introduction

SIX YEARS AGO, WHEN WE WROTE the first edition of this book, mobile and social technologies were still new. Many senior leaders didn't see their value to the enterprise. At best they were considered a broadcast marketing channel—at worst, annoying interruptions in the workplace. In corporate settings and schools alike, educators viewed these social tools as a distraction and a threat to how students learned.

Times have changed. Worldwide, people have more access to mobile phones than they do to running water. Across the globe, people rely on mobile and social technologies to connect and collaborate, share information. and often create change. You need only look at organizations like Kiva or change.org to see how people are using social media to make a difference. People unite around ideas and experiences without regard for geographic boundaries. They connect us with colleagues and friends across the planet. As we connect and build relationships, what captures our attention is more highly valued and relevant because it has been pre-screened by people we trust.

Popular opinion about the value of mobile and social technologies has shifted dramatically. Many of us would feel lost without the swift connections these tools afford. Thousands of organizations and the millions of people within them have made this shift, strengthening and widening a global culture of learning. People ask important questions, observe subtle patterns, and connect previously disconnected groups. We, collectively, are stronger for it.

New Approaches for a Complex World

After the first edition of this book was published, people told us that we brought light to a largely missed opportunity—to learn more, to teach more, and to be more with the aid of new tools. Hundreds of organizational leaders we've met with have discovered that technology that was once considered a distraction is in reality a vital means to engage people in very human ways. Social learning moves organizational practices from rote and mechanical to agile and interpersonal. Social learning becomes learning for a connected social age.

Now it's time to take the next step. It's time we as leaders, educators, entrepreneurs, and intrepeneurs become catalysts—elevating social learning as a key means of achieving more impact. We must shift our perspectives from considering learning across social media as a supplement to our organizations' existing learning initiatives, to one where social learning plays an integral part of how people work together effectively, building upon their individual and collective potential.

It's time to adopt a healthy, inclusive, and resilient perspective of learning where a collective of leaders, workers, customers, and interested onlookers— the people who make up every organization's ecology—generates great ideas and introduces innovative practices. This doesn't take away from the achievements of individuals or small groups of peers. It doesn't take away from the value of face-to-face interactions or formal professional development. It acknowledges that good work isn't created in a vacuum, and that creativity is always in some sense collaborative, the result of unique minds connecting together.

The value we contribute comes not from how smart or talented we are, but rather from the ideas that we share, the quality connections that we make, the emotions we touch, and the conversations we start. Each of us can become an expert curator of interesting stories and facilitator of important ideas.

Beyond Organizational Boundaries

Learning is a never-ending process. It always has been and always will be. The Internet and new social tools provide nearly unlimited access to knowledge and people around the clock, across the world.

To truly create a better world each one of us needs to bring our skills, our talents, and our questions to the conversation. Harvard University professor Howard Stevenson once defined entrepreneurship as "the pursuit of opportunity without regard to resources currently controlled." In the social age, learning is no longer resource constrained. We can be—we must be—learning from everything and everyone possible in order to see the world in new ways and face challenges never before seen.

The best way to get started on the path to social learning is to think about what we want to learn, make a commitment to learning it in front of others, and to share what we learn. This becomes a generative cycle that will keep us informed and curious for the rest of our lives.

It's up to every one of us to model for others how learning can be—how learning should be—and how learning will be far into the future. In the end, the opportunity isn't even about learning, rather it's about what we experience from working with each other, helping one another, and becoming more effective together.

Our hope is that to face today's increasingly complex challenges, society embraces an approach to learning that elevates diverse voices, pursues wide perspectives, encourages collaboration, and values real-time experience. When we grow and improve what we know, organically we create a collective wisdom that can lead to real progress.

Tony Bingham   Marcia Conner
@tonybingham   @marciamarcia
Alexandria, VA   Staunton, VA

Reach Out
and Connect

"A new perspective is changing how we think about society, politics, interpersonal relationships, science, government, and business. New approaches are emerging. Learning and self-expression are exploding. Values are changing. Leadership is changing. The economy is changing. Change itself is changing—it is accelerating and becoming the norm."
—Deb Lavoy, Social business leader and former director at OpenText

PEDIATRICIAN TRACI WOLBRINK, MD, MPH, was in Malawi working with a patient when she realized the approaches she uses at Boston Children's Hospital weren't available, and the practices at the remote hospital she was in weren't working. Having recently been in Cambodia, where she saw a local doctor use a noninvasive ventilation strategy (bubble CPAP) for a child with breathing difficulties, she wanted to try that same approach. She searched the hospital for component pieces that had been discarded from other equipment and created her own bubble CPAP that saved the little girl's life.

When Wolbrink returned to Boston, where she works in critical care, she talked with colleagues about the experience and shared this simple and effective approach with them. She wondered, what if it wasn't necessary to travel the globe to connect knowledge. What if there was another way? She recalled an African proverb that had always resonated with her: *If you want to go quickly, go alone. If you want to go far, go together.*

Wolbrink and Dr. Jeffrey Burns, chief of Critical Care Medicine at Boston Children's Hospital, were working on an initiative to do just that: bring innovative practices out of local toolboxes and into the hands of people searching for solutions. They had begun the project when Burns received a phone call from a pediatrician over 2,300 miles away in Guatemala. His colleague needed advice while caring for a girl with a serious infection.

Burns knew well the cutting edge tools in medicine. When he watched how his son was able to easily connect, build skills, and play seamlessly with others through his Xbox, he wondered why that same level of progress didn't exist in collaboration or learning for medicine. There were too many technical challenges with sharing and exchanging knowledge across the miles.

Wolbrink and Burns created what became OPENPediatrics, a global social learning platform focused on saving lives. Every year close to 7 million children die after being stricken with diseases that are mostly treatable. The challenge is not that more research is needed for new treatments, or even access to drugs and hardware. Instead, it's getting the information needed to treat those diseases in the right hands before it's too late. It was time for sharing medical knowledge at scale.

While watching the Masters Golf Tournament one April, Burns was impressed by the power of digital instruction he'd witnessed on the event's website—where players were coached through weaknesses to find a stronger, more consistent swing, or to deal with specific issues, such as putting or chipping. He aimed to find similar technology for clinicians to receive coaching to improve their practice. Not just video or games, though.

Why not use the power of the Internet to distribute information across the globe with collaborative and social tools? Then clinicians anywhere could be coached through their medical paces, learning from anyone with expertise. Why not use modern capabilities to take a giant leap forward by helping people help their fellow human beings?

OPENPediatrics, founded in 2008, is a free social learning platform for doctors, nurses, and other specialists focused on pediatrics. Over 4,000 clinicians used this private space during its first year, says Steve Carson, director of operations, who joined the team after directing communications for MIT's OpenCourseWare initiative. These clinicians come together around the clock to learn, share, and ultimately improve the lives of children across the globe.

At the core of the system is a library of videos, animations, illustrations, and articles produced by the OPENPediatrics team and medical personnel on the ground who have found a better way to do things than the ways they were taught in medical school.[1]

In the online community, clinicians can structure what they need to learn and share what they're learning each day, unencumbered by space, time, or political boundaries. Over the years, content has grown into a catalyst for conversation. As you watch a video, you can comment or even ask questions of others viewing it. A team of experts is assigned to each video and when questions are posed, they can both answer and create ancillary content to share or to use for updating materials.

> *Sharing something has more value than anything unshared.*
> —Chris Crummey

This is where it gets really exciting. As clinicians become comfortable with the approach, they begin to post their own checklists, protocols, diagrams, and write-ups that can also be shared across the globe. In addition to starting and joining groups around topics of interest, they can receive notification when new content or conversations are forming around topics that matter to them. Through the interaction that follows these connections, they learn from others who are also interested in those topics.

Wolbrink points out that all of the benefits couldn't be known at the outset. For instance, she didn't expect OPENPediatrics would be widely used in Israel, Libya, Iran, and other parts of the Middle East, places where, as it turns out, despite vast cultural disagreements and long-standing animosities, childhood health takes precedence. "The platform has really been able to break down barriers that we never even thought could be broken," adds Burns. "The problem in the medical field is not ready access to information," he adds. "It's how do we manage our knowledge in an era of data overload?"

Clay Shirky, who teaches new media at New York University and is the author of *Cognitive Surplus*,[2] has written about this very disconnect. "It's not information overload. It's filter failure," he says.

Rather than use cumbersome traditional routes to publish, OPENPediatrics makes it possible for doctors to rapidly share information every time there is a new type of medical emergency afflicting a child. Solving this problem across the miles has long been difficult because it hasn't been possible to "load the boat," a phrase used at teaching hospitals to remind medical students they weren't alone. If you had a problem, if you needed help, if you needed to learn something new, there were always people in your immediate area you could call on at any time. OPENPediatrics now makes it possible to load the boat across vast distances.

With OPENPediatrics, Burns says, "our goal was to create a community of practice where, instead of learning together being broad and thin like a MOOC, we would be narrow and much more deep."

OPENPediatrics provides structure to a vast network that has existed for centuries: the medical community of clinicians caring specifically for children. Although online social networks and online communities feel new, they codify and extend a practice used by people through the ages.

Go far, go together. Instantly recall what you know and immediately put it to work. Learn as you do. Engage instead of escape. Thrive instead of survive.

This is social learning at its best. Colleagues turned into collaborators. A modern and brilliant way to work.

The Workplace Has Changed

At this moment, your people are already learning through social media. They're reaching out and connecting in powerful ways. The question is, can you recognize, appreciate, and take advantage of the power inherent in this new level of communication? Do you want to facilitate or debilitate? Do

Between one-third and two-thirds of your employees are meeting their needs by working around you.
—Bill Jensen

you want to play a part in what and how people learn? Or do you want to try to stop them? Will you restrict them? Or will you free them to do the work they were hired to do—and will you do it *with* them?

The 20th century was about leading with technology and tools. The 21st century is about leading into a connected world.

Facebook, LinkedIn, Quora, and their inside-the-enterprise counterparts have enabled an unprecedented number of truly amazing conversations, many of which have led to greater awareness, new businesses, and social change.

We are seeing a new kind of hero who wants to solve some of the world's biggest problems. The new model for capitalism in the world of startups is, "Be helpful. Do something great. Serve."

Gamification is at work in the modern day. The Longitude Prize,[3] the X-Prize Foundation, and the TED Prize offer huge cash infusions to anyone who can solve some of the world's greatest challenges. Our altruism is no longer reserved for after work. It is moving into its proper place, center stage, in boardrooms around the world.

There is an unprecedented desire in people, particularly in younger generations, to make a difference, to make one's life worth something. There is a need to do work that matters.

That need is the tinder of a fire that is now being sparked by the emerging tools and holistic ideals of social learning. Working socially is no longer about just saying "hi." It's now about using modern tools to coalesce into self-organizing groups that are ready and waiting for the call to make things right.

Working socially is not just about rallying around an idea. Social learning is about getting on the same page in a constructivist approach, where every voice is heard and everyone contributes to the solution, where buy-in is endemic to its creation. It's about co-creating the world we want to see, a world we need to see.

Our challenge, at every level of the organization, is no longer just how to beat the competition. We now also have to look at issues of sustainability and restoration from a global perspective. We need to attend to planetary survival as well as the vitality of entire industries and financial markets. We need to accept that learning is produced by society, by us, and that we each play a role in that production.

Social learning resonates with all of us who realize that we can no longer act alone and hope to come up with grand solutions that will work seamlessly across all sectors, across all generations, and across all innovations.

Our world has simultaneously become too complex and too small to do that. We need to come together.

People want to learn fast, as they move through their multidimensional jobs, not just on the rare occasion they attend a class. Senior leaders need to provide their people with vibrant, effective, and cutting-edge tools to support their nonstop learning, which will ensure they can adapt to market forces at the speed of change. Social tools are changing the way people work, often bypassing formal training altogether.

Fundamentally, this book is about how people learn socially, often (but not always) with technology—and how they can do more, learn more, and be more as a result. This book is not a plea to reorganize or dismantle the training department. It's not a pitch to turn off your email, at least not unless or until your company is ready. No one will suggest you move all your work to mobile devices or change your organization's priorities.

Online social tools provide learners with connections across boundaries and over time.
—Baiyun Chen and Thomas Bryer

What this book will show is that learning's value can be recognized across departments and locations, with employees, partners, customers, and suppliers, when social media seamlessly connects people and ideas every day. When people work together, they learn together, in the flow of work.

We won't focus on the tools here. They change fast. We ask you to visit the accompanying website for this book at www.thenewsociallearning.com for details about technologies and where to learn more. There you can also contribute to the conversation and locate fresh information.

Use this book to discover how to extend and expand your interactions with colleagues, and how to use social tools to create something new, powerful, and vibrant—something that could change the organization, and the world.

Amazing things are happening with collaborations that only a few years ago would have been impossible. In this book we make suggestions for how you can become a part of them.

Social learning can facilitate a culture where we get better at getting better. Our work is no longer just about competing. It's now about being stronger contributors and savvier learners, with leaders co-creating the future.

We walk a fine line in this book between being concerned for the future and expressing our excitement about the radical changes in our midst. We provide countless action steps you can take. But it is never our intention to overwhelm. The great thing about the new social learning is that you can start small. There is no need for mass adoption, for total buy-in, or for group consensus.

Social learning is a fundamental shift in how people work—leveraging how we have always worked, now with new, more humanizing tools, accelerating individual and collective reach, giving us the resources to create the organization, and the world, we want to live in.

What Is the New Social Learning?

The new social learning is not just the technology of social media, although it makes use of it. It is not merely the ability to express ourselves in a group of opt-in friends. The new social learning combines social media tools with a shift in organizational culture, a shift that encourages ongoing knowledge transfer and connects people in ways that make learning enjoyable.

"Social learning thrives in a culture of service and wonder. It is inspired by leaders, enabled by technology, and ignited by opportunities that have only recently unfolded."[4] Social learning is the natural complement to social business, connecting people to people, information, and insights within an organization.

Social learning can be defined as joining with others to make sense of and create new ideas. It has been around for a long time and naturally occurs in groups at conferences and among old friends in a café as easily as it does among students online in a distance-learning program who have never met in person.

We experience social learning when we go down the hall to ask a question of a colleague and when we post that same question on Twitter anticipating someone will respond. It can be self-organizing or orchestrated by facilitators interested in encouraging others to learn.[5]

Social learning is augmented with social media tools that bridge distance and time, enabling people to easily interact across workplace, passion, curiosity, skill, or need. Most often social learning is intrinsically motivated and happens as naturally as breathing. It benefits from a diversity in types of intelligence and in the experiences of those learning.

Social learning is accelerated when we give our attention to individuals, groups, and projects that interest and energize us. We self-select the themes we want to follow and filter out those that feel burdensome, all with impunity. No one gets offended when we don't follow a project outside our domain. No one notices when we temporarily filter out the rants of people beating their own drum.

It's because we have independent thought and inevitably spend some time alone that we benefit from the creative abrasion of groups, and it's in pairs and teams in which we can harmonize our

A willingness to keep stretching and moving beyond our comfort zones determine success in this network era.
—Sahana Chattopadhyay

insights with others. Both sides of the African proverb are true and important. *If you want to go quickly, go alone. If you want to go far, go together.* The new social learning assists us with both.

Social media is a set of technologies used to engage two, three, or more people; social business is connecting people to people, information, and insights within an organization; and social learning is working with others to make sense of new ideas. What's new is how powerfully they work together. Social tools leave a digital audit trail, documenting our journey—often an unfolding story—and provide a path for others to learn from.

Tools are now available to facilitate social learning that is unconstrained by geographic differences (spatial boundaries) or time-zone differences (temporal boundaries) among team members.

The new social learning reframes social media from a mere marketing strategy to an approach that encourages and facilitates knowledge capture, transfer, and use, connecting people in a way consistent with how we naturally interact. It is not a delivery system analogous to classroom training, e-learning, or even mobile learning. Instead, it's a powerful approach to sharing and discovering a whole array of options—some of which we may not even

9

WHAT THE NEW SOCIAL LEARNING IS NOT

Another way to think about the new social learning is to compare it with what it is not.

- The new social learning is not just for knowledge workers. It can empower people who work on shop floors, backstage, on the phone, behind retail counters, and on the battlefield.

- It is not your corporate intranet, although features of social learning may be included there. Document management, calendaring, blogs, and online directories may contribute to learning socially, but they are often task oriented rather than community oriented.

- It's not at odds with formal education. Students often use Twitter as a back channel for communicating among themselves or with instructors. Teachers can also use social media before and after classes to capture and share everyone's ideas.

- It's not a replacement for training or employee development. Training is well suited for compliance, deep learning, and credentialing. Formal development programs are still needed to prepare employees to progress through the organization. Social learning can supplement training and development in the classroom or online. It complements training and covers knowledge that formal training is rarely able to provide, and fosters the creation of new knowledge and understanding.

- It's not synonymous with *informal learning*, a term often used to describe anything that's not learned in a formal program or class. The broad category of informal learning can include social learning, but some instances of informal learning are not social— for example, search and reading.

- It's not the same as *e-learning*, the term used to describe any use of technology to teach something intentionally. That broad category can include social tools and, if it's organized using an online learning community such as Moodle, can be quite communal.

WHAT THE NEW SOCIAL LEARNING IS NOT (CONTINUED)

- It's not the approach used with Massive Open Online Courses (MOOC), which aim at bringing pre-packaged content to unlimited numbers of people through open access on the web. While some offer ways for students to interact with one another using ancillary social tools, the programs themselves are largely broadcast.

- It's not a new interface for online search, which could only be considered social because other people developed the content you discover. Finding content with a search engine does not involve interpersonal engagement—a hallmark of social learning.

- It's not constantly social in the same way a party is. Often people are alone when they are engaged and learning through social tools. The socialness refers to the way interaction happens: intermingling ideas, information, and experiences, resulting in something more potent than any individual contribution.

---

know we need—leading to more informed decision making and an intimate, expansive, and dynamic understanding of the culture and context in which we work. "When working in the open, building distinction, and uncovering expertise, social learning makes knowledge relevant and actionable, building the kind of trust, transparency, and agility needed to deliver social business results," says Ed Brill, author of *Opting-In: Lessons in Social Business from a Fortune 500 Product Manager*.

In many ways, the new social learning is far bigger and more transformative than any lens we've previously used to look at learning in organizations. "It is a socio-political, historical shift that is bigger, broader, and much more fascinating," writes social business leader and former director at OpenText, Deb Lavoy. "A new perspective is changing how we think about society, politics, interpersonal relationships, science, government, and business. New approaches are emerging. Learning and self-expression are exploding. Values are changing. Leadership is changing. The economy is changing. Change itself is changing—it is accelerating and becoming the norm."[6]

The new social learning provides people at every level, in every nook of the organization, and every corner of the globe, a way to reclaim their natural capacity to learn nonstop. Social learning can help pilots fly more safely, salespeople be more genuinely persuasive, and doctors keep up to date on current techniques in their fields.

For a long time, many of us have known learning could transform the workplace. We longed for tools to catch up with that potential. Only recently have changes in corporate culture and technology allowed this eventuality to unfold.

Clay Shirky points out, "Prior to the Internet, the last technology that had any real effect on the way people sat down and talked together was the table."[7]

Social learning happens when we keep the conversation going by posting a photo on Instagram and tagging it in a way that elicits more comments from our friends, when we write about it on a blog, during coaching sessions with our mentees, or in a casual conversation with the person on the treadmill next to us at the gym.

Social software has been around for almost 50 years, dating back to the Plato bulletin board system. Network communities included CompuServe, AOL, and Usenet. The WELL (Whole Earth 'Lectronic Link), a dial-up discussion board, was launched when the founders of Facebook were toddlers.[8] Back then, however, it was only technology enthusiasts who used those systems, primarily because their interfaces were difficult to navigate, not terribly intuitive, and didn't readily surface or share the best ideas.

The new social learning moves services, assets, smarts, and guidance closer to people who are seeking answers, solving problems, overcoming uncertainty, and exploring ways to improve how they work. They facilitate collaboration and inform choices on a wide stage, fostering learning from a vast, intellectually diverse set of people.

10 THINGS SAID ABOUT SOCIAL LEARNING . . . THAT YOU SHOULDN'T FALL FOR

1. Social learning is new.

2. Social learning requires digital tools.

3. Social learning needs social learning policies.

4. There's no data to support social learning, and no way to show return on investment.

5. It's always informal (or never informal).

6. A vendor can sell you social learning.

7. Social learning only works for white-collar workers.

8. The talent development department needs to initiate a social learning program before the organization learns socially.

9. For social learning to provide value you need a new LMS. Or an upgrade. Or an LMS.

10. Social learning doesn't affect you.[9]

These new social tools don't replace training, knowledge management, and communications practices used today. They augment them. They introduce approaches that fundamentally change getting up to speed, provide a way to share mockups as easily as finely polished documents, and elicit the participation of departments that previously hadn't considered themselves responsible for employee development at all.

Most of what we learn at work and elsewhere comes from engaging in networks where people co-create, collaborate, and share knowledge, fully participating and actively engaging, driving, and guiding their learning through whatever topics will help them improve.

Training gives people solutions to problems already solved. Collaboration addresses challenges no one has overcome before.

The new social learning allows us, as Stowe Boyd (who first coined the term *social tools* and continues to observe their influence) puts it, "[to grow] bigger than my head. I want to create an idea space where I can think outside my mind, leveraging my connections with others."[10]

Moving Theory Into Practice

A "social learning theory" was first put forward in 1954, standing on the shoulders of John Dewey and drawing on the budding fields of sociology, behavior modification, and psychology applied to understanding and changing conduct.[11] Ideas from social learning theory informed the thinking of later learning theorists, including Albert Bandura, who wrote in 1977, "Learning would be exceedingly laborious, not to mention hazardous, if people had to rely solely on the effects of their own actions to inform them what to do. Fortunately, most human behavior is learned observationally through modeling."[12]

The early focus of social learning theory was learning socially appropriate behavior by imitating others, which is only a small aspect of how social learning is used in practice today. It's unfortunate what was called social learning had such a limited scope. Recognizing this, there will be times we shorten "the new social learning" to "social learning" here, and in our work elsewhere, to describe the broader issues and opportunities now available. Social learning is modeling, observing, sharing, participating, and so much more.

Social constructivism is the theory of knowledge that seems to best describe how people learn together, whether in person or online. When you engage with people, you build your own insight into what's being discussed. Someone else's understanding complements yours, and together you start to weave an informed interpretation. You tinker until you can move on.

Swiss psychologist Jean Piaget laid the groundwork for this approach by challenging the behaviorist notion, popular in the 1950s, implying that people were passive recipients of external stimuli that shaped how they behaved.[13] Instead, Piaget conducted many experiments to demonstrate that people are active participants in their learning. They interpret what's around them based on their unique current understanding of the world, and then they continually modify their understanding as they encounter new information. Piaget's discoveries eventually led to the concept and practice of discovery learning for children and the use of role-play and simulation for adults. Active participation is the key in both cases. [14]

Learning is a cognitive process that takes place in a social context.
—Albert Bandura

We are social creatures. If we play an active role in creating our views of reality, then the groups we participate in also contribute. Our reality is shaped by our social interactions. These exchanges provide context—scaffolding "constructed" of what we have already learned, with what other people have learned, and so on. This generates a virtuous spiral, socially generated and built, and more powerful than any one participant could create individually.

Throughout much of human history any sort of organized learning has been hierarchical. Teachers (and trainers, by extension) have arbitrated learning, and have wielded authority over the students they teach. We often accept this approach uncritically, and it follows us into work. Those who are recognized for holding knowledge are perceived as more powerful than other people who may also know a great deal, but who don't hold that over other people's heads.

But too much hierarchy undermines our ability to learn socially, and there are much better ways to organize things.

Jon Husband, who writes about and consults on social architecture for organizations, realized the power that connections had to subvert and break down hierarchies. In 1999 he coined the term *wirearchy* to contrast with hierarchy to describe how the use of the Internet, hyperlinks, and social technology was going to transform the way we work and learn. The "wire" in the name represents the multifaceted and multilevel connections in a true network, evocative of those in a high functioning electronic device, and based on the natural movement of information between network nodes. In these human-centered networks, sharing builds trust and credibility so the relationships themselves generate value.[15]

Peter Senge, with *The Fifth Discipline: The Art & Practice of The Learning Organization*, introduced a language of change that people within organizations could embrace. It offered a vision of workplaces that were humane and of companies that were built around learning.[16] What organizations learned in the years after working towards embracing that notion was that initiating and sustaining change is more daunting than they'd imagined, and making change happen requires leaders to change the way they think about organizations. Rather than turning to technological metaphors for inspiration, Senge looked to living systems.

"To understand why sustaining significant change is so elusive, we need to think less like managers and more like biologists,"[17] argues Senge.

Dee Hock transformed the credit card industry as the founding CEO of Visa by moving beyond metaphor and structuring the entire enterprise on principles of social learning, evolving systems, and democratic governance. "We are at that very point in time when a 400-year-old age is dying and another is struggling to be born—a shifting of culture, science, society, and institutions enormously greater than the world has ever experienced," said Hock. The ability of individual banks to chart their own courses was protected. Innovation was cherished. Decision making on joint activities was kept as local as possible, among those most affect-ed, so that only the matters affecting everyone were handled centrally. No one knew all that was going on and no one had to. Everyone knew their own parts of the system, what they connected to, and the agreements that held the larger whole together. The system could learn and adapt as fast as any of its parts, large or small, could figure out something better or more valuable to do.

Move from command and control to encourage and engage.
—Jane Hart

Hierarchy won't disappear completely in organizations. Instead, we are seeing an expansion of options and a shift in priorities. As Husband notes, "Business structures founded on command and control, automation, and process are giving way to structures that are less hierarchical and more dynamic, designed to engage people's hearts and minds to make a difference in the world." They can arrive none too soon.

We long for the day when organizing is based on principles, trust, and agreements, rather than on rules, coercion, and authority.

"The person-to-person trust that arises from feeling a connection with people is essential to rapid learning and value creation in a world flooded with communication options," says Joel Getzendanner, the initial director of impact investing at the F.B. Heron Foundation and long-time advisor to social-purpose enterprises. "Any organization that does not actively enhance community—both internally and externally—will be at a severe competitive disadvantage.

"No one is immune from the question of the day, 'How fast can we learn to . . .' with the operative words being 'fast,' 'learn' and most importantly 'we'," [18] adds Getzendanner. The new social learning leverages quick updates, broad networks, content, media, and mobile devices to introduce people to ideas in quick bursts, when and where it suits their workflow—no matter their position in the organization or the perceived power they have from the org chart. Its methods are designed to be compelling and fun, with virtually no learning curve. They support learning in a way that more closely mirrors how groups of people interact in person.

Social constructivism has become timely because for so long work has focused on what's known. To succeed today, we must understand new information and complex concepts—that which hasn't been known before and is often more complicated than one person can figure out alone.

The 21st-century mind is a collective mind where we access what we know in our friends' and colleagues' brains.

"To understand why sustaining significant change is so elusive, we need to think less like managers and more like biologists."

—Peter Senge

Rotterdam School of Management's Karen Stephenson points out, because "We cannot experience everything; other people's experiences, and hence other people, become the surrogate for knowledge. I store my knowledge in my friends."[19]

Together we are smarter. We can address ever more challenging and complex problems. What we store in our heads is not as important as the totality of what we can access through our networks and the breadth of the world we connect into. Together we can go further.

Four Changes That Shift Work

The convergence of four key trends has accelerated change in the workplace and now presents the opportunity for social learning. Although some of these trends have been observable for decades, their influence has grown with time.

1. Accelerated pace of change requires agility.

2. Technology goes where we go without boundaries.

3. Shifting workplace demographics change expectations.

4. People desire personal connection.

These four shifts remind us that the boundary of an organization is no longer meaningful when it comes to what learning is important (to that organization) or where information and experience are available. You don't know what you need until you need it; and it's as likely to come from external sources as those inside. Learning networks need to be both within and across organizations.

The content that needs knowing is potentially universal. Just understanding your industry, country, or company is not enough. Both competitors and partners can arise from anywhere. Business networks must be global and multi-sector, so learning networks must be global and multi-sector.

Learning needs to be continuous and adaptive because the world provides a continuous stream of new challenges. The only learning approach fast and adaptive enough for the new environment is interpersonal, and it uses the tools that in many ways gave rise to the required pace and range of learning we are now faced with.

Learning is a social experience for adventurers.
—Diethild

Accelerated Pace of Change Requires Agility

We take for granted that change is a constant of modern life, and it's getting faster all the time. Then two weeks go by and we realize we missed a whole big thing. Just because we know change is happening, doesn't make it any easier to cope with. Keeping up is hard.

Long gone are the days when you bought the same brands and stuck with them, when you knew what to expect from business, from government, from the economy, from your life. Everything is moving faster, in large part because of the Internet. Companies like Eastman Kodak, which were once titans of industry, have fallen because they couldn't change fast enough.

New companies are popping up all over, at a lower cost of entry than ever before, empowered by global reach. Existing companies are expanding into new markets. Your customers have more choices and more incentives than ever to shift. Outsourcing those nagging parts of your business, like accounting, fulfillment, public relations, and even parts of human resources, has become commonplace, reducing the time it takes to bring new product and ideas to market. Crowdfunding sites have even transformed the way people generate quick cash to work on what's new.

"We cannot experience everything; other people's experiences, and hence other people, become the surrogate for knowledge. I store my knowledge in my friends."

—Karen Stephenson

It's not just the availability of new technologies, but rather a whole new mindset. It's called *lean*, and it has a partner called *agile*.

Lean and agile are the latest concepts in being nimble. They started with "lean manufacturing" and then "lean programs," "lean startups," and "lean learning."

The idea is to look at how people operate and interact together as a system. From this perspective, the people we create for become part of how we design and iterate. Working in tandem, people never work too long on what they're creating before getting feedback—and changing direction if they've missed the mark.[20]

Salima Nathoo, who coined the term *lean learning* in 2010, says, "A lean approach allows us to perfect the art of being human in the age of everything."

When we see learning as the energy that passes between us, it's clear our approaches to learning must be fast, nimble, and relevant. "Learning today," Nathoo says, "ignites at the confluence of limited time and excess consumption. In a world that seeks to predictively analyze what's good for our wellbeing, lean learning places the power and luxury of choice back into our hands."[21]

AGILE VALUES AND PRINCIPLES

Agile is a set of values and principles that often work with lean approaches.

AGILE MANIFESTO VALUES

- Individuals and interactions over processes and tools
- Working systems over comprehensive documentation
- Customer collaboration over contract negotiation
- Responding to change over following a plan.

AGILE PRINCIPLES

- Highest priority—customer satisfaction
- Welcome change
- Frequent software delivery
- Business people and developers cooperating daily
- Building projects around motivated people
- Face-to-face conversation
- Progress measured by working systems
- Sustainable development pace
- Continuous attention to technical excellence
- Simplicity
- Self-organizing teams
- Regular reflection and adaptation.

Rather than months or years in isolation to develop something new, with agile approaches, the developer creates a mock-up in days or weeks to show to the client. That "minimal viable product" (MVP) is the barest functional version of the final product, and may have only one feature. Every step along the way, the client is helping to craft the right product. Almost immediately, each new feature is seen as it gets rolled out. Because each part of the new product is tested and retested before going into production, the new systems and ways of working don't break the larger system.

The concepts of lean and agile are now being used to design and deploy internal culture changes, courses, and even consulting engagements.

People value iteration, the ability to create something quickly, from scratch, and learn about the demand for it before investing much time. You can see if there's interest in buying before you invest too much time.

"A lean approach allows us to perfect the art
of being human in the age of everything."

—Salima Nathoo

If other companies are bringing new products and services to market faster than you can do your initial research, you will be left behind. If younger employees ask technical questions of their network on social media, getting answers faster than you can look them up, you will be left behind. And if other organizations learn how to do "lean learning" and yours does not, then yours will be left behind. It's happening. The world is getting more agile. Will you be?

Technology Goes Where We Go, Without Boundaries

In the past, the best technology was found at work. That's no longer the case. Now it's in our pockets and purses. It's with some of us 24 hours a day. The line between personal time and work, for many of us, begins to blur, requiring new boundaries, limits, and discussions of what makes for reasonable expectations.

In the past, it was rare to be published, for instance. These days, it's the norm. Your words or pictures can show up on a website only minutes after the impulse strikes. This is the age of "living out loud."

We live in a time when it seems everyone has something to say and where feedback is almost compulsive, at least among young generations. Whether your product sucks or rocks, the review

Social media is a tool; social learning is an action.
—Dan Pontefract

gets posted. If you inhibit people's natural impulse to share what they notice about your company, you come across as disinterested, dismissive, and out of touch. And it doesn't matter if they work for you. You become irrelevant, as more and more companies roll out social media programs to capture and embrace such involvement.

Another workplace shift is that everyone's growing technologically savvy. Easy-to-use portable devices and rich media on the Internet, on TV, and in stores have changed our expectations about communication inside our companies, too. We bring our knowledge and assumptions from the marketplace to work. As a result, we are no longer willing to put up with hard-to-manage interfaces, poor-quality events, or questionably useful designs. We now know, and have experienced, better alternatives.

Furthermore, the proliferation of devices means formerly restrictive IT departments are becoming more open to bring your own device (BYOD) policies and providing employees more variety in the tools they procure. Add to that, wearable technology that can interact with personal behaviors at a level never seen before, and technology can help us become more mindful, more capable,[22] and reflective because it makes us more attentive to our movements.[23] The Internet-of-things—where devices are beginning to communicate and assist one another in performing the functions they're designed for—will automate out of our daily mundane tasks, giving us back time to focus on other things.

Workplace Demographics Change Expectations

Think back to the year you joined the workforce. Then reflect on how things were about six months into that job. Did you think you should be given the opportunity to make big splashes and reap rich rewards? Did you consider off hours your own, reserved to pursue your passions? Many of us did. Yet we somehow forget our experiences when we label newcomers to the workforce as unrealistic about advancement or uninterested in working hard.

Some of the qualities associated with the youngest generations in the workforce today are qualities of age, not generation. Brashness, dissatisfaction with the status quo, and constant questioning are characteristics many of us had when we were young. Because we didn't have Facebook connections with friends reinforcing our perspectives, let alone magazines and blogs showcasing young people who became chief executive officers at 19, we abandoned those mindsets to fit in.

Have your expectations of the workplace changed in this newly connected world? Are many things the same as they were as recently as last year? If you were to go to work for your company now, would you not have higher expectations than you had in the past? We certainly would.

Our wide look at demographic shifts has convinced us that organizations of all types and sizes have a lot to learn and do differently if they are to attract and keep the talent—of all ages, genders, and cultures—they need to succeed. It's not all about Millennials—or very soon, Generation Z. Many of us find that social technologies allow us to work in ways we never believed would happen in our lifetimes.

CEOs and industry leaders of all ages are beginning to use status updates to open dialogues within their organizations, throughout enterprises, and with potential customers. By responding to a few words and a question mark, people provide expert testimony, gut-level hunches, and a field view that organizations might never capture otherwise.

Are senior leaders telling their followers what they had for lunch? Probably not. Are they distributing observations while waiting for a delayed flight? Maybe. Do they believe working in social ways offers business value? Certainly.

Bill Ives, a white-haired artist who used to make his living in the enterprise software industry, points out, "These tools allow me to connect with smart people regardless of age or tech-savvy. They honor my busy schedule and let me focus on my business." These shifts are about everyone in the workforce. We don't discount the generational factor; we simply see it as part of the whole.[24]

> *Anyone who stops learning, whether at 20 or at 80, is old. Anyone who keeps learning stays young.*
> —Henry Ford

We believe differences in generation, gender, and culture together provide a useful framework to address a changing workforce and workplace. Success will go to those businesses savvy enough to understand, learn from, and leverage these shifts.

We should aspire to create workplaces that use the talents of everyone, connecting them in meaningful ways, regardless of differences in generation, gender, and culture.

Generation

The biggest demographic change in the workplace is generational. Today, more than half the workforce is made up of Millennials, and by 2030, they'll make up more than 75 percent of the global workforce.[25] Overall, this generation has a high comfort level with technology and broad expectations about using it to learn. The previous generation, Generation X, shares many of these expectations but has learned to navigate slow-to-change workplaces.[26]

Millennials and generations after are not as apt to put up with inefficient ways. Seventy-one percent of 16- to 24-year-olds use online media when they encounter a problem with a product, rather than reaching for a phone.[27]

Baby Boomers, all now over 50, are retiring.[28] Although the perception exists that they do not widely embrace technology, a 2010 survey by ATD (formerly ASTD) shows that 79 percent of Baby Boomers, compared with 76 percent of Millennials, believe social media tools are not being used enough for education activities within organizations.[29]

The swift exit of the Baby Boomers, dubbed the "Silver Tsunami," has far reaching implications on the workplace, leaving skills shortages in its path. Organizations like California utility company PG&E, who realize half of their workforce could retire in the next five years, have begun creating programs specifically targeted at upskilling potential employees to meet the growing demand for skills once more available in the labor pool.[30]

As the cost of college keeps going up, many Millennials are passing up college and the debts that come with it. Instead, they are trying to find new ways into the workforce. Companies, especially with skill gaps and who can teach their new employees the key skills needed for the job, are welcoming these young people with open arms. It's unlikely those companies, which have had mostly older workers in the past, are prepared for the social and learning expectations of their new employees.

Some are revitalizing apprentice programs, certifications, and mentoring networks, made popular before college gained more widespread participation. Companies are also partnering heavily with trade schools and community colleges, bringing specific types of tradecraft into the organization so people can learn on the job. These approaches, too, take on a new flavor when paired with the connected and social sensibilities of younger workers. Maddie Grant, co-author of *Humanize: How People-Centric Organizations Succeed in a Social World* and *When Millennials Take Over: Preparing for the Ridiculously Optimistic*

Future of Business, describes the hallmarks of a Millennial-friendly organization as "digital, clear, fluid, and fast."[31]

However, interesting differences regarding social network use were revealed in a multigenerational study of more than 1,700 employees from organizations across 12 countries and six industries by IBM's Institute of Business Value. According to the study, more than 50 percent of Millennials access their personal social networks for professional reasons less frequently than Gen X employees, who use social networks more frequently (greater than 60 percent) to communicate with colleagues, get industry information, and promote their companies' products and services.[32]

Further, "Millennials have been instilled with egalitarian and participatory values by their parents since birth."[33] These civic-minded, tech-savvy Millennials, accustomed to close networks of peers, also have high expectations that employers will give them frequent feedback, enable workplace collaboration, and provide healthy work-life balance. They want to work at companies in step with their broadminded values. "Millennials favor a corporate culture of inclusion and tolerance and will gravitate toward companies that actively promote racial and cultural diversity," says Ron Alsop, author of *The Trophy Kids Grow Up: How the Millennial Generation Is Shaking Up the Workplace*.

> *Surround yourself with people who light up when they talk about what they're working on.*
> —Grace Garey

Fairly soon, Generation Z will begin entering the workforce. They are even more intimate with technology and have higher expectations for instant answers and constant connectivity than Millennials. With them will come the ability to influence world events through sizable communities rather than large pools of capital. They will also create exponential hyper-connectivity among people, computers, machines, and objects. They will take shortcuts through systems to focus on outcomes rather than processes, making meaning and purpose the center of personal and professional experience. If you think the Millennials change everything, they will be eclipsed by the shifts brought into the workplace by Generation Z.[34]

Gender

To add to the demographic shift, estimates suggest that within this decade nearly 60 percent of the workforce will be female, a group more likely to turn to its social networks for insights and perspectives than males.[35] Studies show that women experience a physiological and emotional change when they connect verbally. Combined with new ways to easily maintain, organize, and create new connections, these networks demonstrate value to women more quickly because they feel more like experiences that take place off line.

Perhaps that's why 76 percent of women online use social networks at least weekly and the rate of social network adoption in the past year has been especially strong among older women.[36]

The impact of women and economic growth has played out quietly for centuries despite impressive results and may well be the dominant source of economic growth in the near future. Organizations that are able to capitalize on the roles women play in the economy will most likely have a competitive advantage as the world pulls out of the global recession. To this end, where organizations have invested in the development of women, the results have been both profound and dramatic.[37]

There are implications of shifts in family, too. According the U.S. Census Bureau, married couples currently make up only half of the population and in most couples both adults work.[38] This means that unlike in years past, there isn't someone at home to be there to wait on a cable repair service call, or to pick up a sick child from school. Flexible work schedules and the ability to connect from anywhere grow in importance.

Culture

Race, natural origin, ethnic background, religious differences, and cultural upbringing influences organizational culture too. Culture refers to the values, norms, and traditions that affect the way people typically perceive, think, interact, behave, and make judgments. Culture even affects perceptions of time, which can impact day-to-day scheduling, deadlines, and how long we expect change to take.

Being a country of immigrants, the United States has a very culturally diverse population made up of people from every part of the globe. Workplaces have become multiracial and multicultural. Today, the workplace of most organizations is more culturally diverse than

A culture of learning often produces great achievement but a culture of achievement rarely results in great learning.
—Drew Perkins

at any time in history because leaders understand diversity provides wider perspectives and greater chances to look at work in new ways.

"A major cause of many of the conflicts in the world is our intolerance of difference," says Mary Gordon, author of *Roots of Empathy: Changing the World Child by Child*.[39] "Though Americans, especially, like to proclaim independence, our health, creativity, productivity, and humanity emerge from our interdependence, our history of relationships," add Maia Szalavitz and Bruce D. Perry, in *Born for Love: Why Empathy Is Essential—and Endangered*.[40]

Studies show a focus on cultural competence can improve the ability to interact effectively with people from different cultures; such competence depends on our awareness of our own cultural worldview, knowledge of other cultural practices, tolerant attitudes towards cultural differences, and cross-cultural skills.

Culture also has a big influence on the workplace. People across the world now have access to technology, which can help them connect with new customers or a remote workforce. Out of the world's estimated 7 billion people, 6 billion have access to mobile phones. Those numbers demonstrate just how ubiquitous these tools have become—only 4.5 billion have access to working toilets.[41]

Organizations that are cross-generational, cross-gender, and cross-cultural will be more capable, agile, thorough, and empathetic—understanding, and supporting their community members. They will be stronger and will contribute more to their organizations than either integrated teams or any other group of employees.

Expanding Desire for Personal Connection

Let's get to the core of our challenge, though. We have always been social creatures. We have been naturally driven to communicate, converse, and have shared with one another since our ancestors came into being. This is part of our survival mechanism, as well as our natural preference, and our ability to converse and share with one another continues to expand.

"A global social conscience is one of the biggest trends to have emerged in the last decade," says Amilcar Perez, president of telecom/mobile worldwide at Nielsen. "Global consumers are collectively speaking out and demanding that corporate make a positive contribution to society."[42]

"During past tough economic times, there was a decrease in volunteering," says Patrick Corvington, then CEO of the Federal Corporation for National and Community Service, "but today there's a 'compassion boom' of people helping others."[43] That compassion boom echoes around the world. "Despite the [economic] downturn, across the globe people's sense of commitment to helping others—and to brands and companies that share that commitment—remains strong," says a series of reports from public-relations firm Edelman.[44]

In an Intelligence Group Cassandra Report, 64 percent of Millennials said it's a priority for them to make the world a better place.[45] A global study by

Deloitte showed that greater than 47 percent of those under 40 years old world-wide believed that the purpose of business is to improve the world around us.[46]

When people on the farm worked with their neighbors, putting up a barn or exchanging wheat for corn, they shared information about a harvesting technique or a new recipe. They created and sustained social capital—the stock and flow of social trust, norms, and networks, and the reciprocity drawn upon to solve common problems. Social capital became financial capital as two farmers who exchanged tools could do more while buying less.

The opportunities ramped up as transportation enabled us to become more mobile and broadened the number of people we could socialize with around town. Then the phone let our voices do the travelling and negated the requirement for us to be in the same place as those we wanted to talk with. As telephone lines expanded globally, distance became even less of a barrier for conversation and connections. As satellites and cellular and computer networks came online, we became able to communicate with anyone and everyone, anywhere and anytime.

Communication and collaboration reached a tipping point with email and online forums, then instant messaging, then voice over Internet, then video. Just as we thought we couldn't possibly be any more connected, our social nature fueled another expansion as we formed alliances and human networks of distributed organizations using social media tools. Finally.

These connections represent more than an expanding volume of conversations. We are witnessing a dramatic increase in our collective thinking, collaboration, and capacity to grow. We are seeing a previously unachievable human network effect, where our growing connectivity is enhancing everyone's ability to know.

Doug Engelbart, the father of personal computing, and inventor of the computer mouse, was prescient when he pondered a collective IQ half a century ago:

> What if, suddenly, in an evolutionary sense, we evolved a super new
> nervous system to upgrade our collective social organisms? [What if]
> we got strategic and began to form cooperative alliances, employing
> advanced networked computer tools and methods to develop and apply new
> collective knowledge? [47]

We may now be realizing this dream. An opportunity to raise personal, organizational, and collective IQ has arrived. As stressed as our communication capabilities seem today, history shows this trend will continue as we figure out how to more effectively connect, collaborate, converse, and learn. We need to embrace the opportunity for personal connections and be willing to evolve.

As Harlan Cleveland, former U.S. Ambassador to NATO and contributor to the Marshall Plan wrote:

> If we raise our periscopes for a 360-degree look around, we see that the pyramids and hierarchies of years past are rapidly being replaced with networks and uncentralized systems. In these systems, larger numbers of people than ever take initiative, make policy, collaborate to point their organizations' ways forward, and work together to release human ingenuity and maximize human choice. These people's actions are not, for the most part, the result of being told what to do. They are the consequence, not of command and control, but of consultation, of relationships that are intermixed, interwoven, and interactive. [48]

Is This Learning?

Often, when we talk about these trends and technologies, people ask us how we define *learning*. We define learning as the transformative process of taking in information that—when internalized and mixed with what we have experienced—changes what we know and builds on what we do. It's based on input, process, and reflection. It is what changes us.

Learning is what makes us more vibrant participants in a world seeking fresh perspectives, novel insights, and firsthand experiences. When shared, what we have learned mixes with what others have learned, then ripples out, transforming organizations, enterprises, ecosystems, and the society around us.

Pamela Moss at the University of Michigan says:

> From a sociocultural perspective, learning is perceived through changing relationships among the learner, the other human participants, and the tools [material and symbolic] available in a given context. Thus learning involves not only acquiring new knowledge and skill, but taking on a new identity and social position within a particular discourse or community of practice.[49]

Étienne Wenger, co-author of *Digital Habitats: Stewarding Technology for Communities* and author of *Communities of Practice: Learning, Meaning, and Identity* asserts that human knowing is fundamentally a social act.[50] By hearing about the experiences of others, you mash up snippets of data, add them to your own, and fit them into your sense of who you are and what you can do— together and with others. Learning "changes who we are by changing our ability to participate, to belong, and to experience our life and the world as meaningful."[51]

Content and communities are shaping how people find and connect with each other.
—Gautam Ghosh

Training, knowledge management, good leadership, and a whole host of organizational practices can add to an environment where people learn, but people can learn without this assistance, too.

The 70-20-10 model explains that the vast majority of learning occurs as part of daily work. Seventy in the model refers to the learning and development that takes place from real-life and on-the-job experiences, tasks, and problem solving. Twenty denotes development that comes from other people through our networks, informal or formal feedback, mentoring, coaching, and other social activities. Ten refers to formal training and development activities.

The numbers originated in a study by Morgan McCall and others at the Center for Creative Leadership. A group of successful managers reported this ratio as the way their own development happened. "This isn't a rule," says Charles Jennings, former chief learning officer at Thomson Reuters and co-author of *Working Smarter: Informal Learning in the Cloud.* "Learning and development is always context dependent. Research over the past 40 years has increasingly shown that informal and on-the-job learning is pervasive and is a key indicator of success. People who actively and regularly carry out on-the-job learning through their experiences, through practice, through conversations, and through active reflection will outperform their peers who don't do this."

Studies have shown that the performance increases can be as much as threefold, and that employee engagement can be more than doubled.[52]

Reiterates Jennings: "70:20:10 is not about the numbers. The numbers simply remind us most learning happens naturally as part of the daily work-flow, through doing our work, and through conversations with colleagues and with experts."

"... most learning happens naturally as part of the daily workflow, through doing our work, and through conversations with colleagues and with experts."

—Charles Jennings

To help see learning in a broader way, think of five people you communicate with and then identify at least three things you learned from each. Most people find this easier than recalling information they learned in a formal setting—not because they weren't offered useful topics to learn—but because when we connect with people, the exchange sticks with us. That engagement calls up something from within us or connects with an emotion, and that mental dance leaves a footprint we can walk in again. Reflecting on it later improves learning even more.

Some formal training programs are designed for gaining new skills or competencies. New emergency medical technicians may not remember all the steps for CPR, but when they need to use it, they know what to do. That learning is about more than recall, too. It's also about building muscle memory and a warehouse of options when the need to resuscitate someone arises.

Other training programs are for expanding our thinking or capacity to deal with situations ahead. The same is true of learning with people. This also comes from the community around us, in person or online.

The traditional model of corporate training, where experts disseminate knowledge in one-time training events or all-day presentations, is being modernized. It needs to take full advantage of the larger opportunity for incidental learning, learning from interacting with others, and learning along the way in the course of work.

A social learning culture thrives when people don't fear feedback. This is when people ask other people to be part of their ideas.
—Sumeet Moghe

"To learn is to optimize the quality of one's networks," says Jay Cross, author of the Informal Learning Blog and co-author of *Working Smarter: Informal Learning in the Cloud*. "Learning is social. Most learning is collaborative. Other people are providing the context and the need, even if they're not in the room."[53]

"Over 60 years ago, W. Edwards Deming encouraged management to drive out fear and break down barriers between departments, and still worry and walls are the two constants that most organizations share," says corporate trainer Steve LeBlanc. "If a culture is truly focused on service, the most pressing question to ask is, 'How can I help you?' How can I help you succeed? How can I help you ask strong questions, take wise risks and deliver great content? How can I help you prosper? Most importantly, how can I help you learn and make new connections? How can I help you serve the larger group, of which we are both a part? Yet in most classrooms, people are prevented from helping each other learn and succeed."[54]

Organizations and individuals will not be sufficiently served by only receiving formal training. Diverse backgrounds and learning styles, and especially the complexity of people's jobs, also determine what and how they learn. More critically, much of what needs to be learned is moving faster than we can create relevant, structured learning opportunities. Traditional training methods may be useful for teaching highly specific tasks or safety procedures, but evolving practices require more. Ad hoc and self-directed learning becomes a key strategy when we need to move fast.

> "Learning is social. Most learning is collaborative. Other people are providing the context and the need, even if they're not in the room."
>
> —Jay Cross

The new social learning, which centers on information sharing, collaboration, and co-creation, not instruction, implies that the notion of training needs to expand. Jane Hart, founder of the Centre for Learning & Performance Technologies, points out that "workplace learning is no longer something that is wholly owned and managed by L&D; everyone now has access to resources and tools to solve their own problems. So the [new] role of a learning consultant is to work closely with teams and individuals in order to enable and support solutions that best suit them."[55]

"Learning has always been social. That's not the innovation here. It is our relationship with the learning process that is the innovation," says Allison Anderson, curator and long-time corporate educator.

Studies show that we learn what we need to solve problems and inform decisions in the real world. Learning and work strategist Harold Jarche often says, "Work is learning and learning is the work.[56]

Knowledge acquired but never put to use is usually forgotten. We may act as if we care about learning something and go through the motions, but we will forget it unless it is something we want to learn and it fits how we work.

Social learning is especially good at showing us that for any crisis, or just to satisfy our curiosity, there is a network to support us at any time. We can load the boat. It's what Howard Rheingold, who teaches about social media and *virtual community* (a term he coined) and is the author of many books, including *Net Smart: How to Thrive Online*, describes as the "online brain trust representing a highly varied accumulation of expertise."[57]

Social learning is also very good at giving people a view into the little moments that happen between big activities, modeling behavior for others to observe, retain, and replicate—or avoid.

> New behaviours emerge as work is done in new ways.
> —Harold Jarche

We look across the tweet stream and tuck away lessons of finessed customer service calls, graceful endings to overlong presentations, and recoveries from cultural faux pas in front of visiting clients. Together we are better.

Social learning creates a way to remind us at work that people are not things to be manipulated, labeled, boxed, bought, and sold. We are entire human beings, containing the whole of the evolving universe, limitless until we start limiting them. We must examine the concept of leading and following, learning and knowing, with new and focused eyes. We must examine the concept of superior and subordinate with increasing skepticism. We must examine the concept of management and labor with new beliefs. And we must examine the nature of organizations that demand such distinctions with an entirely different consciousness.[58]

How to Respond to Critics

One of the largest roadblocks for organizations struggling to get started is having the courage to face those who think what you're doing is dangerous or dumb. Maybe they have heard a story of someone doing something that scares them. Perhaps it's the unknown itself. In chapter four we uncover just about anything that could go wrong and address how to turn that around. Here are the most common stumbling blocks we hear about with regard to social learning and ways we believe you can address them.

> "If a culture is truly focused on service, the most pressing question to ask is, 'How can I help you?' How can I help you succeed?"
>
> —Steve LeBlanc

Critique 1: Using social media at work is a waste of time and productivity. Socializing can seem frivolous to people who haven't connected it with the benefits of building relationships, accessing information from untapped corners of the organization, or feeling connected to co-workers so work seems like less of a chore.

Even in the most progressive organizations we talk with, at least one or two people said they didn't want their staff to waste time on platforms like this. "They should be doing their work, not be on online or reading social media streams."

An extremely security conscious organization, very worried people would use social tools to waste time, invited a consultant in to speak to their senior leadership team. These leaders were anxious to learn how other organizations were addressing social media concerns. It soon became obvious they were not interested in allowing these tools into their halls, so much as they were in learning how they could provide services to those in other organizations in order to mitigate what they perceived as inordinate risks stemming from the use of such tools.

As the speaker entered their building, she passed through a metal detector, then was required to put all of her electronic devices into a locker from which she could retrieve them on the way out. These people were serious about not giving access to their workforce. The speaker gave her talk and had a lengthy sit down meeting with the leaders. At that point, when she often mentions people are using these tools with or without permission, she stopped, noting this was the first organization she'd been in where she knew that was not the case—but that it would likely be the situation with any organization they partnered with.

> *Social learning tools can make hidden practices and knowledge available to an org. Like buried treasure.*
> —Jason Willensky

After collecting her belongings and getting into her car, a noise caught her attention in the vehicle beside her. A worker was in his car, typing on his smartphone's keyboard. Out of the corner of her eye, she noticed another employee in her car, and then several more. As she drove through the car park, mid-afternoon on a weekday, she realized that despite the organization's most diligent policies, people were accessing social tools from the privacy of their vehicles.

It doesn't matter what policies or extreme precautions are put in place. These tools are now ubiquitous, with more people across the world having an active presence on Facebook than comprise the populations of Russia and all of the European countries combined.

How much productivity was being lost by these people in their cars, having to physically go around the system to connect in a way that met their needs? While we will provide many benefits to using social tools in this book, the bottom line is that people will use these tools even if you, personally, or the critic you work with (or for), don't find value in them. There may be no way to provide any more evidence than their listening to the words of people they know and trust who do find value.

Critique 2: People will say inappropriate things. If someone puts inappropriate content on the office door, you don't remove the door. If someone makes a tasteless joke over the telephone, you don't take away the phone. Social tools are often held to higher standards than traditional business tools because they are new, and bad stories circulate—go viral—quickly.

Rather than blame collaborative systems, educate people how to use them effectively for work. Social tools are the future of collaboration and learning at work, so the more you prepare people for how to use the tools respectfully, and how to apply good social practices, the better.

Andi Campbell, vice president of human resources at LAZ Parking, responds to this criticism simply, "If we don't trust our employees, we have a much larger issue here."

> "Learning has always been social. That's not the innovation here. It is our relationship with the learning process that is the innovation."
>
> —Allison Anderson

Critique 3: People will post incorrect information. One leader we spoke with expressed his concern this way, "Our employees may someday graffiti versions of our logo all over town, but we don't want to hand out spray paint." He feared that encouraging the use of social tools would encourage his people to write posts he wouldn't approve of.

We asked in return, "Would you rather give people a chance to surface what they know and get it corrected by their peers when it's wrong, or for them to continue believing (and likely repeating) incorrect information over time?"

Details of wide-ranging inaccuracy have always spread between co-workers and the market you serve. Information (both true, and not true) about your organization seeps out when people talk in restaurants over lunch or speak on a mobile phone while waiting in line at the post office. When you provide venues where people can share peer-to-peer and be accountable, the best information rises to the top because many people have rated it as useful. Different voices can weigh in and correct what's wrong. If anything, organizations have more stories about how people rectify misnomers quickly, rather than how people make statements that are untrue. When questions and answers take place in public, people are more apt to correct misrepresented facts, old data, and rumors or speculation and, realizing their responses will be widely seen, work toward accuracy (or at least what they perceive it to be).

A network is the structure of culture.
—Karen Stephenson

In an age of transparency, giving people a way to work together toward achieving greater accuracy of information makes more sense than keeping inaccuracies under wraps.

Critique 4: Senior leaders won't embrace social media for communications. We often hear this critique as a reason not to pursue social approaches. This year it's very possible executives (and perhaps people at different levels throughout the organization) won't see value or understand how using social tools can actually create more time in their overburdened lives. For many, those objections will fall away as, over time, working in these ways becomes the norm across society.

For others, active participation is simply a matter of time and economics. At least one organization we know created a way for people to share their thoughts without spending much time learning all the ins and outs of the social platform. Although they also created incentives for people to master the tools, they created less high-touch approaches, too.

For instance, they created an email address where anyone within the company could send what they'd written (in an email, a memo, or even—

with good penmanship—on a napkin), which would be received by a team of writers who would turn the message into a blog post and publish it on the sender's behalf.

"Work is learning, and learning is the work."

—Harold Jarche

At first this approach received criticism from some employees for not being authentic, a cornerstone principle of working socially. When a senior leader addressed this head on (with the help of one of the writers), those in the organization empathized. He explained that he had written the gist of the messages and even provided a calculation of the cost of his time. It wasn't cost effective for him to also master social-platform tools. He hoped to someday, but not amid his current priorities. He also pointed out that almost all of his correspondence was routinely edited, and that editors also were available to those in more junior roles who didn't have confidence in their writing skills.

People may prefer to ease into working socially. Status updates work their way in because an enterprise tool that can be implemented for free gets added to the intranet. Employees may be encouraged to comment on company blogs or to blog on their own. Perhaps an employee directory goes online and then someone creates a wiki to take notes at meetings. In some organizations, many adopt it, some even sponsor it; it needn't be universally supported to be effective.

This is what embracing social media and the new social learning looks like. It's a process of adapting and adopting. Begin where you are and build where it suits your culture and environment. Learn as you go.

Critique 5: Social learning will distract from the changes we need to make in our business. Inevitably, every organization needs to change how it works in some fundamental way. That's the nature of progress. The trouble is, many change efforts fail in large part because the people being asked to change aren't included in the process.[59] Social systems give people a view into the organization and what their colleagues are doing, which can bring them into the heart of the change itself.

Ben Brooks, business coach, describes change management as an arc or a journey, getting people to move from point A to point B. "Some leaders will obsess about the route or the distance, but they fail to think about what it takes to actually get people in motion, in the same direction. At the beginning, change within an organization is like beginning a 5K race with every one of your staff. While leaders may like to believe everyone will start at the same place and will go in the same direction, at the same pace, your people will behave more like cats than roadrunners. Some will barely even notice or care that there's a race going on. Some will scatter, some will go backwards; few will move at the same pace. Change requires planning and allowing humanity to occur, not assuming people will behave like programmed, compliant robots," says Brooks.

Conversation + concepts converge on social learning.
—Kare Anderson

"We have different attention spans, comfort levels. We create complicated project plans, and then only think about people at the end. It's as if the people who are impacted by the change deserve no more thought or support than a dollop of sour cream on the top of a loaded baked potato. In reality, empathetic and practical change support needs to be embedded into the process, not a layer you smear on at the end."

Brooks, who personally was responsible for a very large corporate transformation, sees four distinct stages of change, each of which can be accelerated when an organization is in the habit of working together in social ways. These are focused less on the range of emotions we can expect humans to have in the face of change. Rather these are like mile markers on the journey between point A and B.

First there is awareness. Have people heard about the change? Do they directly have it in their ambient awareness? Next, understanding. Do people have a detailed understanding of it and does it make sense to them? Do they understand why the organization is making this change? After that is embodiment. Are people internalizing the changes—starting to run the race? Are they doing something differently than before, becoming walking-and-talking examples of the change, pulling other people in? Has their behavior started to change? Finally, there is accountability. Are people being recognized and feeling accountable? Are early adopters being celebrated and treated like champions? Is there now a social upside to working in new ways? And are the laggards being identified and addressed?[60]

"Change requires planning and allowing humanity to occur."

—Ben Brooks

These are the types of shifts organizations can excel at as they work out loud, with one another, in the flow of work. Each of these stages can be deepened and accelerated when people can see their peers also participating in the journey. No matter how comfortable people feel with change, knowing they are not alone can improve the situation. Sensing people are working together spurs them on as they take action.

Critique 6: People need training, not socializing. Learning socially does not replace training. It may overlap a little and complement a lot, but it can address the knowledge transfer that training may never get to.

Ellen Wagner, partner in Sage Road Solutions, notes that "workplace success has shifted from individual accomplishment to teams, communities of practice, and collaboration. Today we assess personal mastery of knowledge and skills with how well people can leverage their interconnected networks of resources, information, and subject matter specialists."[61]

"The most significant thing going on in workplace training is that we have punched through the walls of the classroom to allow experts and peers to bring their messages closer to work and life through technology," adds Allison Rossett, professor emerita of educational technology at San Diego State University. "I had my doubts about the 'learningfulness' of social networks until I began to use one in a graduate class on performance consulting. My students worked in teams, conducted research, created presentations, sought experts, stirred up conversations—even conflict—and engaged hundreds of people beyond our registered classmates. It was much better in almost every way."[62]

> Focus on Social Business and Social Learning will follow.
> —Terrence Wing

Critique 7: Collaborative systems compromise classified information. Organizations such as the U.S. Central Intelligence Agency (CIA), Boston Children's Hospital, National Australian Bank, and the Mayo Clinic use social media widely, even though their data are very sensitive. Rather than pronounce this new approach unfit for their environments, they practice good governance. They remind people to participate in online information-sharing communities with a full understanding that they bear responsibility for protecting sensitive or classified details.

As Chris Rasmussen, in the intelligence community once pointed out, "If you bring too many locks into an overly cautious culture, that's all you get: locks."

Critique 8: Social practices can't be governed. Rather than start with a large, heavy-handed policy condemning the use of social media, put in place simple rules stating when people should use which tool to communicate, create, or share specific types of information. Make it easier for people to classify information they create. Specify which data and content are appropriate for what use—especially use within the company. Also, the fact that people can see what others share provides a reason to self-monitor and for people to monitor each other. See the Appendix for examples of governance policies.

> ## "If you bring too many locks into an overly cautious culture, that's all you get: locks."
> —Chris Rasmussen

Critique 9: Social practices can't be measured. People who say there is "no way to measure this social stuff," are often really saying it seems too tacit and ephemeral. However, there are dozens, if not hundreds, of ways to measure and analyze newly surfaced value in their organizations, which derives from people working in social ways.

Understanding and using this analysis to make smart decisions requires focusing on what you aim to accomplish and the many factors that led to where you've arrived. There's a fundamental disconnect—perhaps several—between new social and collaborative practices, and the leaders who are interested in measuring their value.

Most social platforms used within enterprises include some analytics capabilities. At minimum, they can tell you how many people logged in (initiative), how many people came back, presumably because they found value (persistence), how the network expanded (connection), and how technology use changed; for example, if there were fewer documents sent across email (transition).

You can analyze what people are searching for and map what they find. You can analyze not only where people go with their social tools, but also how they get there, how long they stay, and what they do when they are there. Although this does not verify the transfer of knowledge or skills, it is a pretty good indication.

Good measures look at functional outcomes rather than simply asking, "Did they learn?" or "Were they social?" There is little value to the organization if people don't apply what they take in. The best measures go the next step and connect the use of new skills and knowledge with how it affects numerous measures, including the bottom line.

There are now approaches to measure the network, the ripples of impact, the engagement, and even the goodness of an organization based on how people are interacting, collaborating, and working together.

Chapter 5 is dedicated to the many ways it is possible to analyze and understand the connection between social learning and returning value to the organization.

Critique 10: Employee engagement efforts don't improve the bottom line. Engagement is situational, and varies by firm, region, and organizational culture. One-size-fits-all models rarely work in actually engaging people who are already fighting a culture that doesn't value people's perspectives or that doesn't look at the underlying factors that support company growth.

Laurie Bassi, co-author of *Good Company: Business Success in the Worthiness Era* and CEO of McBassi & Company, points out that increasing employee engagement alone doesn't lead to increased business performance. "To drive better sales results, an organization should focus on those items that are actually driving sales," she says.

When you ask people if they would refer your company to friends as a good place to work and if they intend to stay with your organization, you're looking less at engagement, more at the drivers that engage people at work.

DEFINING THE SMART WORKER

Jane Hart, at the forefront of social learning, describes the smart worker this way:[63]

- The Smart Worker recognizes that she learns continuously as she does her job.

- The Smart Worker wants immediate access to solutions to his performance problems.

- The Smart Worker is happy to share what she knows.

- The Smart Worker relies on a trusted network of friends and colleagues.

- The Smart Worker learns best with and from others.

- The Smart Worker keeps up-to-date with what is happening in his profession and industry.

- The Smart Worker constantly strives to improve her productivity.

- The Smart Worker thrives on autonomy.

A connected workforce may increase the likelihood sales people feel connected to their co-workers so they have less interest in changing employers, but it's not guaranteed to increase sales. Leaders who "measure engagement without also understanding what's driving business results are missing an opportunity to align their efforts with the efforts to address organizational business challenges," adds Bassi.[64]

Organizations that value and develop their people will be more successful than their competitors, not because of some engagement score, but because they are addressing the roots of personal drive and doing good to become great.

The Next Level

Senior leaders consider employees' knowledge a strategic priority, yet they often leave the topic of learning out of strategy discussions because years ago they relegated it to the training department. Over the past 20 years, companies have strived to transform organizational learning by streamlining the training function and moving courses online. That doesn't address the deeper dilemma: Training and learning are not the same thing.

In our view, training describes an outside-in approach to providing known quantifiable content, while learning describes an inside-out process that originates with the learner's desire to know, either long held or spontaneously arising from recent events or a moving interaction.

A community is about having passionate members that belong.
—Sandy Carter

The new social learning fosters an environment where people readily and easily pick up new knowledge and skills as the world shifts around them, meeting the demands of a constantly changing mobile world.

The new social learning transcends social media, training, or workplace learning practices of the past because it offers 1) more information sources: access to people who can lessen your uncertainty with vetted data, presentations, research, and wide perspectives that can help make your case (or your decision) easier; 2) more dissemination points: people can self-serve their needs by accessing your resources, giving you back your time and simultaneously meeting their needs; and 3) an open approach: wide networks of communicators and collaborators who can help work flow.

If this is your first step into social media for learning, you are not alone. And if you're one of the veterans, please leverage these new tools and technologies to share your knowledge and collaborate with us all.

Informing Decisions

Many of the following chapters begin with a case study from an organization deeply engaged in using social media to learn. We end this opening chapter, intended to provide context for the specific approaches addressed ahead, with the story of an organization using social media to offer context and make decisions clear.

Although your organization and the CIA may seem to have nothing in common, their objectives are not so different from those of every organization.

In 2006, a team of analysts at the CIA was tapped to replace an old print-based publication, primarily containing information from the president's intelligence briefing or about a crisis that had come to light. Like a newspaper, a certain amount of space was reserved for graphics and the rest was used for text. It worked, but it never shined.

Rather than build on what they already had, they started fresh, creating a new structure with social media sensibilities and a brighter vision.

The result is a daily electronic publication to update senior policy and security officials on trends and news overseas that have the potential to affect U.S. interests. The analysis in the publication is classified, noting the methods used to acquire the information and the sensitivity of the topics it contains. More than just a newspaper, it anticipates developments and makes projections about the future.

The CIA calls it the CIA World Intelligence Review (WIRe) because the world is what they cover, intelligence is their vocation, and review is what they do.

The WIRe is the CIA's collective and dynamic online presence. The WIRe leverages innovative tools and processes to make the richness of the CIA's content, including text, multimedia, graphics, and video, accessible wherever and whenever needed. Updated throughout the day, the WIRe's front page is dynamic and customizable, and it delivers reader-specific intelligence in a timely manner. The WIRe makes it easy to navigate volumes of reporting by linking analysis with source materials and providing robust search and feedback capabilities to support knowledge management.

For the CIA, being "central" doesn't simply reflect the title of a director, the name of the organization, or its role for legislators. It refers to being central, being essential to their particular customers. The organization aims to lead the way, at the center, pioneering in times of change through demonstrating applied leadership.

In creating the WIRe, the team followed four "tracks." These objectives mirror those of many organizations pursuing a new vision: Retire and replace what no longer works. Get better. Learn from errors. Commit to getting it right.

> *Keep it open, searchable, accessible. There is no evolution in an echo chamber. There is no oxygen there.*
> —Jeannette Campos

Embrace the best of what's being done in the private sector and apply it to intelligence, providing it in a user-friendly, online way. Customers accustomed to the BBC.com or Google News would know how to use this.

1. Develop a relationship with customers.

2. Communicate with them; don't just transmit information to them.

3. Pay attention to how they interact with the information and make data-driven improvements because of it.

4. Recognize that we won't always know how social media tools fit or how they will apply to us, but innovation and flexibility are part of our mission, and we'll weave them into our activity.

Although these four objectives have grown over time, the team still lives by them, mindful that customers don't purchase the WIRe with money; they invest in it with their time. And invest they have. The new system has eclipsed the old system that had about 750 viewers a day. The system now has more than 100,000 registered users across the globe. It has become the gold standard for information sharing in the U.S. government. It is printed out as part of the president's briefing, read at the cabinet level, and added to and read online by sailors and soldiers implementing national security. In these ways, it's as far reaching as it is impactful.

The WIRe's purpose is to inform decisions, revealing what people think about as they make decisions. The WIRe is the CIA's voice, expressing as an institution its perspective on a topic. Now it also provides a means to express knowledge in a collaborative space others can link to and from, add to, and learn with, so it no longer represents discrete, isolated data. It expresses personal interaction attached to relevant information that with a few clicks connects to all other relevant information. It's interconnected and put into the context of what's going on in the world.

Rather than tell the story of a leader in an emerging government through words or a few static images, the WIRe can show a video clip, perhaps captured by a spectator, of how the leader whips up the crowd with a passion and a presentation style that reaches into the hearts of his audience. Anyone seeing that clip can understand why he is so powerful.

With that, producers of intelligence can make points more vibrantly, creating presentations with great impact. Conveying the message goes beyond basic audio, video, and text sharing. Media are integrated from multiple sources and delivered and constructed by many people. People can discover a framework of intelligence relationships and see that everything is connected, for the most accurate representation.

In addition to shared intelligence published by the WIRe team, those viewing the information create new knowledge through the paths they take in their discovery, the comments they leave, and the tags and social bookmarks they create. Each intelligence gatherer—"learner" as it were—can see what someone else navigated to or tagged from a particular point of departure, then see what else she or he tagged as relevant for making informed decisions. By observing one another's tags and navigation, people can also discover other people and groups interested in similar topics, potentially making decisions about similar things. This facilitates new relationships and new perspectives.

The WIRe becomes a combination of daily intel-
ligence and a grouping of topics, trails of interests, and search queries, leaving an archive that can satis-
fy a series of needs from customers that may not exist yet. Rather than try to tailor a presentation to meet those various needs, the WIRe becomes a diamond

Networks are present everywhere. All we need is an eye for them.
—Albert-László Barabási

that in its raw form has value in itself. What gives it sparkle is the ability for each decision maker, each person seeking timely information, to cut in and look at it through an individual lens, looking for different facets. It might be that the detail you want is on the homepage, the highlights presented by the WIRe team, or through an RSS feed you create and view. A regional page gives you another aspect, and topic areas a third.

What makes it unlike systems that have come before it within or outside government is that it works in seemingly conflicting worlds—that of wide-open sharing and that of the highest security. Both extremes are dangerous. As founding editor-in-chief of the WIRe, Geoffrey Fowler, says, "Share too broadly, and people can die. Hold your information too closely, decisions can be ill-informed, and people can die. Our responsibility is to share broadly and securely—to make certain that these two critical needs are not viewed as incompatible extremes. The truth of the intelligence business is that information sharing and information security need to co-exist."[65]

The WIRe provides openness and security in tandem by building on the CIA's security clearance system. Although there are restrictions, people using the system can search all the data holdings and discover trails leading to information they didn't even know existed. The organizational culture is moving from one focused exclusively on the need to know to one recognizing that success depends on the need to share. The WIRe focuses more on intelligence than the locks and walls between groups.

Fowler adds, "When I look back over the past few years, I see the evolution and the growth of a program, of an organization, and of a community. I see learning. I see dynamic interaction among experts in social and online media and those involved in the creation and conveyance of intelligence. It's time to expand that conversation, to talk about innovation beyond tools—to talk about innovation as an art, as a behavior, and as a necessity for survival and progress. Growth and adaptation are part of a journey, one that cannot be successful if taken alone. And so we come together."

The CIA's ongoing interest and work with social media tools inspires us in our work. Its attention to both security and distribution reminded us as we wrote this book that systems should be facilitators for learning, not gatekeepers or megaphones. Social media can and should provide a medium for what people need now to make educated decisions. Working together, each of us, like pebbles tossed in a pond, can make both ripples and waves.

Go far, go together.

Embark on the Journey

What's your business problem, what isn't working, why are you change-oriented in the first place? When [what isn't working] is clearly defined . . . then we can ask the question: "Well, given the culture, is that going to help you solve the problem or hinder you," and it always ends up being both. There are always parts of the culture that help solve the problem and other parts of the culture that get in the way. Then you're finally at the point of saying, "Well, maybe I need a culture change program," but you got there by thinking about the business problem you are trying to solve.

—Edgar Schein[1]

ORGANIZATIONAL CHANGE REQUIRES CULTURE CHANGE, but that's not the place to start. It's time to look hard at the aspects of your business that aren't working and aren't leading to the results you desire.

For some readers, the problem may be that people in the organization have no modern-day way to work together across standard lines of business, or work effectively with external collaborators and allied organizations. That means they're disengaged at work, growing increasingly uncomfortable with old-style management. The problem is exacerbated when no one in the organization is stepping up to initiate a large-scale social approach.

For others, collaborative systems may be rolling out, but those who focus on innovation, talent management, human capital, or learning and development haven't been invited to the table so no one's making sure discovery and learning are prioritized.

It's time to lean in. We've been there ourselves and have worked with many leaders in similar spots. We know the challenge can be daunting.

In this chapter you'll find the guidance you need to move forward in either a central or supporting role. Trial and error can be useful, but it can also be terribly painful, and we're pretty sure you don't have the time and money to stumble all the way through.

You need a plan that will help you address your organization's problems, weaving learning into your workplace processes. Designed properly, this won't make your job more complicated or take more time. It will change how the entire company works and succeeds.

You especially don't want to create or develop illusory or provisional goals that either disappear or aren't seen as serious. It's time to work on the hard problems, to join your colleagues in joyously tackling the most vexing issues, and to come out of the shadows to work out loud.

Euan Semple, who introduced blogging to the BBC and is author of *Organizations Don't Tweet, People Do: A Manager's Guide to the Social Web*, puts it this way:

> The days when you could get away with not being noticed at work are passing. Being seen, and being seen to know what you are talking about, are becoming more important. This will be a wrench for some and a liberation for others. It has never been easier, or more fun, to share what we know. Being willing to share and help others is becoming an important factor in successful business.[2]

As with any new initiative, taking action is critical—even if you know there are umpteen obstacles in your path. New ways of working—and the technologies that come with them—can be challenging, sometimes even frightening. Getting past those challenges requires systematically looking at those barriers and removing, or going around, them.

Get started by figuring out where you are along the social learning spectrum. Does one of these most closely mirror your situation?

Don't ask.	We're more likely to stare at our shoes than share openly with other people online.
Toe dippers.	We use social media for marketing, but only a few departments do anything inside the organization with social tools.
Just beginning.	We have a plan in place but haven't rolled it out completely (or, we had a plan we rolled out but have cut it way back).
On a roll.	We are becoming more social and collaborative each day, but it's a slow process.
We've arrived.	We actively use social tools throughout our organization, our work practices are now relationship oriented, and we're learning nonstop.

Whichever stage you're in, it's time to move further along.

People often struggle to embrace change, but organizations as a whole find it even tougher. Just like the human body, which replaces most of its cells during the course of a few years, organizations regularly handle significant turnover of employees without disruption. Policies and procedures, not to mention surrounding co-workers, are in place to keep things running smoothly when a newcomer shows up. They have co-evolved to reinforce one another, and respond creatively to unexpected events.

Anything less could threaten the organization's survival and the employees' livelihoods. So, like the body, organizations have the ability to "heal" from efforts to change from the outside and have developed an "immune system" to resist and recover from changes that have found their way inside.

The more frequently change efforts are tried and beaten back, the stronger these defenses become.

Your opportunity is to work within your unique organizational culture, carefully and consciously navigating your organization's defenses, to help your colleagues understand and embrace a more collaborative, transparent way to work.[3]

"The days when you could get away with not being noticed at work are passing. Being seen, and being seen to know what you are talking about, are becoming more important."

—Euan Semple

We aim to help you do that. By looking at hundreds of social implementations across a wide range of industries, taking into account the humanizing element of working in social ways, we have determined the steps we believe you need to take (and not take) in order to break through.

Think of the following list not as a lock-step process, with each stage carefully following the previous one. The order in which you take these steps is only marginally important. Look at them instead as a recipe; one that is flexible and requires you to modify the ingredients to satisfy your local tastes, the available ingredients, your dietary requirements, and climate. Ultimately, what you're cooking should foster a healthy climate where people can thrive.

Just be sure to start with a clear idea of what you're creating. As with a recipe, there's no point beginning until you know if you're looking for an entree or side dish. Everything else you do should depend on your specific situation.

One-size-fits-all approaches never quite fit right. Your organization gets work done differently than any other. How people communicate and share with each other, and how the relationships between management and staff are structured, sets you apart in every way.

It's from this unique vantage point—through your own lenses—that you need to look at the work ahead. These are the doors you'll be going through.

- Get clear about your challenges.

- Determine what's in it for people.

- Reach out to your partners and stakeholders.

- Identify quick-win opportunities.

- Initiate, seed, and spur on activity.

- Encourage champions.

- Differentiate benefits.

- Establish guidelines and road rules.

- Serve as a positive, visible example.

- Measure things that matter.

- Trust people and share, share, share.

Along your way, you'll discover many other areas, some seemingly insignificant and others massively important. Provided that you notice when you run into one of these and find a way around, you're ready to be on your way.

If you're in that *don't ask* phase of the spectrum, this might be where you get off the trolley. Consider looking for a new job with an organization actually committed to moving ahead. While we can't say the road you're on is too bumpy for travel—after all, we were all there at some point—there are likely other forces at play.

Maybe your industry is so mired in bureaucracy nothing ever changes. If the CIA can find a way to work in a social and collaborative way some of the time, we no longer accept "we're in a too tightly regulated industry."

If you're in a *toe-dipping* company, consider there's a chance it's not just your marketing department using social tools. In 2014, more than 93 percent of corporate recruiting departments used some social tools.[4] Look around to find if other groups may have dipped their toes in, too.

START BY EXPLORING

In her book *Business Common Sense: What's Old Is New*, futurist and change agent Ayelet Baron encourages people to begin their journey by exploring.[5]

- Always ask: What is the problem we are trying to solve? Spend time with as many people as possible to clearly define the problem. Tap into any internal and external connected networks. Assess what is not working. Where does it stem from? Don't jump quickly to the solution, creating a Band-Aid approach.

- Identify the stopgap solutions already in place. Explore the assumptions and look hard at what's really happening. Put your concerns, and "the smelly fish," on the table to really acknowledge and address the problem.

- Ask: what happens if we solve it? What is the opportunity? Do you continue to go on for a few years, or have you created new markets, products, and services?

- Understand your own culture. Listen to people. Go have conversations (not meetings). Ask questions and listen. Find business partners who can help you analyze what you are hearing. Uncover the uniqueness of what is in the hearts and minds of people beyond the presentation decks and marketing slogans. Assess the gap between what leaders are saying [words] and what they are doing [actions]. Understand what would motivate people to help the organization get stronger holistically.

- Don't waste time with the best practices of someone else's diagnosis. Please don't go to the latest and greatest hyped solution on the market, as your people will call it the "flavor of the month." Find leaders who have gone through similar problems, who may be outside of your business sphere, and connect with them for conversations. Look for thought leaders who solved similar problems in practice, not theory. Listen and learn about what worked and what didn't for them. Remember your culture and prototype with the right people.

START BY EXPLORING (CONTINUED)

- Don't initiate another re-organization [please]. Go back to the drawing board and evaluate your mission, vision, strategic frameworks—and ask yourself, "What's our purpose?" Invest time in simplifying and leading with purpose. A re-org is a stop-gap solution, so take the time to identify and address the systemic problem. If your strategy is simply to build an organization without vision and purpose, prepare to fail. Too often, leaders explain why they decided to change by talking about the organization chart before bringing people toward the vision and purpose. Don't be like them.

- Create shared purpose. Forget the different departments and functions. Be very clear about what you will achieve together across the whole body of the organization and make sure the parts are functioning together in harmony. Once you are clear, then and only then, figure out the people, technology, and process you need to enable that purpose through a connected network with trusted internal and external communities. What's your shared purpose? What will make people jump out of bed every morning excited about achieving it? How do you tap into the hearts and minds of your killer app for the 21st century: people?

Those organizations *just beginning* are further along than an organization in a similar stage five years ago. With greater than 85 percent of the adult population in North America and Europe using social networking websites, organizations are filled with people who at least understand the value of connecting to learn. Your challenge is to consider how your organizational needs can be addressed in a social way and bridge the gap between capabilities and working solutions.

Organizations we've worked with that are *on a roll* are the most likely to be using social media with parts of their workforce, yet may not have taken the step to focus their attention on learning. Oftentimes, someone has initiated a program to get people talking without actively considering how, with just a little additional effort, they could be identifying what people know and need from one another to make better decisions and go further together. You're in an ideal position to make that leap.

If you've *arrived*, we invite you to visit the conversation online with others reading this book to talk about what you're learning and telling us about the amazing journey you've been on.

Susan Scrupski, founder of Big Mountain Data, who launched both The 2.0 Adoption Council and Change Agents Worldwide, points out that social software has been used widely in enterprise organizations for nearly a decade. She says, "It's like a generation has gone through high school and graduated. This isn't something new anymore. We know what works and what doesn't."

With that experience, she says, "The biggest lesson learned is about dealing with the uncertainty that comes from choice. When people have so many choices of where to impart their coveted experience and their precious time, it's hard not to get distracted from delivering on the organization's goals.

"You need to create a careful, delicate balance of group interest and self-interest, or the invisible force that holds the network together falters, destabilizes. That invisible force, that magnetism, is trust. It's up to leaders to discover and foster individuals' real motivations and work with them on how those can align and support the organization. People are messy, and they can't be programmed like robots to support company goals that don't align with their innate human aspirations."[6]

The following sections outline the work required to begin the journey. Many steps will happen simultaneously, but none can be skipped. They can also all be used again and again to help move your current efforts further along.

Get Clear About Your Challenges

If you don't know where you're going, any road will take you there. We've all heard this cliché and know its inherent problems, yet we launch into projects before we clearly look at why we're setting out in this direction. What's the pressing business problem, as Edgar Schein asks, we must address to go on?

For OPENPediatrics, the problem was that clinicians didn't have a way to connect across vast distances. At the CIA, the problem was that people needed to share intelligence at the speed of change. In chapters ahead, you'll learn more about the problems people have to solve in getting help quickly from peers, how to build a talent pipeline, or understand what leadership looks like. You'll see how a workforce can learn how to surface innovations and how a global youth movement can create an atmosphere where fresh ideas thrive. At just about every organization we've learned from, the overarching theme has been to create a great place for outstanding people to work in smarter ways.

If you're struggling to figure out which are your most pressing problems, ask yourself and other senior leaders what causes the most heartache or requires the most time and energy to accomplish. What spurs on griping or rework and constantly seems to create new problems? What situations are costing you money, people, and time?

Content curation is an art, not a science. The most useful tool is you.
—Jonathan Henley

Once you list the problems you need to address, pair them with your desired outcome by describing the strategic benefits you expect your company to achieve using social tools.

Trisha Liu, former community manager at Google and HP says, "I learned to always ask, 'Have you sorted through the noise to discover what's really important? Can you state your goals?' If yes, your job will be easier. If not, how can you expect to make good design or program decisions?

"There are two types of goals: organization goals and participant goals. Why is the organization investing time and energy launching, supporting, maintaining, and working in social ways? What does the business hope to get in return? Then, what are people hoping to accomplish by building community and coming together?

63

COMMON GOALS, COMMON RESULTS

Here are a few common results articulated by other social learners:

- Finding solutions to customer problems often takes days, not hours or minutes. This creates low-satisfaction ratings and loses us business. By aggregating, then curating insights and great practices directly from people on the front lines, we will respond more rapidly to customer and competitor developments. We will also decrease call-center response time by accelerating the rate at which agents can find the answers to repeated questions.

- With a shortage of people in key leadership positions, there aren't enough hours in the day to look after management issues, work strategically, and get through email. By reducing email volume and giving leaders a way to "manage by virtually walking around" the halls of their teams, we will increase productivity and the time people have to focus on the most important tasks.

- Our top accounts and project teams have to fend for themselves during our peak seasons, creating frustration, lags in project progress, and almost no new sales. By creating an online community across the ecosystem, key clients, account reps, and project teams will have a space where they can share ideas and ask questions at any time. Interacting seamlessly with our top accounts will keep our eyes open to new opportunities and likely raise far more questions than we ever could using the traditional means.

"When you know the participant's goals, you can design the experience, calls to action, and product features to support these goals. People will feel like they are in the right place to do what they set out to do.

"Organizational and participant goals can overlap, even if they don't look the same on the surface. A corporate goal might be to reduce the number of support tickets in customer support. A participant goal might be to find an answer or solve a problem. The member may not care about ticket deflection, but finding an answer meets both the participant and organizational goal."[7]

Just looking at the obvious problems isn't enough, though. Ask yourself and those articulating the problems if the assumptions are correct. Spend a little time gathering real evidence to refute or prove some of the assumptions before you make plans based on what they are. For instance, is the real reason you're losing young employees because you don't have modern tools to help them get their work done or, upon talking with 20 employees, do you discover your tools are fine, but your cafeteria food is unhealthy and you expect everyone to put in 70-hour workweeks?

Once you're clear on the problem you're trying to solve (and you've cleared out the noise), it's time to consider how and why people will want to join you on this journey and how you will align with their goals.

Determine What's in It for People

The French pharmaceutical company Sanofi Pasteur named its social initiative Project M. With a focus on what's in it for the employee, M stands for "me" or "moi." They realized, while their approach provides approximately 600 people across three countries a learning-lab experience with an experimental feel, it was important to encourage employees to think about themselves.

Although some people at Sanofi may think they'll work at the company for the rest of their careers, fresh perspective comes from looking to the big and open future. Project M provides such a perspective by including an online community called M-Connect, global brainstorming meetings, mentoring, and numerous opportunities for people to connect differently. Through serendipitous interactions and conversations, new ideas are born and take hold.

With artificial intelligence and the likes of IBM Watson on the horizon, there is the very real possibility global competitors will soon have the ability to automate routine tasks and look across vast signals to identify emergent patterns and trends. Those who do will have a significant advantage when it comes to innovation and creativity.

There will be a need for people with higher-order skills. Individuals can choose to go with the flow or they can realize they need to learn new ways of working, with people in different cultures. This will encourage people to make an investment in themselves.

"Have you sorted through the noise to discover what's really important? Can you state your goals?"

—Trisha Liu

One of the nonnegotiable boundaries that Dany DeGrave, senior director of strategic alignment, expertise, and innovation at Sanofi, and one of the creators of Project M, was given at the outset was that Project M could never be the reason for missing key company milestones or experiencing any delay in deliverables. (They were also not given either funding or head count, which he considers a great advantage because it also means no one can take those away.)

These resource constraints focused DeGrave and his team on fostering an atmosphere of cooperation and collaboration. They found a way to update and redecorate their workplace; for example, with people motivated to put in extra effort, finding discretionary time amid other priorities. DeGrave says, "We want people to have an influence on our environment, which makes them feel good, perform well, and the company will be better off for it."

Project M removes barriers that people had previously experienced in their work. For example, if something goes wrong, that's seen as an opportunity to learn, reflect, and share what you and others can do differently next time or in similar situations.

DeGrave, who also has vaccine-related responsibilities, adds, "We want to avoid the typical situation where people are asked to contribute ideas on how to work differently into an idea box, and then never hear about it again. If someone wants to set up a new initiative or test a new approach, if they can find several people who think it is a good idea they have permission to test it out. It's a 'Go,' provided that it is a new way of working, inspiring engagement or unleashes our talents."

Project M's primary purpose is "personal learning and engagement—and each of our roles in all of this," adds DeGrave. "When you go to a party, the host can create a vibrant atmosphere, but if you stand in the corner, you won't really experience the environment." Sanofi provides the environment and opens the door to something different, though it's up to each person to engage and benefit.

If you're going to start a transformation process, the first question to answer is what you want to become.
—Dave Gray

Sanofi uses what Kevin Prentiss, a speaker and executive advisor on engagement, calls the "Dance Floor Theory." Prentiss knows that people who are the most engaged aggregate towards the center of the dance floor, close together, where they radiate the most energy. In contrast, people on the edge stand apart from one another, arms crossed. They don't participate at the same level, nor emit the same energy.

When people who opt in to work on Project M share with their co-workers news of what they're learning and how they're working in new ways, they are inviting others on to the dance floor by example. Through self-interest in working in new ways, they're enhancing group interest, too.

With both the interests of the organization, and those of the people without whom it would not exist in mind, you can now create your roadmap. You wouldn't dream of building a house without a blueprint to guide its construction or going on a trip without a map to help you find your way. As well, nowadays most of us wouldn't consider working on the house or going on that road trip alone.

Embarking on the journey requires you to plan to head in the right direction. While you can't account for every contingency, or document every step, if you do your planning with others, spend some time gathering requirements, and talk through what you're trying to accomplish together, you can also begin to envision how to get closer to your destination.

Look at the Tools You Already Have

Assess if you have tools in-house that you can use or if you'll need to get new (or additional) ones. Are you starting from scratch or do you have some tools that can serve your purposes? Do you have a learning management system that really doesn't support social learning among people or a social network not explicitly for learning—but surely could be used for that purpose, too? Think about how you can leverage what you already have in place and how people familiar with those tools could pitch in.

Also look for technology where, once employees touch it, they understand it because they are familiar with the Internet; because they have used Facebook or Twitter; or because they have already made a personal investment in the learning curve and can immediately begin to use the tools, greatly speeding up adoption.

Rally People for What's Ahead

Just as looking at the technology you already have is key to gathering requirements, so is considering the people who already have a stake in working in social ways. They have a stake in your success. People are more apt to participate in something they've taken an active role in supporting.

One organization created a petition that was posted widely on the intranet and in the halls. It said, "We are in the early stages of creating a social network with blogs, group forums, and status updates for our employees. What will you write about?" Within one week they had hundreds of responses, demonstrating to their senior leaders there was groundswell support for the program and also giving their workforce something to look forward to participating in.

BUILDING AN EMPLOYEE PLATFORM

Better knowledge sharing initially drove the decision to revamp Cigna's employee collaboration platform. Karen Kocher, Cigna's chief learning officer, said the company originally had two separate self-service intranets in use; but in use was somewhat of a stretch. Out of nearly 50,000 content pages, fewer than 500 had been used by more than 100 people.

The company aimed to replace the intranets with a single system and change their model of participation from passive self-service to active collaboration. But many of Cigna's 40,000 employees weren't ready to dive in when Cigna rolled out the platform. "People don't instantly understand the value. We think because they use Facebook, employees will naturally become collaborators in the workforce. It doesn't happen," Kocher says. "It's so different from anything we've ever expected of people or enabled them to do that they just don't naturally do it." For that reason, Kocher encourages leaders to set reasonable adoption goals and avoid judging the initiative's success by initial participation.

Another hurdle to adoption was that employees at first found the platform too open, because blogs could only be published on a company-wide scale. "Employees were uncomfortable posting to everybody, but initially we didn't have a way of doing it on a smaller scale," says Kocher. Cigna finally modified the technology and created smaller collaboration communities that allowed employees to post items only to specific groups.

Even though all employees retain the ability to post whatever they want to the entire company, Kocher says Cigna doesn't mandate significant oversight. During the planning stage, Kocher sought advice from other large global companies who had deployed similar systems, and found that several launched successfully with little governance or control. Despite hands-off approaches, none of those Kocher spoke with reported any epidemics of inappropriate use—only a few isolated incidents.

BUILDING AN EMPLOYEE PLATFORM (CONTINUED)

Another tip she picked up from talking with peers was to prohibit anonymous posting. Employee names are pulled from the company's enterprise resource planning (ERP) system when they log on to My Cigna Life, thereby ensuring all comments are attached to names.

Although Kocher "isn't ready to ring the success bell," she cites a few important benefits. For instance, the time spent vetting learning content has fallen drastically thanks to ratings. People show one another which content they find valuable. "Do you have any idea how many people I used to have to consult with to determine if content was accurate, current, and interesting? Now we do a basic screen and make sure it meets the objectives and put it out there," she says. "Very quickly the community distills down program options into the one that's best, and they give you details as to why."

Kocher says she also learned the importance of not neglecting the search function, as content will only be used if people can find it quickly and easily.

The system has also enabled collaborative problem solving. "An employee in a very remote office needed to find a piece of information because she had a customer meeting that afternoon. She posted a status update, and 37 seconds later the response came . . . and the person who sent it was someone she'd never met," Kocher says.

Today the company is working on beefing up waning executive sponsorship and identifying change agents through network analysis. Overall, Kocher knows working together across the organization means people are learning together—and that's healthy for everyone.

Reach Out to Your Partners and Stakeholders

So much of what needs to be done is in creating the right environment. Not the technical environment, although it's important as well, but the overall environment. This includes culture, communication, traditions, policy, procedure, processes, incentives, and much more—an environment where people partner and look to one another.

THE MOTLEY FOOL'S JINGLE

Although financial services and media company The Motley Fool scored consistently high overall on the biannual Gallup employee engagement survey, there was one area in which they needed improvement: communication.

To address the problem, their chief people officer, Lee Burbage, decided to roll out a new collaboration platform to the company's 300 employees to replace the segmented system it had—an intranet built in 2001, plus assorted applications used by various departments. They named it Jingle for the sound of the bells on the hat worn by the court jester in the company's logo. It has now been in use for two years.

Burbage listed five steps in the deployment process that, though largely tactical in nature, served their limited deployment quite well:

- Shut down the existing systems.

- Preload content into Jingle.

- Orchestrate content for the first 60 days after launch.

- Guide individuals on how and when to use it.

- Provide continuing education.

In addition to choosing to place enticing, can't-miss content exclusively on Jingle early on—such as invites to an office pizza lunch—Burbage also said he intentionally launched the system at bonus time and forced employees to use Jingle to find bonus information. These measures served to drive adoption.

Landing pages are personalized for employees with news, frequently used items, and group updates. Employees also have the ability to construct a personal page that displays their self-defined purpose and objectives. But the biggest win is the increased communication efficiency from the reduction of email.

"With email, I'm just pushing it out. But everyone has different levels of tolerance about what you want to get with email. There are people in the office that really don't want to know that the printer is down in the south corner," he said. "With this tool, we're able to have you choose what you want to get signaled for. It's an opt-in process."

THE MOTLEY FOOL'S JINGLE (CONTINUED)

Burbage said managers are actually able to send more communications through the collaboration platform, because they no longer worry about items getting lost in an email deluge and employees have the ability to define their own bandwidths. Videos of executives explaining company issues or ideas help inform the workforce of important happenings in near real time.

"We are fast and loose—governance by community," Burbage says. "If you post or do something that's inappropriate, you'll hear about it from the people around you before HR."

And although he analyzes activity through built-in reports and Google Analytics, Burbage has a clear anecdotal measure of success. "The day I knew we were winning is when I heard the word Jingle used as a verb."

People are like water—in a tight spot they will always find the path of least resistance. But if you intentionally create a path for the water, it will flow naturally.

Rather than viewing people as a necessary part of the organization, see them as the organization itself. External partners and internal stakeholders are fundamental to your success.

Many organizations we've worked with find that a steering committee proves very helpful early in their journey. Representatives from different parts of the organization, each with a different sort of stake in the initiative's success, can help you work through the challenges. Someone from a line division may not immediately grasp how this will affect their interests, but soon they'll see connections to their goals and be able to align with your desire to address the problems you've laid out.

There is no magic formula for how many people, or what departments, or what levels must be involved. Be open to exploring the right mix for your organization and be open to changing that mix frequently until it works. A team of diverse and committed people can serve the interests of not only the individuals who use it, but also the organization as a whole.

Some organizations invite their gatekeepers in right away. Others develop a full plan and then share it with those most likely to want to halt your progress so they can't stump you with questions for which you haven't yet considered the options. For

Don't fear the unexpected, embrace it, and use it as your muse.
—Zachary Oxman

some organizations those gatekeepers are the legal or compliance teams. For others it's human resources or procurement, and for many it's IT.

Although both early and late approaches can work, we've seen one approach that's especially effective. That's to invite key people on board at the outset, not inviting them to your introductory steering committee meeting, but as soon after that as possible—once you feel comfortable in the capabilities your approach will provide.

Simon Terry, former CEO of HICAPS, a healthcare-focused division of National Australian Bank (NAB), recalls almost immediately going to meet with the general manager of the bank's tech security team. He had to make sure that any cloud-based collaborative software he wanted to use would be on the company's whitelist. If it were put onto the blacklist, it would in effect be unreachable by people in the organization. He asked what would be the biggest issue the tech security team would have. They said publishing identifiable customer information. If there's customer information going across the network and out of the network to the cloud, there will be a problem. Terry knew that had to be priority #1. No customer information could be within the online community.

Then he asked the GM, "What are you trying to achieve?" He needed everyone in the organization to understand the company's Internet usage policy and how to prevent phishing, practices that applied to everyone at NAB. "What if we explain to everyone joining the social network that they need to first read through the Internet usage policy and that there would be forums to talk about ways for people to ensure they were both abiding by the policies and coming up with even better ways to work?" The security team thought this was a great idea, knowing that it would put something important (and previously unattainable) to work, and improve tech security across the company. Before a technology was rolled out, the tech security team tested the system and reported it proved better than their penetration testing. What could have been an ongoing struggle, created a team of allies who were respected throughout the organization.

Terry's team did this again and again, each time with different groups, refining their arguments and their strategic goals, showing what collaboration could help with, and drawing new groups in. They chose to talk with their lawyers last, and found little argument. The legal team could see the benefits of a thriving community and wanted to create one for themselves, too.

Identify Quick-Win Opportunities

Every organization has people who are more likely to benefit quickly than others. That's where you should begin. Identify what developers call "use cases"—the ways and means people will use these new approaches to clearly articulate who and how. Some use cases could be specific to individual groups (for example, project team collaboration), while others should be company wide (for example, cross-silo discussions).

Their purpose is to catalyze rapid, even if low-impact, results. Of course, if you can identify a use case where success would change something in the organization dramatically, these instance would be a powerful signal you're moving in the right direction and others would want to join in. Just be careful your reach doesn't exceed your grasp. A spectacular failure would be as memorable as a wild success.

CREATE AN ADVISORY GROUP

While at EMC, Jamie Pappas created the Social Media Advisory Council to bring together the people responsible for setting and executing the social media strategy for their organization or geographical areas. The council comprised a cross-functional, cross-geographical team of people who met virtually on a monthly basis to collaborate on the company's social programs and initiatives, exchange ideas and best practices, solve challenges, and work together to increase awareness of social media in the organization. Now that she's at Akamai Technologies, a similar model is in place with a governance team of key stakeholders and executives who have a vested interest in seeing their community succeed. They are committed not only to help lead adoption, but also to remove roadblocks that may arise and brainstorm the best ways to approach each phase of the launch.

"Embarking on a community initiative is not easy and requires patience and hard work to succeed—but it's a worthy pursuit," says Pappas. "Clearly define your goals and take a keen interest in the individual business needs of your audiences and tailor your message according to their needs and top priorities. You must also commit to developing real partnerships with employees and stakeholders, leveraging the people who have a true passion for community and collaboration as your strongest advocates. If you do this, understanding that flexibility and change are must-have ingredients, you will find the support you need to continue to pave the road that will provide your organization with benefits you have only just begun to imagine."

Company-wide use cases deliver broad exposure within your company, while group-specific use cases can generate deep business value. Here are some we've found deliver the greatest, and quickest, value in organizations:

New Hire Onboarding

Provide new hires a small corner of your intranet full of pointers to information they need to help themselves get started. Not just paperwork to fill out from HR, but where the best places are to get lunch in the area, or what the best way is to let recruiting know you have a friend who would be a great fit, too. If you don't have a social network already in the organization, add to this space a way for other employees to contribute their favorite suggestions and to make the new people welcome with information they wish they had when they'd just started.

Research shows that in strong culture companies it usually takes three to five years for newcomers to become influential in networks and replicate the connectivity of successful people in that organization. This timeframe has been dramatically shortened by organizations that have developed processes to help newcomers more rapidly integrate and replicate the networks of high performers.[8]

Photo Collections

Does your marketing department spend big bucks on contracts with stock photo services? Sponsor a photo contest using a photo-sharing tool where employees can upload their personal photos that showcase the types of images you often need. Write up a simple sharing agreement, explaining you'll credit them for the photo, and launch with a company-wide contest for the best photos across the globe. Let your employees offer their best and ask them to help you determine which resonate most with people to gauge what prospective customers will also enjoy.

Employee Suggestion Box and Ideation Space

Launch a public conversation by asking, "What should be done to make this a great place to work?" Host this on an intranet site if you don't have a social network, or put it on a giant bulletin board in the cafeteria. Move it online as soon as you can, helping people get in the habit of both making suggestions and offering help to address the request themselves alongside leaders also committed to the cause.

Tweet Through Class

Encourage participants in training courses to tweet with one another, to the instructor, and to the larger world across Twitter to ask big questions, seek more updated information, and garner stories of how various approaches have

Remember: social technology is not just to promote but mainly to connect. Be personal.
—Benjamin McCall

worked in other organizations. Begin with a hashtag and a list of everyone's Twitter ID in the class, give a quick introduction to TweetChats, and start at the first class break. You'll get immediate interest from people realizing this isn't learning as usual, and you'll get the larger insights from people everywhere.

You might be surprised by what takes off and what doesn't, so approach this in a spirit of experimentation and discovery, allowing it to happen dynamically and by asking yourself if there are insights that can be applied to other projects along the way.

Initiate, Seed, and Spur on Activity

Eventually it will be time to get your social tools up and running. You'll likely accomplish this through a combination of the vendor you're purchasing tools from and your IT department, who will also shoulder responsibility for ensuring these tools integrate with your current systems and can be kept up and running.

Once this has been done, your first order of business will be to figure out how to turn the social implementation into a social *learning* implementation. Here are some suggestions we believe will help ensure your success.

TRIED-AND-TRUE PRACTICES

If you're taking on the responsibility of launching a social effort from scratch in your organization, there are some tried-and-true practices you should consider, too.

1. Get to know the big providers and the new entrants by doing some online research.

2. Ask people in roles similar to yours in other organizations what they've used and what they'd use if they could start from scratch.

3. Seek out lists of vendors in the space you're looking for, being careful to realize that new solutions appear weekly that might challenge the market positions of the most established players.

4. Sign up for a week of demos. Compare what you like and don't like, ask others you work with for their takes, too. Don't ignore concerns you might have overlooked before like "clunky interfaces" and "limited functionality." There are well-designed, easy-to-use solutions coming to market every day.

Inventory the tools already used inside your organization. Does a team in customer service use Yammer and Lync, Huddle, or even a Google group? Talk to someone using these systems and ask what they wish it could do that it doesn't do already. Would they be interested in making it company wide? What are people learning there? What more could they learn or share if changes were made?

Ask people what they use to get their work done that's not sanctioned (or at least provided) by the organization. Are there Facebook or LinkedIn groups being used between departments? Did you find someone else in your company looking for similar data through your personal Twitter accounts? And what about the learning as a result of this? Consider "seeding" content from leaders and others who are interesting to the organization. Also, look beyond content knowledge. What decisions can be made faster? Which people are rising to the occasion by introducing new practices?

To benefit from the open and real-time nature of social tools, embed tutorials and tips directly into your social space. Establish "rules of engagement" and highlight examples of how people use the space to align with your organization's goals.

Social learning is the team sport of informal learning.
—Kelly Garber

Akamai has created a robust set of tutorials, best-practice guides, and 101 introductory modules that serve as a starting point to help employees feel comfortable with engaging. They've also included social media awareness and smart practices in their new-hire training so employees are aware of the guidance from the outset.

One of the first reactions of many people is to ask, "What's in here?" You can answer that question simply and effectively by building a lobby area for your social space. This public entryway can serve as a place to share openly by default and a "one-stop shop" where new entrants can branch off into other, more specialized areas. If you were in a college or a student union or a community center, this would be the area you start out in, without the disoriented feeling you'd have if you went in directly to the break room or swimming pool. The lobby should be accessible to everyone in your organization and should host most, if not all, of the following elements:

- Announcements

- What's new

- Knowledgebase

- Discussion forum

- Q&A and FAQs

- Rules of engagement

- Group/team lists

- How-tos

- New-hire onboarding

- Standard collateral

- Links to other workspaces you've built or plan to build

- Links to where to get help.

Populate these sections with content people will appreciate finding. This should be content colleagues already have, in the form of existing emails, documents, or personal knowledge easily available—which aren't circulating already and that people will see value in right away. Spend time also seeding conversations on topics that will attract more people. You're aiming to get people saying to one another things like, "Ooh, did you see that conversation in the online community? I hope you'll contribute what you told me about last week." Create conversations around the topics everyone is talking about right now as well as a few specialty areas that will remind others there's value in addressing both the broad and the deep.

Here are a few fun and novel ways to bring newcomers in and encourage them to engage:

Dangle an Information Carrot

At an electronics company in Asia, the social learning leader stopped writing full emails. Instead, he began with headlines like, "Report Now Available on Social Progress." In the body of his email he'd write, "We're thrilled to report we've made huge strides with our social platform. Within the month of October, we had a 15 percent increase . . . ." And then include a link in the email to where he'd written the rest of the post online. Everyone wanted to see the results and clicked on the link, finding themselves in an online community where, after they read his post, they saw other valuable content they wanted to read, too. Within a few minutes, they understood why the space was growing quickly, and they wanted to be a part of it.

Develop Treasure Hunts

When a media giant's board welcomed a half-dozen new directors, the personnel chairman created a treasure hunt to help acquaint them with the organization, fellow board members, and the local area. Three teams of four received hastily drawn learning-treasure maps before a self-guided tour of

Social is a marathon: go slow to be fast, run your own race, be willing to redefine success.
—Gina Minks

the corporate campus, a local shopping area, and a park. As they came across each clue identifying a person, place or thing, they used tablets, cell phones, texts, and cameras to capture what they found. Two teams even collaborated to find a missing clue. By the end of the day, they felt more connected and knowledgeable than with their participation on any other board. Why not try the same approach with new hires or business partners in town for a long meeting?

Turn Out-of-Office Messages Into FAQs

Chris Crummey, worldwide executive director of engagement and evangelism for social business at IBM, uses the out-of-office message in his email system as an opportunity to redirect the attention of people contacting him. The message says, in effect:

I'm out of the office and you've probably asked me this question before. Rather than wait until I'm back at my desk, consider doing the following:

1. Look through old emails to see how I answered the question last time.

2. Go to my online profile to see a list of frequently asked questions with links, including presentations and articles on how I've answered these questions in the past. [He includes a link to his profile.]

3. Search on my name in the company social network to find hundreds, perhaps thousands, of links to every topic I've ever worked on, with supporting information on how you can take action on your own.

4. Post the question on my wall so that others in my network can answer it for you while I'm away.

5. Ask your network if they have additional ways to solve your problem, discovering your network's breadth and depth.

I'll be back next week.[9]

Provide Ways for Lurkers to Contribute

Not everyone feels comfortable commenting online at first—and some will never be ready. The silent majority who rarely make the time to post can still gain tremendous value from the breadth of the organization they can glimpse online. They can learn from those who are participating more actively. In communities with tools that automatically recommend content based on what others read, lurkers become contributors without even having to chime in.

To engage people who wouldn't naturally share publicly, have at least one group that doesn't require public action in order for someone to get value from it. For example, while serving as Tyco's community manager Phoebe Venkat started a public corporate news group. The majority of people who joined the group simply read the articles. They didn't have to "like" or reply to feel part of something important. She found that the lurkers sometimes became active participants, but she realized it was more helpful for them to promote their experience to others who may have been wary like them. She says, "Keep in mind that lurkers may be getting a lot of value out of their experience, too."

Listen Intently

You will not convince anyone to join you in this social adventure by ignoring or dismissing critics. By listening, you may find opportunities for improvements, further exploration, or even education on misinformation or lack of knowledge or understanding. If you can anticipate and think of a response to some of the objections ahead of time, you may be able to keep the conversation on point, and it will help you to illustrate the benefits for that group with meaningful examples and case studies.

Many organizations now even create groups expressly for critics. Rather than people complaining just anywhere, they can huddle up. Just be sure to have a few people check in periodically to calm the flames before they get too high, by answering questions, diplomatically taking matters offline, or alerting the right people to make fixes when the situation warrants it.

Social media isn't enforcing old ways, rather enabling new ways.
—Jane Hart

In a similar way, one of the most effective techniques we've seen for culture change is to create a group all about rumors: From "Is there a merger on the horizon?" to whispers that headquarters may move to another state, this is the place for people to talk about what they've heard. What's unique with this approach is that it's more than water- cooler gossip. Organizations who use this approach make a commitment to answer all speculation with honest information. Rather than people wasting time wondering, they know there is one central place to learn what's really happening. Anecdotally, we've also seen that people who had no interest in joining the conversation online are drawn to a place full of rumors. Once they're there, they often find out that the online space provides value they'd never before considered.

Encourage Champions

Ready to start reaching out to other departments and groups? Take time to identify local champions and ambassadors who can share their enthusiasm in hands-on ways that motivate others to join in. Focus on those who are already on board. They'll want to help you. They will look forward to helping their group. They just may not know how. Sit with them or connect online to explain what they can do.

Some people will naturally become advocates of social initiatives in your organization. Welcome these people and make it easy for them to share their knowledge, experiences, and expertise with others.

> "Keep in mind that lurkers may be getting
> a lot of value out of their experience, too."
> —Phoebe Venkat

The online community at EMC, EMC|ONE, launched with a voluntary mentor program that encouraged people to add their names to a list of people whom anyone could contact for assistance, advice, or brainstorming. Champions emerged from all parts of the organization, with the diversity of experience to share what worked and what didn't in different parts of the company as well as with customers, partners, and the larger ecosystem the organization serves.

When you introduce social tools into your organization, you are not simply introducing a new piece of technology; you are also ushering in a new way of working. That's going to require some internal evangelizing, and you're going to need some help from colleagues who are the first ones to get it. These are your early adopters, and they will play a crucial role in the success of your effort.

It may take some looking to find those early adopters. Either publicly or privately, you will need to recruit them. To do that, you'll need to show off the technology. Even more importantly, you'll need to provide answers to the following questions:

- Why are we bringing this technology in?

- How will we use it?

- Why is it better than what we're doing now?

- What value will it deliver, and how will we realize it?

These are fundamental questions we recommend you address at in-person interactions with your colleagues, rather than relying exclusively on emails, posters, or other mass-marketing techniques. Ideally, these interactions are done face-to-face, but live screen sharing presentations may be more pragmatic for distributed groups.

I'm working on continuously improving my social ground game, learning out loud.
—Aaron Silvers

Time is tight, and you will need to focus your initial efforts on groups that have the greatest likelihood of embracing social learning. So where should you start? The strongest early adopter candidates are groups with the following characteristics:

- There's at least one energetic and enthusiastic local champion inside the group who will encourage participation.

- Group members who are frustrated due to their inability to access updated information from their colleagues.

- They're geographically distributed because they're in global teams or distributed divisions.

- They're technology friendly and likely comfortable with the changes new systems can go through before they get established. This could be IT or media departments, for instance.

- They're innovation oriented, for instance, innovation centers or new product developers.

- They're engaged in project based work like R&D teams.

- They're new to the organization, so they don't have established routines of how things are done.

Of all these characteristics, the strength of a local champion should be your top priority. As a core implementer—especially within a large organization—you cannot be everywhere at once. Time and again, we have seen how an enthusiastic and energetic individual can make an enormous difference. These local champions can come from any role, junior or senior. They need not have technology expertise, but it is very important they have personal credibility and daily engagement within the group they champion. They must also be willing to spend real time—up to 15 to 25 percent of their time for two to three months—to help you get their groups focused and learning.

Differentiate Benefits

You can't sell the same value proposition to every group. What works for telemarketing is not likely to work for programming. Take time to understand the group you're talking to and adapt the message, making it relevant to them. Don't just say social learning is great. Tell people how it benefits them, how it can broaden their unique networks and enable them to do new things. Tailoring your message to your audience is at the heart of enabling them to see value in the new tools and the new ways of working being proposed.

Keep in mind the benefits you will see are not confined to those directly affecting business processes. There are many benefits available to those who participate that are more subtle, yet no less important to the long-term success of your organization.

As you move away from the push of information to the pull of learning, you will liberate creative powers in people, helping them to succeed in a fast-changing environment. Making it easy for them to inquire and announce activities and projects, both professional and personal, creates an environment where people are not afraid to fail, emboldening them to ask the really hard questions. You also begin to get answers you never would have found otherwise.

Research is quite clear about this: The more engaged people are, the more effectively they learn.[10] In other words, the more questions they ask, the more they care and believe what they have to say matters, and the stronger their learning process becomes. Social learning is about making it easier for people to find both their questions and their voice.

Take, for example, Ben Brooks, a young man in an old profession. He worked for a large global insurance company—a company that insures other businesses that face complex risks around the world like cyber-security threats or political instability in emerging markets.

To help turn around the firm and grow its sales, he needed a way to interject modern practices and what he calls "sexy approaches" into a business that was flat-out risk averse.

Share is the new save.
—Jane Bozarth

When C-suite executives at the firm challenged him to train and educate the very experienced employee base, he jumped at the chance to up his game. The firm had amazing employees and provided white-glove service to their elite clients. Yet it had no way for employees to share or showcase their knowledge outside of their narrow product silos. And when it came to learning, the firm leaned on outside trainers to educate their deeply experienced employees, which didn't make much sense to Brooks.

He conceptualized an approach for staff to share knowledge across silos in an effort to increase share-of-wallet of clients. But before rolling out a way for people to work collaboratively across the organization, he needed buy-in from the company's legal team.

He began simply enough. He described to the lawyers an initiative that would bring social media tools to the company's workforce, for internal use, and would train them on how to use these tools effectively. He then asked for the lawyers' thoughts. They rattled off the risks involved and why they had apprehensions. They covered important points and conveyed thoroughly why they were unlikely to support his plan.

Brooks then broke out each of the risks they laid out, at an even more granular level, and showed them unrelated things that they were lumping together.

They said, "People will post inappropriate comments."

Brooks asked, "Is our view that colleagues are bad people? If that's so, shouldn't we be taking action now, to weed out the rotten apples if you think we have some? Or instead, should we assume great behavior from our colleagues?"

"People will make inaccurate comments."

Brooks asked, "Which is more dangerous, that they post something to their colleagues that's inaccurate or that they believe and repeat something that's wrong without them or us knowing? What are we doing now to ensure all the information in our organization that's shared is right? We reduce our risk by having greater visibility across our 400 offices in real time."

"Is our view that colleagues are bad people? Shouldn't we assume great behavior?"

—Ben Brooks

He went on, intentionally showing value and necessity. He asked, "If we want to expand our business, would it even be possible for just the marketing and communications department to share information? We need our thousands of sales people, who are the ones who actually speak to our customers and know our business, to be talking with one another."

Rather than come across as a freewheeling innovator, he showed them how in comparison to the way people were currently working that using social media would actually help de-risk the firm.

Brooks, now a business coach, points out that it's natural for people to compare new opportunities with previous experiences, as if they're looking into a rear-view mirror. By doing that, they can convince themselves they understand what's being introduced and how it fits into the lexicon they know. In some ways, it's a natural defense mechanism for feeling equipped, comfortable, and looking smart, even when we're in new terrain. "It's incredibly important to consider how you define things, and how you frame them so people can make the leaps with you rather than tattoo old thinking onto the organizational brain. That doesn't mean to create a whole new vocabulary, mumbo jumbo that makes you sound smart and those to whom you're appealing to feel dumb. Really think about what you're trying to get accomplished and put it into the vernacular people you're appealing to will understand."

REPUTATION, TRUST, and SOCIAL CAPITAL are becoming the true currency in the workplace.
—Tricia Ransom

There's more upside than anyone would recognize if you only look at the downside. In insurance terms, Brooks showed the risk/reward ratio. When they could look at the two in tandem, they could see both the potential downside and desired upside. This shifted the conversation from speculating on potential risks to a business-based analysis of total potential risk exposure in relation to the overall benefit of the change. When he compared the risks, most of which he had plans to mitigate, to the upside of revenue growth that would move the stock price, it was a no-brainer. He had differentiated his message.

Few people agree to new things they don't understand or see value in themselves. People you work with may already see benefit to working in a social way but don't know how to proceed. By explaining how working in a social way serves their interests, you might open the door to getting started.

A corporate study from the Society for New Communication Research, called the "Tribalization of Business," found that the greatest obstacles to making a community work were not about technology or getting funding, but about getting people involved in the community (51 percent), finding enough time to manage the community (45 percent), and attracting people to the community (34 percent).[11] Management was not cited as an obstacle. Just 9 percent of the respondents said that their management was unwilling to share with community members or support the initiative.

Lois Kelly, co-author of *Rebels at Work: A Handbook for Leading Change from Within*, managing partner at Foghound, and one of the Tribalization report researchers, pointed out that a common fear—losing control—"may not be as big an issue as [people] think. The bigger challenge is focusing the community around a purpose that people want to contribute to and be involved with—and devoting the right resources to promote and support the community."

Establish Guidelines and Road Rules

Phoebe Venkat, who was at Tyco and is now director of community engagement at salesforce.com, says in her experience the best policies are like "bumpers, guiding, helping, connecting, leading, driving, but not dictating. They establish the rules of the road."

"At first I wrote our social media policy," says Simon Terry. "Then the champions in our community told me I'd missed the mark. They used a wiki to write up a policy that was focused more on what people could do and less on what people couldn't do."

They helped Terry realize that he could mandate a tighter policy or enable a daily conversation about how to make good decisions. At times there were raging discussions about how stuff in their business works; at other times there were lingering and provocative exchanges about helping one another ensure confidentiality and how their actions provided greater support to their clients.

Because people in the community created the guidelines themselves, they talked to people joining the social network about them, using them as educational materials, rather than the fine print that could get them in trouble. When topics came up that either hadn't been addressed in the guidelines or where people could see there was a better way to work, they'd work together online to revise the guidelines, applying what Terry describes as, "fitness to purpose." Overall, they tried to maintain policies that recognized that social collaboration was nothing special, it was just another way people worked in the organization. Normal policy and behaviors should apply.

Organizations often start with a long, heavy-handed policy restricting the use of social media, then put in place simple rules stating when people should use which tool to communicate, create, or share specific types of information. It's important to make it easy for people to understand which data and content are appropriate for what use without being so prescriptive as to inhibit creativity. Then, when people can see what others share, they will self-monitor and begin to see how to thoughtfully monitor one another.

Clark Quinn, author of *Revolutionize Learning & Development: Performance and Innovation Strategy for the Information Age* and an engaged learning consultant, captures the essence of good guidelines this way, "The best social media policies are only slightly less terse and irreverent than 'don't be an idiot.'"[12] Well said.

We've included examples of several very good governance policies in the Appendix for your reference.

Serve as a Positive, Visible Example

The best way to help is by modeling the behavior you want to instill across the company—in other words, by using social tools themselves. When the organization sees its leadership "walking the walk" and not merely "talking the talk," it sends a powerful message that the new process is real. If you want a culture that takes more (calculated) risks, you can't convince people that it's OK. You must show them.

Trisha Liu believes in the Golden Rule of Community Design: Do unto participants as you would do unto yourself—and work toward ensuring senior leaders are doing it, too. Any action that you want people to take, like filling out their profile or posting a question, ask yourself, "Would I do this? Would the CEO? If not, why not? If yes, why? Write down all your answers. These become your training materials and objection handling guides."

SAMPLE CODE OF ETHICS

The following is an example of a short-form code of ethics for use in your online community. This example reflects one company's personality so it should be adjusted to reflect your company's culture.

- We will write openly and honestly, on relevant topics about which we are knowledgeable and passionate.

- We will not embrace controversy simply to drive attention to our posts, nor will we shy away from it when it is called for.

- We will credit others and clearly indicate when we're quoting others' materials.

- We will not disparage our colleagues or competitors in any way.

- We will respect the privacy of employees, customers, business partners, and others we work with.

- We will disclose all affiliations in order to avoid any opportunity for misunderstandings as to our allegiances.

- We will quickly and forthrightly acknowledge and correct all errors.

- We will not take ourselves too seriously, or not seriously enough.

- We will work with one another to amend this code and our views as time and perspective changes.

Executive participation can be one of the most powerful drivers for adopting social approaches, when it's done in smart ways.

Laurie Ledford, chief human resources officer at Marsh & McLennan Companies, walked through the halls of her organization, taking candid photos of employees (with their permission) to populate their profiles and give the network a personal touch. Many of the employees didn't have a photo they really liked or didn't realize it was important, so they'd left the photo field blank. Ledford's enthusiasm and playful spirit as she snapped photos showed both her commitment to the organization's social network and her personal stake in helping to make it succeed.

HOW TO CREATE A PERSONAL PROFILE

If your organization already has an online community and you haven't done so already:

- Create a personal profile, complete with a picture of yourself, making sure you fill in every field available.

- Configure your personal information dashboard.

- Create a new page in the social workspace, and link to it, showing others the topics you care most about.

- Invite five colleagues in and offer to guide them.

- Start using updates to communicate with others.

While she knew adoption wouldn't grow through executive mandate, seeing her active participation in other people's success contributed to the culture she aimed to foster.[13]

Our experience is that when executive sponsors simply tell their organizations to use social software, adoption is short lived. We have even seen cases where heavy-handed, top-down directives hindered the success of grassroots adoption campaigns.

A community is like a shark. To live it must keep moving. If it stops moving it dies or becomes a group.
—Kelly Smith

What's most important is active participation from influence leaders. Sometimes those are executives, other times those are leaders because of their insights and enthusiasm, not by position.

Research shows that leaders can speed adoption of change by 20 to 25 percent by working through opinion leaders to facilitate uptake of initiatives such as formal restructurings, cultural change programs, deployment of technology, or adoption of new work practices. Network analytics help identify both critical change agents and points of resistance that can derail change invisibly.[14]

"It's incredibly important to consider how you define things, and how you frame them so people can make the leaps with you rather than tattoo old thinking onto the organizational brain."

—Ben Brooks

Typically, leadership values transparency and the ability to drill-down to understand what people are working on, as well as to see the underlying assumptions. When leaders occasionally monitor open collaboration and perhaps bring attention to valuable contributions of others, contribution tends to increase across the board.

When you see you're getting traction across the organization, that's the right time to recruit other executives who will do their work in social tools and further build momentum to the larger initiative. Here are some of the most effective things an executive sponsor can do:

- Use social tools to replace the monthly status cycle by encouraging everyone to use them to report on their activities and then regularly monitoring their progress.

- Use status updates to tell the company what you're doing and to seek input from everyone who might have something valuable to say. This can prove especially powerful when issues that will affect everyone need to be understood and weighed.

- Provide opportunities to answer questions posed by anyone within the organization.

- Post critical information, such as meeting agendas, in a shared workspace, instead of emailing them, and encourage the use of shared calendars.

- Blog internally on the social platform.

- Start a shared workspace for the executive team so the full leadership team has an opportunity to directly realize the value of your implementation.

- Post group- or company-wide announcements in the social space.

- Comment on workspace pages with observations and follow-up questions.

You may need to invest extra time with executives to mentor them personally. By modeling the behavior expected of everyone in the organization, they can rapidly accelerate your organization's rate of adoption.

Measure Things That Matter

You've built it. Are people showing up? Are people learning from one another and affecting the problems you set out to overcome when you began? Monitoring use and practice delivers insights into how your organization is using social tools.

Social learning can't be enforced by leadership, but it does need leadership endorsement & participation.
—Kay Chappell Wood

With a little additional effort, it can also help you understand if it's being used for learning, too. Focusing on change will also help you gauge the impact you're having. Most importantly, it will enable you to build on your successes and identify initiatives that need your help.

Social networking or online community workspaces provide administrative capabilities to generate weekly and monthly usage reports. Look at these reports weekly and ask yourself a few diagnostic questions that will help focus your time on where it can make the greatest difference. As your implementation progresses, you will likely find interest in different metrics to gauge the health of your organization's use. Here are a few early indicators you should monitor.

> "The best social media policies are only slightly less terse and irreverent than 'don't be an idiot.'"
>
> —Clark Quinn

How Is Overall Adoption Going?

Overall adoption is the most basic high-level snapshot of impact. While there is no universal standard for healthy adoption, here are some useful benchmarks:

- If at least 25 percent of your organization visits monthly, you're starting to have significant impact.

- If at least 50 percent of your organization visits monthly, social tools are becoming an ingrained part of how you do business.

- If you're using your social implementation as an intranet or other content publishing platform, you should see a relatively low rate of contribution (for example, 5 to 10 percent of unique visitors are also contributors).

- If you're using it for project team collaboration or other interactive work, you should see a higher rate of contribution (for example, 25 to 75 percent of unique visitors are also contributors).

- You can expect a large percentage of people will log on to the system but will seldom participate. Rather, they will lurk. This isn't a bad thing. Lurkers read and learn; not everyone needs to be an active participant in order to receive value from the overall experience of your organization.

Keep in mind that these numbers may vary significantly by department, group, or use. Also remember that trends are as important, if not more important, than absolute numbers.

Are There Strong Pockets of Adoption?

You should leverage your strongest pockets of adoption to spread the value across your company. Reach out to your most active participants in heavily used workspaces. Ask them:

- How are you using these social tools?
- What business value are they generating for you?
- What have you done to integrate them into the daily flow of your group's work?
- Where else in the company can you see a valuable role for social tools?
- What are you learning?
- What else would you like to learn—and what would be helpful along the way?

In particular, when you collect anecdotes of generated value, share them publicly and refer to them as you enhance the business case of your social implementation. Encourage the people you talk with to share their stories, too. Showcasing success from more than one perspective strengthens your efforts and encourages others to join in.

Are There Places Where Adoption Is Low or Declining?

You can proactively help workspaces or groups that are struggling. Reach out to them to understand why adoption is low or declining. Specifically, ask them:

- Is there a clear and compelling business objective for your use of social tools?

- Have they invited in everyone required to make your use successful?

- Is the experience attractive and compelling?

- Do they use the social tools daily, posting meeting notes, to-do lists, documentation, FAQs, and pictures for others to see?

Trust People and Share, Share, Share

Although the use of social tools grows each day, we still often hear, "We limit what we offer to keep people from playing all day." Somehow it's assumed the software can cause misbehavior.

Rather than agreeing, turn the assumption around. Gently remind such doubters that if people are wasting time, there is a management and talent-vetting problem, not a social learning problem. Some people will always find ways to waste time.

Ben Brooks compares collaborative platforms to metal detectors. "In addition to helping you find the jerks more quickly, you can find the people who are hidden gems you didn't know before. The kind of emergent talent that's buried under layers of management or in smaller offices."

Social approaches to work also bring to light intangibles that haven't found a way to show up yet on the balance sheet. You "illuminate all sorts of assets your staff has that you didn't realize they had," says Brooks, "their connections, their experiences beyond their roles, their passions, and their willingness to take the firm to the next level. This is the organizational value you can't see in the two-dimensional structured data of an HRIS system."

Once learning is traversing around and across groups, encourage repeated participation and entice people who are more reluctant to step in. One of the most effective ways to do this is to route more and more of the organization's work through the social space. Remind everyone why this is being done and show them how it works.

Present at regular team meetings, first in one group, then in another, until you've moved across your organization. This enables each group to talk and brainstorm about the specific ways they will use social tools, and ask questions they may have. As you engage with each group, aim to:

- spur on excitement about the power of social software to improve the way the company runs and how each person learns.

- connect social learning with the larger objectives of each group and work with them to figure out additional ways they can replace their boring tasks with more modern (and fun) ways to work.

- identify several potential champions within each group who can energize further participation.

Once you have a few successful groups up and running, it's time to scale up your success to the rest of your organization. Here are some of the most effective ways to let the rest of the company know what you're up to:

> *Social isn't something you do;*
> *it's something you become.*
> —Mark Oehlert

- Expand your road show. Talk to more groups once you have had more practice and you can point to internal success stories.

- Harness your company's internal communications group. Use your corporate communications vehicles, like newsletters and internal video channels, to spotlight early adopters.

- Integrate social tools with other websites your company uses, and with social tools from your intranet, knowledge management system, document management system, and others. Cross-link, build custom dashboard widgets, or integrate curated lists wherever people can benefit from them.

- Present to senior leadership, who can help turbocharge your efforts. When you're really proud of what your early adopters have done, share it and ask for active participation from the highest levels in your organization. Executives also benefit from learning fast.

- Encourage those enjoying success to share it from their perspective. This works particularly well if they were reluctant in the beginning and are now advocates.

By going public with your early success, you will start expanding beyond early adopters to the rest of the organization. Then you can repeat the process with more and more groups. Each follow-up group will have your early adopters as a template and model for how to proceed.

> "If you post or do something that's inappropriate, you'll hear about it from the people around you before HR."
>
> —Lee Burbage

As implementation and use of your platform grows, and you begin analyzing change, you will want to start finding out how the people who are using the system interact with other organizations, including suppliers, customers, and your local community.

Much of what you learn may not be immediately useful. As time goes by you're going to want to reach out to your customers and suppliers, the former so you can respond to problems and issues quickly and in a transparent way, and the latter so you can improve on your supply chain and your ability to iterate your systems more effectively.

Most organizations also wish to be good corporate citizens and, as a consequence, they make efforts to be involved in community activities. Frequently, these activities are limited to merely holding fund-raising events and donating money to a local charity or helping organization. As your organization and people build experience and gain expertise in social learning, you may find you can provide local organizations with more than just money. You may be able to share some of your knowledge of collaboration to help them be better as well.

You are embarking on a journey that will be rewarding and (dare we say . . .) fun. You are opening up your organization to a whole new way of working. You are bringing your colleagues together in dynamic and exciting ways that will reduce drudgework, make your company more productive, and strengthen your colleagues' sense of community and connectedness. That's exciting.

The best ideas come from the many thousands of people around the world who use social tools every day. Once you're on your way, discuss the ideas, techniques, and resources in this book with your colleagues and please reach out to us and other people interested in these themes in our online community, where people post new ideas, questions, tips, practices, techniques, and more. Come join us at www.newsocialearning.com. We look forward to learning with you.

Transition and Engage

"People are held together by anecdotes, impressions, observations, and narratives, which map the shape and substance of their world. Then community becomes a diverse garden of connected stories; the more deeply people know the stories, the more deeply people know the community and themselves."

—Dan Pontefract, chief envisioner, TELUS

UP YOU CLIMB. Fixing the telephone line for a customer who has been without service for hours. He's called customer service twice. You've done this a hundred times, but this time the weather is worse than usual. A tree is precariously close to the pole. Something just doesn't feel right. It's not as though there's someone else who could get to this remote site whom you could ask how to proceed.

You walk back to your truck, get out your handheld device, point it toward the pole, and narrate the situation you're facing. Three minutes later you upload the digital footage to your company's in-house learning and collaboration system, and you ask for eyes. You're feeling a little better already, knowing you're not alone. If two minds are better than one, why not thousands?

Within 10 minutes, colleagues from across the country have commented. One points out a wiring issue you hadn't noticed. Another suggests a new technique she'd used that you hadn't heard about. The third reminds you of a similar sticky situation you'd been in and how your instincts helped you through.

Imaginative story or on-the-job learning? If you work for TELUS, the Vancouver, Canada–headquartered telecommunications company, this is more than science fiction.

Dan Pontefract, author of *Flat Army: Creating a Connected and Engaged Organization* and TELUS's chief envisioner, was hired to modernize their training function into a media-rich, collaborative, and customer-focused change engine. Rather than develop an expensive proprietary system, he worked with internal stakeholders to source multiple technologies that created a highly usable system—TELUS Habitat Social.

At its core, Habitat Social is a means for the 45,000 people employed by TELUS around the world to tell stories of experiences that are instructive, as well as to quickly seek assistance from their peers. These are the people responsible for 13 million landline, wireless, satellite, and digital connections across Canada.

Frontline technicians need fast information, accessible from their trucks while on-site with customers, to learn quickly as they change routers, set up home phone systems, and perform custom installations they may never have done before.

By equipping the technicians with a media mindset and a culture of collaboration, everyone shares responsibility for educating one another and giving each person an opportunity to seek focused help. The workforce becomes the organization's lifeline to what's happening in the field right now. The same can be said for call-center support agents or team members in the sales organization.

Alongside easily digestible bits of text, photos, and video created in the field capturing setting and context are documents, recorded broadcasts, and simulations. People throughout the organization can make and review comments, rate content "thumbs up" or "thumbs down," and offer recommendations to other team members regardless of the department they work in.

Updates in quick-access form can be searched by topic, category, or keyword. There is a formal taxonomy and an informal *folksonomy* (a term coined by information architect Thomas Vander Wal, combining the terms *folk* and *taxonomy* to convey an organic, ad hoc, and friendly way to tag, categorize, and locate content based on the terms people use in ordinary speech).[1] For example, a video of a TELUS OPTIK TV installation could be tagged as relating to the TV business, installations, media content, or wiring.

> *Content powered communities need social learning, good UX, search, semantic analysis and well planned analytics.*
> —Megan Bowe

This defies any preconceived idea of who is a producer and who is a consumer of learning at TELUS. The organization's goal is to build workforce competence and acumen, enabling everyone to make good judgments and quick decisions to better serve customers. All content is readily available in an easily contributed and consumed format, used by people in multiple countries 24 hours a day.

After 14 years of leading large organizational change and learning programs, Pontefract knew that the first things to prompt cultural shift are the stories people tell one another. It's why media sharing was always so central to his plans. But people won't share if the culture doesn't support it.

He knew the culture transformation would require more than adding an interface and tools. The organization needed to change its own practices, too. For example, they decided to implement the TELUS Leadership Philosophy (TLP)—an open and collaborative leadership model for all 45,000 team members at the company. The TLP runs parallel to their learning strategy, where leadership and learning are thought to be equal parts formal, informal, and social.

When the TLP launched in 2010, alongside Habitat Social, behaviors and tools were bridged, and the culture began to become more open and collaborative. Employee engagement rose from 53 percent to 85 percent, and customer complaints against TELUS decreased by 26 percent, representing only 5.8 percent of overall industry complaints, despite TELUS's owning 28 percent of the wireless market share in Canada.

Since assisting the creation of TELUS Habitat Social, Pontefract has been tasked with the mandate to help change the culture of the other TELUS organizations. In his new role, he takes this social concept further, into the hearts and minds of people not just where they aim to learn—but as they aim to work on issues that matter most. As he often says, "We're not here to see through each other; we're here to see each other through."[2]

Set Your Sights High

Once you have a sense of how to introduce social learning into the daily practices in your organization, it's time to dig in and widen your horizons.

Set your sights not on just getting to the next phase, rather on focusing your attention on working toward the right sorts of objectives, ensuring you're meeting the goals you set out to achieve, and creating less work (and higher value) for yourself and your colleagues as quickly as possible.

> "We're not here to see through each other;
> we're here to see each other through."
>
> —Dan Pontefract

This chapter introduces how organizations across the globe have grown their social learning approaches and used them to transform their workplaces in ways that feel natural and deeply human.

"We have moved past the early adoption phase of holding hands and sharing files" says Ed Brill, author of *Opting In: Lessons in Social Business From a Fortune 500 Product Manager*. "Today, we need to create an environment that focuses on company results and personal joy."[3]

Once people get out of the habit of going it alone, and in the habit of sharing and building on what we know individually and collectively, we can create connected teams, working and learning together across the miles.

> *Alone we can do so little; together we can do so much.*
> —Helen Keller

Strategy 1. Invite People Onto the Dance Floor

"We've created a wonderful environment for people to work together, and this new guy took a document that a group of us had been working on, and started sharing it with other groups as if it were his own." This was the dilemma of a real-world leader-in-transformation we spoke with, aiming to bring her organization into the social world. She was exasperated both by his behavior and that of others who were excited that a high-visibility colleague had come on board. She wanted to explain to her team, people who had little experience working collaboratively, why his behavior wasn't cool, while also not dampening their enthusiasm for the project or calling the offender names.

"I wish I had a way to explain this in terms everyone can relate to," she said. "I've seen things like this happen for years, and they're just not right." They are, however, the sorts of real experiences along the path to organizations working in new ways, which requires new skills to handle. Kevin Prentiss, a speaker and executive advisor on engagement and supporting technology, likens patterns of change to your first high school dance. Inevitably, there are people hanging around the walls of the gym who haven't any idea what to do with themselves. Those wallflowers may not be on the furthest edges to examine the paint; it's more likely they don't have the skills or personality to jump into the fray.

Dance floors have patterns that represent our basic humanity. We all have experience with them. Looking at the introduction of social approaches as the precursor to organizational change can seem too complicated for some and too scary for others.

If we think about the challenge as a school dance, we immediately have a shared framework to make sense of what is happening so we can begin to take action. The dance floor seems simple enough so everyone can discuss it or, even better, act on their own.

If there were someone at the center of the floor dancing wildly, thrashing his arms around, making people around him fear they could be whacked in the face, how would people handle that? How do your long-since school-dance sensibilities tell you to respond? This isn't about the dance for people with more energy than finesse. It's very likely they don't have the skills or personality to appreciate the dance any more than the wallflowers.

Between those hesitant to participate and those dominating the spotlight because they don't yet know how to engage in healthy ways, are people moving towards the dance floor and those truly benefiting from dancing with one another.

As you move your organization further along the social path, it's important to "be able to observe the development of an engagement pattern, the curve of participation," says Prentiss. It's up to each of us to differentiate the various stages people are in and help them work in the interest of others and the organization. To increase engagement, create an environment where those along the wall aren't being pushed towards the center of the floor, rather to the edge of it, where they can talk with other people, perhaps about how awkward they feel.

Likewise, the people already at the edge of the floor might be seeking a dance partner who can coax them further in. From there, people will naturally gain comfort and confidence, without feeling overwhelmed, literally, by those in the center.

Prentiss adds, "Be the spatula. Scoop the edges, gently stirring those who have similar levels of engagement with each other by making introductions and finding commonalities."

Imagine the dance circle that instantly forms when someone is genuinely a good dancer and does something extra special. Everything works out as long as the skilled dancer relinquishes the center prior to the watchers in the circle feeling intimidated beyond recovery. Someone else could even jump in. Circles of attention are like bubbles that form, and only become bad if they get stuck.

The people working in the organization's best interest are those people who are engaged and who aggregate towards the center, move close together, and radiate inviting energy.

Engagement is not the announcement your company's throwing a dance or an indication you've hired the right sorts of individual personalities. Engagement is a measure of shared energy in each moment, engendering a feeling of comfort and belonging that leads to people wanting to do the right thing.

It doesn't matter what we cover; it matters what you discover.
—Noam Chomsky

When people get in that conductive dance floor place, it is their peers' activity that triggers them to see possibilities in themselves. People are influenced by those they consider their peers, people like them, people who are always making their way through the dance.

"Small dance circles make up the whole. Relationships trump music. Some people are conductive and some are resistant by personality. Resistant personalities tend to drink more in, in an effort to become conductive," says Prentiss. "The best dances are those where a chain reaction leads to a self-amplifying positive loop of participation. The best dances are where everyone loses their self-consciousness, dances a bit, and has a good time even though they are typically stiff and hate that kind of thing."

What can you do to invite people onto the dance floor, encouraging them, by example, into being the spatula?

- Reach out to members of your community at random, getting a sense of how comfortable they are working this way, and if they would benefit from knowing others who are a little closer to enjoying the dance.

- Pay special attention to people who post once and then retreat to the walls, encouraging further conversation by comment on what they've written, directing them to someone else asking questions or providing insights on similar things.

- Get to know the people sweating up a storm, finding ways for them to talk with one another, creating more air space on the floor . . . and where they can feel the attention they're craving. With some care and attention, those in the middle might just learn to build rapport with (instead of intimidating) those around them.

- Work to create an environment where people across the space— perhaps because they are of a different nationality, ethnicity, age, or simply have a unique personal style—begin to identify how they (and the community) can benefit from working in new ways, with no expectation they'll be radically changing who they are in the process.

- Most importantly, realize this isn't for any one person to do alone . . . or that whatever your role, your job is to manage all aspects of the dance. It's a far better practice to work on creating the environment where people can coach and coax one another to engage.

This is a personalized approach that can easily be scaled when many people are working together toward creating a safe and welcoming environment.

Welcome Everyone

With social tools, each person has an opportunity to provide her distinctive perspective on a broad range of topics. Everyone in an organization, regardless of role, title, or focus, can contribute insights to the conversation. The more people that come together, the more information is shared, the more ideas are generated, and the better-informed people's decisions can be.

All of this discussing and collaborating together leads to an invaluable online, searchable resource for everyone who participates. John Walton, Symmetrix engineer and EMC fellow emeritus, says, "I cannot think of a time during my 20 years at EMC when I felt more informed, involved, and confident in myself and the business before EMC|ONE." Kevin Prentiss adds that the changes in our workforce, and the expectation of people to have highly customized environments, means that authentic engagement can no longer hide behind words like, "It's too hard to personalize this for everyone." If anything, it's so easy we look incompetent when we don't. For example, if a small startup can use inexpensive (or even free) mailing list software to address their newsletters with your first name, it's no longer OK to welcome people with "Dear employee."

> *It's never all or nothing.*
> *It's everything always.*
> —Megan Murray

Wayne Hodgins, a global futurist now sailing around the world after spending decades focused on technology, standards, and knowledge creation, coined the term *snowflake effect* to describe the exponentially growing trend toward extreme mass customization for every person, every day. [4]

Be Sure to Ask

At a large financial services firm, the team rolling out the collaborative system repeatedly told the consultants working with them that many of the influencers in the organization were never going to get on board. Knowing that would prove problematic very early on, the consultants fanned out through the headquarters campus to personally visit a few of the "doorstops."

After explaining in general terms what was coming, and asking what the team could do to gain support, one consultant received quite a surprise. A manager, who had been said to be opposed to any program like this, became very flustered, then put his head in his hands.

When asked if everything was OK, he pulled his hands from his face with tears in his eyes. "I've worked here for over 30 years," he said. "And you're the first person who has ever asked." Together they talked through a few ideas the manager had on how to engage with people in his organization and how asking for people's thoughts—and then truly making changes based on them—could fundamentally alter how he felt about the company, making it one he would be interested in working in for years to come.

Another perceived holdout also provided an unexpected response. One of the company's most well-respected researchers opened a drawer at the bottom of her desk. In it, she'd been keeping reports and papers throughout her career, "waiting," she said, "for an opportunity to share this with people who have probably thought I couldn't help them in their jobs." The notion of a company-wide network where anyone could connect and share with anyone else, she said, "takes my job in directions I only dreamed might some-day happen."

We have the capabilities and need to invite everyone in the dance.

Strategy 2. Obsess About Getting Back Your Time

At a meeting of a team of leaders at Standard & Poor's, a woman asked this question with a look of exasperation on her face: "When do you expect us to have time to learn from all this social content? We're all so busy. Even if the system had all the answers I needed, I'd never know how to find it or how to put it into use—let alone find the time to even think about looking."

With 34 gigabytes of data—1,005,000 words, 147 newspapers-worth of information—available to each of us every day, it's hard to imagine any more of anything, content or collaboration, could move us in the right direction.[5] With such powerful advances in technology thanks to Moore's Law, we have become overburdened with information while seemingly having difficulty sorting through what might actually help us perform. Declining capabilities reduce organizational value.

Social systems done well should give us our time back. They should replace the outmoded, the time consuming, and the inefficient.

Sheila Babnis, global head of strategic innovation and product development at the biotech firm Roche Pharmaceuticals, says at the beginning of her journey she thought that if she adopted social approaches to work, it would be easier to share information. "Then I realized I could either go to meetings where I'd talk with four people, or I could gather people together online, talking with 4,000 people. We could get input, make

Keep your baby eyes (which are the eyes of genius) on what we don't know.
—Lincoln Steffens

decisions, and iterate in real time, all with a similar intimate and connected feel. That's so much more valuable than just sharing," she says. "Now I know there's a whole world I can connect to and want to be part of, solving problems with other people who care about health care. I don't have to do it anymore by myself and with my tiny group."

For her, this was a huge "aha," after growing up thinking she should solve problems herself. Eventually, though, she says, "I learned those behaviors were no longer useful and I no longer had to work that way. I can use my time far more valuably." She cut down meeting times by 50 percent and found that accelerated her work by at least 50 percent by spending time having more meaningful conversations that led to co-creation.

Shifting how they worked, Babnis says, "we also created a much stronger bond amongst our team." Having never been co-located, there are people in San Francisco and Basil, Switzerland, leaving only three hours of overlapping workday time.

In a company with more than 80,000 people, and a division of about 5,500, across five sites, and another 55 affiliates in additional countries, it's hard to even know who to go to. Using this network approach made a large company feel small.

Working with her team and with other parts of her organization was just the beginning, though, for Babnis. Facilitating meetings online, talking with people across various social channels, and creating new processes out loud, with others in the organization, led her to realize this might be an approach to extending the circle of those who affect her work.

> "... I realized I could either go to meetings where I'd talk with four people, or I could gather people together online [and] talk with 4,000 people."
>
> —Sheila Babnis

With her team, Babnis began looking at how the company could work with patients, clinicians, innovators in very different fields, academics, and even the regulators, "anytime anyplace anywhere. We can broaden our work from being internally focused to looking at ourselves through the eyes of people externally as a global business," she said.

When the company's chief medical officer talked publicly about how critical innovation has become and how connected networks should be at the center of how everyone in the organization works, Babnis knew a critical threshold had been crossed. "Pharmaceutical companies have been working in the same way for the last 25 years, and a large percentage of employees in any of the companies out there could say they've never had firsthand interaction with patients. Design thinking and human-centered design are critical to gaining empathy and co-creating solutions."

Just as the shift in her thinking transitioned from sharing information outward, this work shifted everyone in her organization's perspective, away from just listening and hearing from others.

They began with interviews of 75 people, each who had a stake in what the company offered, aiming to understand what could be changed in this modern, connected world. What came out of those conversations was an empathic understanding that they had an opportunity to build and expand relationships far beyond the subset of people they had been talking with in the past.

Then, rather than gather all the information they had before taking action, they could begin implementing what they heard as they heard it. They didn't have to wait or wait to be invited. They could initiate conversations and also join those dialogues already going on around what people were doing, finding concrete approaches to solving problems weighing on people's minds.

> Let the network do the work.
> —Dion Hinchcliffe

In a connected network, through trusted relationships, they could all focus on engaging the right people at the right time, to create new value and bottom-line impact. This changes how quickly they can uncover solutions for patients. Rather than look at themselves as a drug company, they could become a solutions company.[6]

Harness Discretionary Time

Engagement is often considered a measure of the emotional commitment employees have to the organizations and its goals. When employees care, they tend to use more of their discretionary effort towards helping their organization and those they work with.

"This means the engaged computer programmer works overtime when needed, without being asked. This means the engaged retail clerk picks up the trash on the store floor, even if the boss isn't watching. This means the TSA agent will pull a big suspicious bag to be searched, even if it's the last bag on their shift," says Kevin Kruse, co-author of We: How to Increase Performance and Profits through Full Engagement and author of Employee Engagement 2.0: How to Motivate Your Team for High Performance.[7]

This focuses leaders on asking themselves how willing their employees are to contribute time not blocked off for specific activities. Social approaches provide a means to capture effort—in effect increasing the organization's labor capacity.

Business coach Ben Brooks encourages leaders to look at discretionary time in a similar way to a carbon sink. In the same ways these reservoirs actively capture and store carbon-containing chemical compounds, "A capacity sink," says Brooks, "is the capturing and pointing to untapped effort in your organization. Ask yourself if you're creating an engaged environment where people spend their discretionary effort cleaning their desks, horsing around in the break room, or prepping for their daughter's bake sale—or are they utilizing that extra capacity to help to drive your organization forward." The choice is yours.

Filter and Focus

Time-wasting systems are devoid of context. Content, often more than you could ever wade through, was practically thrown at us, completely unrelated to our daily flow of work. These repositories were separate from where we spent our time, from the searches for clues to what we needed and what was important to us.

One challenge social technology can solve is the idea of filtering. For example, how does an organization use social technology tools to find its own expertise?

Online communities and blogs can help identify subject matter experts or workers who may have information pertinent to a particular decision. But determining what is relevant is still the responsibility of each of us individually. Although the environment can create automatic data collections, the human touch provides necessary context.

Online communities can bridge the gap between the climate you have at work today and the one you want to foster—one in which people want to learn from each other because they trust one another. They want to hear from people like them, facing the same decisions, the same challenges, and the same options. As Babe Ruth once said, "You may have the greatest bunch of individual stars in the world, but if they don't play together, the club won't be worth a dime." The way the team plays collectively determines its success.

Make the value gained by participating its own reward.
—Jeannette Campos

Rather than use social systems to duplicate programs and processes that are working, look at your organization's weaknesses. New modern approaches are most useful when they address failures or inadequacies in the old ways work was done.

As a society we moved through the divergent phase of networked technology in the 1980s, when people learned to share information within work groups and across organizations because they could. Within the silos, there was a limited amount of context. Between silos, there was less.

Then, in the early 2000s, organizations began working in a convergent way, attempting to present and share information with intention—by design. Content increased, but the information was still not as relevant and accessible as it could be.

Now we are in the middle of a new phase—where relationships between people, and between topic areas and people, are becoming more explicit. There are online groups to meet with in online communities. There are blogs to follow and comment on around topics people care about at work. Social gathering spaces become the means for finding what's relevant.

Getting a sense of the people who are contributing provides the additional context. "Oh, if Natasha is paying attention to this topic," you may think to yourself, "and I know she's just begun working on that new project, then it would be good for me to track and learn about this, too." With this additional context, people can confront and reduce information overload, now having a way to sift through—based on social relationships—what's more important than something else.

Be Compelling

In an age of too much digital noise and not enough value, getting and holding attention is pivotal if you want people to learn. If you can't get people's interest, what's the point in even trying to connect with them? Old-school ways of communicating with employees and customers are often ignored altogether in the engaging and entertaining social media world.

Although some argue that social media keeps people from paying attention, research shows that it can be a big part of the solution.

A survey of more than 60 executives by Thomas Davenport and John Beck looked at what got their attention over a one-week period.[8] Overall, in rank order, the factors most highly associated with getting attention were:

- The message is *personalized*.

- It evoked an *emotional* response.

- It came from a *trustworthy* source or respected sender.

- It was *concise*.

Social sharing excels at all of these factors. Messages that both evoked emotion and were personalized were more than twice as likely to generate a response.

The best ideas for improving your organization often come from employees, partners, and customers because they have a vested interest in your success and know your organization best. Harnessing their collective wisdom through social means can be both compelling and attention getting.

Social sharing encourages and enables a community where people can see and learn from one another and get contributions from everyone and anyone. Video messages that allow for comments help bridge the gap between leaders and the larger ecosystem. People can provide feedback, ask questions, and send their own videos through the platform's commenting, tagging, and sharing features.

For example, an employee who is planning to retire could create videos and content about her areas of expertise. A senior executive could create mentoring videos, giving advice to newcomers. A

> *Stories are like a catalyst for processing meaning.*
> —Clark Quinn

technical employee could create a step-by-step video to explain a procedure. The training department could ask employees to create videos to incorporate into a learning program.

Videos are especially good at presenting things sequentially (this happened, then that) and showing causality (this happened because of that), so they're a powerful way to show people what happened (the sequence of events) and why (the causes and effects of those events). In a world of hyperlinking and twitter bits, seeing the whole picture, even a small slice, offers "what" and "why," which are critical but often hard to discern.

Turn executives' messages into short video or audio streams. Post them on the intranet, web portal, or online community; pipe them to screens in the entryway; and offer the videos to customers who want to hear the CEO's perspective.

When seeing isn't as important, or for sharing information that can be listened to without having to take your eyes off of other things you're working on, audio podcasts can be used to share valuable historical and explanatory information and knowledge. They can be recorded by individuals as mentoring moments or by two or more people in either interview or panel discussion formats.

Because shared spaces need people to start conversations, consider starting with topics that you care deeply about, things you want others' perspectives on and that would help in your work. These are the topics you will be the most motivated to invest time in.

Ask hard questions. Asking a dull question takes as much time as asking a meaningful one, so ask those that get at information you and your organization need. "So, how far along are you with this idea?" Or, "Has anyone else succeeded in doing this?" Those who make the most effective members of a collaborative team are those who get to the heart of issues and facilitate effectively and honestly.

Strategy 3. Foster a Sense of Community

Social networks might get more media buzz, but online communities provide something extra special. Community, the place where we live, work, and do things with other people, is a concept most of us learned and put into use when we were very young. Coming from two Latin words meaning "with gifts," the term *community* suggests a general sense of reciprocity, altruism, and benefit that comes from doing something together.

The old town of Mombasa, Kenya; the Green Bay Packers fans who watch games wearing cheese-wedge hats; or fire spinners worldwide all comprise examples of communities. Each type has its own shared language, rituals, customs, and collective memory. In most cases, sharing is the norm and people choose what information they share.

When people speak of community today, they are usually calling up the hope of reviving closer bonds among people that seemed to occur in ages past. Don Cohen and Larry Prusak, authors of *In Good Company: How Social Capital Makes Organizations Work*, point out that when we talk about community in business, we nod to the reality that companies and the individuals who run them don't exist in a social vacuum devoid of ties, histories, loyalties, and values that might influence their actions. There is also a similarity between the way people have learned in communities throughout time and how people in organizations learn.[9]

If you are interested in creating a rich and vibrant connected network of people across your organization, you're looking to encourage more than a group of people to use social tools. You're aiming to create a community—one that meets and engages online.

Research from the Network Roundtable, led by Rob Cross at the University of Virginia, showed that people use communities to find others who provide resources, career development, personal

Community is not a website.
Don't build it like one.
—Trisha Liu

support, and context. The depth and breadth of these relationships, whether they are serendipitous or planned, predicts performance, innovation, employee commitment, and job satisfaction.

You're spurring on a *community of practice* (CoP), a name coined by Étienne Wenger and Jean Lave in the pre-Facebook era to describe a form of social network whose participants "share a passion for something that they know how to do, and who interact regularly in order to learn how to do it better."[10]

One study of a community of practice within a critical business unit at Halliburton showed that within one year they were able to lower customer dissatisfaction by 24 percent, reduce cost of poor quality by 66 percent, increase new product revenue by 22 percent, and improve operational productivity by more than 10 percent.[11]

Vedrana "V" Madiah, vice president of enterprise communication and colleague engagement at Marsh, Inc., points out, "Community helps bring colleagues together to discuss, collaborate, and share common interests."

Jamie Pappas, director of global brand communications and social media at Akamai Technologies, says, "One of the key strategic benefits of community is connecting people who might have never crossed paths, let alone learned valuable lessons from each other. Breaking down information silos and enabling your employees, customers, partners, and advocates to exchange information that makes their lives easier and enables them to enjoy more of the things they are passionate about provides huge benefits to the business when it comes to employee productivity, satisfaction, and retention; not to mention customer and partner engagement and retention benefits."

Based on 10 years of research at over 100 organizations, Rob Cross, at the University of Virginia, and those who participate in the Connected Commons Consortium have identified five network management principles successful leaders use to bridge formal structures and ensure they benefit from key talent and expertise:

- Managing the center: Minimize bottlenecks and protect hidden stars.

- Leveraging the periphery: Rapidly integrate newcomers and reengage underutilized high performers.

- Selectively bridging collaborative silos: Target key intersections in the network and leverage opinion leaders.

- Developing the ability to surge: Ensure that the best expertise in a network is brought to bear on new problems and opportunities.

- Minimizing insularity: Manage targeted relations with key clients and external sources of expertise.[12]

Rachel Happe, principal at The Community Roundtable, a professional services organization for community managers and social business practitioners, reinforces this point, "Communities are fundamentally about relationships and learning from peers, so online communities must be created around individuals. The more they participate and share, the more value they get because that sharing creates serendipity, bringing people and knowledge to them that they didn't even know they didn't know. In turn that serendipity saves them time, makes them smarter, and surfaces opportunities for them."[13]

Because online communities are not constrained by the need for anyone's physical presence, we have greater flexibility with our ability to join, learn, and congregate with people who have similar interests no matter their location.

Being part of a community—whether online or offline—offers the benefits of belonging, commitment, mutuality, and trust. These are environments where people are free to learn.

"Just be sure not to re-create the silos you already have in your community," warns Trisha Liu. "This is an easy trap to fall into. The existing structure is familiar. But didn't you undertake this project because you want something better?"

Questions to consider:

- Have you made it clear that anyone can create or join a community, and have you opened the process up to everyone? If not, do you have a really, really, really good reason?

- Are you participating in the "gardening" of your organization's communities by at least occasionally participating and commenting?

- Has your organization created a policy that can be used not as a hammer, but rather as a flashlight, providing guidance and encouragement, as well as the opportunity for everyone to participate in expanding, explaining, and improving?

Community Members Look Out for One Another

More effective than rigid policies, a group can help keep its members on track by reinforcing good practices, building and communicating guidelines, removing inappropriate material, and having continual dialogue about the right balance.

On rare occasions, organizations need to take action, but those are few and far between and usually, in the end, reflect more positively than negatively because they demonstrate the power of peers managing one another.

One example of this is on the social collaboration platform at Home Depot. After the system had been in use for a while, managers found that groups became self-policing. According to one member, "Inappropriate behavior just isn't tolerated, so you really don't have to worry."

"One of the key strategic benefits of community is connecting people who might have never crossed paths, let alone learned valuable lessons from each other."
—Jamie Pappas

That's not to say people don't gripe a little bit, which helps the community's space feel real. It also enables managers to address employee concerns before they take a larger toll on the workforce. For instance, Home Depot originally prohibited employees from wearing shorts after Labor Day. While this was reasonable in cooler areas, employees in warmer climates were displeased, and took to the collaboration space to sound off. As a result of the comments, management changed the policy.

Community Online Connects People Across Great Divides

We've been working side by side with people since sandbox days, but there were limits to how much and how far we could share. Email, instant messaging, and text began a movement beyond the walls that separated us. Now we share what we're doing, ask questions, post details, and mingle our ideas online.

Yet this still leaves out tacit knowledge—things that are hard to communicate by writing and speaking, but can be learned by watching others and actually doing them.

People crave the opportunity to learn from one another, side-by-side, gaining hard facts and wisdom in context. What else could account for the use of classroom learning decades after people realized its inherent limits? We value opportunities to see we are not alone; there are people we can lean on, learn from, interact with, and rely on to help us.

In a landmark study, Richard J. Light of the Harvard Graduate School of Education discovered that one of the strongest determinants of students' success in higher education—more important than their instructors' teaching styles—was their ability to form or participate in small study groups. People who studied in groups, even once a week, were more engaged in their studies, were better prepared for class, and learned significantly more than students who worked on their own.[14] These students, in their own way, created small communities.

Demographics research at Deloitte uncovered something similar: People who could look to other people online for support felt more connected than their nonconnected counterparts, stayed with their employer longer, and produced stronger results.[15] The creators of Deloitte's online community, D Street, recognized the benefits of nurturing a culture of reciprocal learning and continue to make sure that's central to what they do.

Exponential growth comes from the phenomenon of "compound learning curves."
—Chris Anderson

Community Builds Your Internal Brand

David J. Birnbaum, who supports 101,000 independent sales agents at CENTURY 21 Real Estate in 78 countries, understands that his organization's social portal is key to building the company's brand value proposition. As vice president of learning, Birnbaum points out, "our sales professionals are very independent and they could go to a different brand in a second, if we didn't provide a great platform for them. While the training and information they can get in the portal brings them back again and again, it's not nearly as important to them as feeling like they are part of a community that supports their development, and ultimately helps improve their business."

While in the past, a training class brought dispersed co-workers together for a short period of time, and at the end they had a certification with a company logo to hang on a wall, social learning approaches provide an ongoing relationship. Birnbaum adds, "Our agents used to leverage training one to three times a year. Now they log into the portal one to three times a month to learn and much more. After a class, they stay in touch virtually, they continue to follow the instructor, they create groups in the portal, and even set up alumni groups on Facebook. Their learning never ends because they belong to a community, a community of learning and sharing. That community ultimately strengthens our real-estate brand even more as they talk with new agents about the benefits of the portal, and their franchise owners are reminded the brand has ongoing value."

> "The more they participate and share, the more value they get because that sharing creates serendipity, bringing people and knowledge to them that they didn't even know they didn't know."
>
> —Rachel Happe

Salima Nathoo, talent development leader and founder of RocktheGlow, says, "When used inside an organization, social media offers all parts of HR an opportunity to raise their game in influencing people, process, and profits of an organization—beyond policy. It is the face of the company's internal brand as the organization recruits, hires, and on-boards the next generation of leaders. Not convinced? Ask yourself what the cost is of being unknown, disliked and worst, ignored in the industry and job market?"

Nathoo adds, "Let your employees know the influential role each of them plays in writing the brand story and contributing to collective success. Make it easy for existing and new employees to learn, understand, and communicate the core elements of your brand promise and value proposition. Existing internal social collaboration and communication tools are a great way to accomplish this, crowd-source ideas, and run a pilot. Make it fun with some gamification. Finally, recognize those who do it well."

Questions to consider:

- Does your system provide "gathering places" where people can participate ad hoc, or spur of the moment, in group activities that will serve to build trust, camaraderie, and morale?

- Do you take pains to advertise and promote, through other, nonsocial media, the opportunities that exist for group activities and collaboration?

- Do you make it clear by what you participate in and support that cooperation and collaboration, not individual competitiveness, are the goals?

Strategy 4. Identify Value Markers

The power of collaborative work is a trusted and repeatable activity, where people can bring their ideas together, vet them with their peers, and publish them in a way that can be revised and revisited, representing multiple viewpoints.

For codifying the multifaceted nature of information, Don Burke and Sean Dennehy, social evangelists in the U.S. intelligence community, have identified three qualities that stand out as markers of success: vibrancy, socialness, and relevance.

Vibrancy

Working socially online should be measured by vibrancy and the ability to energize the people who work in a social way. Social spaces showcase people's needs, interests, passions, and emotions—so they need to mirror the vibrancy humankind can provide.

Vibrancy characterizes the inviting, energizing place where people want to be. The space is jumping, alive with energy. People come back because they find value.

Envision a party. When you walk in, it takes only a few seconds to judge if you want to be there and if it has taken off. People are exceptionally good at assessing this. It's primordial. We have millions of years of evolution in our DNA telling us to be wary of a dead place where we stand out, where we wonder, "Is it precarious for me to be here?"

When a collaborative space is hopping with activity, form follows content, not the other way around. Planning revolves around how to get more "eyes on content" to improve accuracy, add perspective and subtleties, and show it has captured what's new.

This poses a chicken-and-egg problem, though. Someone has to create the vibrancy, open the space, and welcome the guests. Someone has to get the ball rolling. OPENPediatrics and TELUS Habitat Social became successful because initially a core group of people was willing to contribute before there was any reason to do so, before the other participants arrived.

Sometimes the party host or hostess is an organizational leader. Just as often it's the people working on the front line who have been waiting for their opportunity to invite others into a vibrant conversation that matters, creating ambient awareness, which is what social scientists call this continuous, low-level, background connectivity. It is, they say, very much like being physically near someone and picking up on his or her mood through actions—body language, sighs, stray comments—out of the corner of your eye.

Clive Thompson, a contributing writer to the *New York Times* and author of *Smarter Than You Think: How Technology Is Changing Our Minds for the Better*, calls this "the paradox of ambient awareness. Each little update—each individual bit of social information—is insignificant on its own, even supremely mundane. But taken together, over time, the little snippets coalesce into a surprisingly sophisticated portrait of your colleagues' lives, like thousands of dots making a pointillist painting. The ambient information becomes 'a type of ESP,' an invisible dimension floating over us."[16] It's a new dimension of energy floating between us.

Clay Shirky, author of *Here Comes Everybody: The Power of Organizing Without Organizations* and *Cognitive Surplus: How Technology Makes Consumers Into Collaborators*, refers to "algorithmic authority," meaning that if many people are pointing to the

> *The currency of real networking is not greed but generosity.*
> —Keith Ferrazzi

same thing at the same time, it's probably worth paying attention to.[17] Think of it like in-real-life trending. Does constant updating sound like a vice of vain people with nothing better to do? Paula Thornton, a design thinker focused on humane ways to work, points out, "In the machine world no one would imagine doing away with the conveyor belt. Updates are the conveyor belts of information in a service organization."[18]

That conveyer belt of information should be interesting to any organization with a large distributed workforce because it supports the dynamics, efficiency, and agility of a small company. It raises awareness of others within an organization and, with this, opportunities for learning, collaboration, and innovation.

Online spaces rich and vibrant with ambient information increase the quantity of tacit knowledge shared because they make you aware of what people are doing in a way that was not possible before.

Burt Kaliski, former director of EMC's Innovation Network, and his team started planning for the company's annual Innovation Conference by brainstorming ideas about the focus of the event on EMC|ONE. As that was settled, the team moved on to posting and refining event details. Then they launched their innovation submission process on EMC|ONE and received more than 900 submissions from passionate EMC employees throughout the world who felt so comfortable in the community that they were even eager to post their submissions on the site for others to review, comment on, and provide suggestions.[19]

> "In the machine world no one would imagine doing away with the conveyor belt. Updates are the conveyor belts of information in a service organization."
>
> —Paula Thornton

Questions to consider:

- Have you provided a method that makes it easy for people to have complete, interesting, and useful profiles, including pictures?

- Do you allow tagging of files and other artifacts, and does your system provide for a loose "Folksonomy", rather than a rigid taxonomy?

- Does part of your system allow for continuous, in-line, and real-time updating and are people encouraged to share what they're doing; that is, to "work out loud?"

Socialness

If, as Woody Allen said, 80 percent of success is showing up, at least 10 percent of the remaining 20 requires engaging with those around you who can contribute to your success.

If people don't talk and support each other and build off one another, social tools don't provide much benefit. Interaction among people amplifies individual contributions. Articles on similar subjects can change from noise to sound when they're synthesized and cross-linked.

The first and largest integrated not-for-profit medical practice in the world, the Mayo Clinic employs more than 57,000 physicians, scientists, researchers, allied health professionals, and residents. The world-class staff, deeply entrenched in labor-intensive intellectual work, aim to create a culture of collaborative care—with social media as a new and vital resource.

Monty Flinsch, who has led technical initiatives at the Mayo Clinic's central campus in Rochester, Minnesota, for more than a decade, sees the endless potential of social learning to establish and support relationships between people and departments. He doesn't see these tools used to develop knowledge, rather he sees them as a critical component for Mayo clinicians to make vital connections.[20]

A physical scientist by training, Flinsch likens status updates to cloud seeding, the distribution of silver iodide that changes the energy in clouds and leads to rain. When people ask a question or post a link to a resource across Mayo's internal social tools, their open sharing creates a place where ideas get crystallized. Ideas ignite more sharing and then

> *Social learning is simply to learn with others and through others. This is natural, omnipresent, collaborative learning.*
> —Frédéric Domon

normal human relationships take off. People go to lunch, talk on the phone, or invite each other to see something they are working on.

Because this happens more frequently and sooner than if someone had to make introductions, or they read about the challenge on a piece of paper near the elevator, people at Mayo are making more substantial contacts. They spark off of one another's ideas. Connecting again online or in person reinvigorates the process and brings new energy to their communications. For busy people who need to find ways to manage their attention stream, updates seem little enough to not feel like a burden. It's akin to having vibrant conversations without the time commitment. It's sufficiently lightweight to fit into the spaces between the critical work people do.

Physicians at Mayo, like people in many professions, face a huge number of system alerts begging for their attention. Updates can become their unified activity stream, which they can look at through the corner of an eye and receive alerts and gain an ambient awareness of conversations going on. Rather than being bombarded with notices that blood work is complete, a room is ready, or a package has arrived, this unified stream is there when they are ready to review it. Although some people believe that updates add to chaos and perceive it as just more noise, others find threads of relevance in their first few experiences. They use it as a digest, checking in once in a while and getting an idea where the institution is on a topic. One more blip isn't distracting; they view updates when they have time. They can engage when appropriate.

Ideas get tossed out, and some fall to the bottom of the pile (when a reply or conversation isn't required). Others stick, and engagement ensues. Messages touch a nerve or mix with threads that keep popping up, forming a pulse of the institution. When there's internal rumbling, you can sense it across the stream. Ideas are refined in the space, issues get aired, and people feel connected to one another and to the vibe of the organization. They feel connected and social in a way that reminds them they're colleagues, not just people working at the same place.

Monty Flinsch says, "These technologies create energy that is self-sustaining. Social sharing provides a simple way for people to connect, set ideas on fire, and make ideas rain."

Questions to consider:

- Does your system utilize a micro-blogging or status update component so people can see what their colleagues and teammates are doing during the day?

- Does it allow for the integration of updates and alerts into its communications stream, so people can "pull," rather than have "pushed" the information they need?

- Are you using a wiki or some other form of web-based collaborative tool that can preserve portions of your organization's more explicit knowledge and information?

Relevance

What good are vibrant social exchanges if they aren't pertinent to the people and mission of your organization?

The Jacksonville (Florida) Sheriff's Office (JSO) strives to protect and serve its community by preventing crime and disorder, while guarding personal liberties. With a population of approximately 875,000 residents, 1,600 officers serve a consolidated area of 844 square miles. In order to effectively serve its citizens, all of the units within the office must work together, share information, and collaborate in real time, but the JSO found this to be difficult with only a static internal website.

By taking a social approach, they now have a central knowledge portal, making relevant resources accessible to the officers and detectives who need them. The JSO has improved the accu-

Think big and think different.
Then connect it all.
—Gina Minks

racy and value of crime analyses by increasing real-time collaboration between officers and analysts. Crime patterns and trends are easily searchable with tags. Former crime analysis unit manager Jamie Roush says, "By incorporating social, we shifted the crime analysis and distribution process from one-way communication to a collaborative effort, creating an efficient feedback loop."[21] For crime analysis, the key to effectiveness is having accurate information and making sure the detectives and officers receive the information and can contribute to the analysis process.

When Roush decided she wanted to implement a social solution that would eventually be available agency wide, she bypassed the top-down method of change management that often exists within law-enforcement agencies. She made the officers and detectives an integral part of the change by showing them the technology, highlighting the benefits it offered them, and providing full access. By explaining the reasons behind, and the benefits of, using the technology, and then allowing employees to play a critical role in making the change, the Sheriff's Office increased communication and collaboration that became a part of the officers' daily flow of work.

Traditionally in law enforcement, crime analysts distribute their reports through email or a static internal website. The JSO realized that with these distribution methods, the reports spiraled into a "black hole." The email recipients often deleted the emails because they didn't see the value. Sometimes, the analyst would receive a phone call from a recipient and would then incorporate the feedback, rewrite the analysis, and start the entire cycle again. The JSO wanted to ensure that the right information was distributed to the appropriate people and wouldn't just be deleted.

Now, a crime analyst posts information to a wiki page in a workspace, officers provide feedback in real time, which the analyst then incorporates and immediately shares with all of the officers. Using social makes this process more efficient and accurate, because all of the officers can contribute, view each other's suggestions, and work together to build a complete analysis.

Roush called their new platform Wikid 94. She wanted the name to be catchy and relevant; the "94" speaks to the actual signal used for collecting information. It has links to all the main patrol and investigative areas. Officers enter all patterns and series information onto the appropriate pages, so the most current updates are always available. Tagging helps information on crime trends, and patterns get to the relevant pages for officers to view. Even those who aren't frequent social media users off the job recognize the value Wikid 94 adds to their work, and its use has become second nature.

Success requires more than brilliant analysts and the understanding of policing and police managers—it requires a system fueled by information and data. JSO's strength is their work environment, their system. Prior to taking a social approach, JSO's analysts spent at least half their time extracting, cleaning, and coding data so that they could analyze it. They needed a system that is fast and flexible because "speed is the currency of law enforcement analysis."[22]

Social approaches are being used for law enforcement, public engagement, and for investigative purposes.

Studies show that 87 percent of the time social media, when used as a probable cause for a search warrant, holds up in court, and 67 percent of people believe information obtained via social media can help solve investigations more quickly. Social media may be one of the best modern tools to improve police work. In one case in Jacksonville, Roush, who was monitoring Twitter, saw tweets about a shooting at a mall. Only after a little while, she said, did she get a ring from her traditional police scanner, saying the shooting had occurred.

The interconnected, interactive nature of social learning exponentially amplifies the rate at which crucial content can be shared.
—Abhipsa Mishra

Questions to consider:

- Did you communicate with, and do you continue to communicate with, the people who you expect will benefit from a collaborative, social learning environment?

- Do you know what their needs are or which of their processes are responsible for the most aggravation and disruption in the organization?

- Have you carefully scrutinized how your system works, and what components are available, with an eye toward the specific ways in which they'll be used by your people?

Taken together, an online community or social network's degree of vibrancy, socialness, and relevance offer a distinctive way to measure the success of a collaborative environment. More powerfully though, these criteria can serve as objective measurements of the quality and reputation of a person's or group's contributions. Are people contributing? How, when, where, and how often? Are they interacting in a positive way? Sentiment analysis could even be applied. Does editing have a positive tone? Are people discussing, cross-linking, and debating in a healthy way?

Such measures allow organizations to evaluate employees not by their direct output (number of reports, accounts won, or hours on the job), but by how well they facilitate and enable a virtual collaborative community and contribute to something larger than themselves.

Strategy 5. Ensure People Are Digitally Literate

Organizations often find that some of their employees aren't working in social ways because they don't know how. Find catalysts to make their experience more positive. Some just need hands-on training, as they may not currently use social tools. Others will benefit from coaching on how to work in relationship-oriented ways.

It's only after you're deeply into your work that you may realize some people need to increase their overall digital literacy.

A Dutch-based financial institution had set as a corporate priority to transform their IT department across the globe. Central to that was creating a collaboration platform. With it, they created an ambassador program and a consulting practice only to realize that digital literacy had to be addressed.

Alvaro Caballero, who was collaborative program manager, recalls, "we realized one of the reasons for the low adoption rates was not a lack of awareness about the tools, but a lack of understanding on how to use them productively. When employees said they didn't know how to use any of this, they really meant it."

Putting into practice the approach pioneered by Sugata Mitra, education researcher from India and winner of the 2013 TED Prize, Caballero and his team created a series of six-week programs for anyone in the company to steep themselves in the digital age. They put out an open invitation through their usual communications channels and organized everyone who applied into cohorts with specific start dates.

In a company of over 50,000 people, and an IT department that made up one quarter of its global workforce, the aspiration was for those who went through the program to teach others what they'd learned.

Caballero worked with a small team to create digital spaces for dialogue and reflection around key topics of digital use in an enterprise.

Networks are the new companies.
—Nilofer Merchant

The program was composed of weekly topics, starting with a conversation. Connected together in a closed community inside the company's social platform, which Caballero describes as "sort of a TweetChat or stream of comments," the people in the group talked about what they wanted to learn.

By admitting in this small private group that you didn't know what hashtags were, let alone how to use them, or what was the difference between a blog and working out loud, people began to trust one another, knowing they weren't alone. Something one person didn't know might be well understood by another, so they also could begin thinking about how they might help each other.

Then participants received a trigger question about one of these topics. They stepped out of the conversation to investigate on their own and came back to contribute to the ongoing live discussion. Some brought back links to posts they found particularly useful. Others came back with more questions, videos, comments, and experiences.

The program facilitators, two in each session, didn't use materials or lessons, per se. They followed the exchanges closely, asked interesting questions. They pointed out how people were building on one another's answers, and how to say something for others to build upon. They also asked questions to surface how participants could apply what they were doing into their daily work.

After the group session was over, participants were assigned a series of collaborative tasks and it was their responsibility to decide how and when to do them within the following week—together whenever possible.

One task was to create a profile in a social platform. While just filling out a form could be seen as completing the task, the teams chatted between themselves as they did it. That prompted them to begin also seeing the benefit in writing short descriptions of their work, something that wasn't asked for in the profile, and adding links to materials other people might get value from.

The profile question alone prompted the groups to have more in-depth conversations about additional digital literacies. For instance, "Is it OK *not* to include a picture?" and "If you need one, what makes a good picture?"

Other collaborative tasks included looking back through blog posts and comments, replying to status updates and commenting, asking questions of their networks, working out loud, and identifying the value of connecting with others.

The goal of this reflection was to help participants connect personally with the content as they talked about it with their cohort mates. It also ensured they began feeling like they could work with others, passing this knowledge along to others interested in increasing their digital literacy. The post-discussion analysis and teaching mindset were key to the program's success.

The facilitated sessions lasted for an hour and usually generated 90 to 120 comments. Although the design team tried various size groups, they learned over time that a cohort of seven to eight people worked best. They created groups of 10 and, inevitably, two or three didn't attend each time.

Participants were also encouraged to consider themselves future instructors. Whatever they ended up creating would be used as guidance for the next group. This helped everyone practice in the co-authoring process and instilled a sense of pride among the participants, knowing they were building something of value for their colleagues. Most importantly, they made sure there was time for personal reflection and analysis, core to their retaining and using what they'd learned.

At the end of the program, the facilitators picked out of the homework some of the groups' breakthrough moments. After a little bit of styling and editing, Caballero and his team created booklets with pictures in them on nice glossy paper. They gave each participant several of the booklets so they could share with colleagues or family. The books bridged the digital and physical world, providing each participant an artifact to prompt additional conversations about digital literacy and working together online.

> *Social Learning: because situation beats instruction.*
> —Charles Jennings

Strategy 6. Focus on Increasing Collective Smarts

Watch a group of 4-year-olds build a skyscraper made of cardboard, and you might think anything is possible. One offers up her vision, another gets the boxes, and a third clears the space in anticipation of something big. No one taught them their roles or pointed out the opportunity. They each saw something greater than they could do alone (or at least in the time before playgroup ends), and they joined in, *collectively*.

While social learning may at times feel foreign because of our years learning alone at school, collaboration is something we've known how to do our entire lives. Working together to produce something more significant than one person can do alone is timeless. Relying on one another to get smarter is part of our DNA.

Modern collaboration tools, when used by several people simultaneously, enable a shift in individual thinking about the energy and intelligence we can produce together. Add to that the complex nature and urgency of problems facing organizations today, and we're reminded there's no time to waste.

"If you ask someone what data they want to share with whom, in a general fashion, people give up, overwhelmed," says Adina Levin, collaborative software visionary. "But when tools enable people to share information about themselves, their organizations, and the urgent issues they face right now in the context of who they are meeting with and what they are working on, people make pretty good decisions and create real digital social networks."[23]

Ask people what they know and they'll be hard pressed to articulate it. Put them in a situation where they are required to use their knowledge and recall is often immediate and complete.

Working together isn't something new, but capturing perception, thinking, and the ideas needed to understand the full context of a problem to produce something that remains up-to-date is revolutionary.

Doug Engelbart, the father of personal computing and for over a half-century an advocate for the creation of collaborative tools to augment collective work, believed the answers are right in front of us—if only we could reach them.[24] What if groups of people could access their collective knowledge quickly when facing a decision, sorting through all other noise, and keying in on the most relevant information? It would vastly improve our ability to deal with complex, urgent problems—to get the best possible understanding of a situation, including the best possible solutions.

The success of any size organization or team is based on its collective IQ, a measure of how well people work *collectively* on important problems and challenges—in other words, its collective smarts. It becomes a measure of how effective we are at tackling complex, urgent problems and opportunities and how effectively a group can concurrently develop, integrate, and apply its knowledge toward its mission.

Questions to consider:

- Have you made it clear, and do you reinforce the notion, that collaboration is not seen as "cheating" and that everyone is not merely allowed to work together, but is also actively encouraged to do so?

- Have you identified specific work-related processes you know can be made better through the active cooperation of the people who touch it?

- Have you thought of developing occasional challenges and opportunities for people to work together toward a goal that isn't necessarily work related?

Make Informed Decisions in Real Time

Good decisions are the heart and soul of any successful, fast-moving organization, and the more informed the decisions, the better they are likely to be. Although most people say they want input from co-workers and staff prior to making a final call, often it's just too hard to do in a timely manner. Real-time input on decisions is yet another way that social learning facilitates what people learn. Being able to access tacit knowledge from a wide range of people in the organization allows us to solicit opinions; ask questions; get pointers to more information; and see referrals, testimonials, benchmarking, and updates that relate to what we need to decide.

Question to consider:

- Have you created opportunities and methods whereby feedback can be sought from everyone in your organization who wishes to offer it and have you actually sought such feedback?

Create Opportunities to Reflect

Social media, by its nature and even its name, implies an outward connection. Look out. Look up. Look around. What about looking in? Online communities offer intrapersonal benefits for those paying attention to what they can learn about themselves.

Although the public visibility of an online community can be unsettling, there is a very positive result of incessant updating: a culture of people who know much more about themselves. Many of the people we spoke with about their social media use described an unexpected side effect of self-discovery. Stopping several times a day to observe what you're feeling or thinking can become, after weeks and weeks, a sort of philosophical act. It's like the Zen concept of mindfulness.

Having an online audience for self-reflection can prompt people to work harder at it and describe it more accurately in more interesting ways—the status update as a literary form.

Laura Fitton, microsharing maven and co-author of *Twitter for Dummies*, points out that her constant status updating has even made her "a happier person, a calmer person" because the process of, say, describing a horrid morning at work forces her to look at it objectively. "It drags you out of your own head," she says.[25] In an age of virtual awareness, perhaps the person you see most clearly will be yourself.

Whom do you influence? Look at the people who have chosen to follow what you're writing, and you'll begin to get a picture of who takes an interest in the areas you focus on. Someone you have admired for a long time may be looking at what you do; someone you'd never considered talking with about a topic near to your heart might be chiming in when you don't expect it. Someone who follows you may consistently ask you to clarify or dig deeper into a theory when you explain something. This may help improve your writing or steer your work to assist more people.

Garden and Weed

Just as some people are terrific at encouraging their friends onto the dance floor, communities benefit from gardeners to nurture and tend to the proverbial soil. Plot out a community objective with a clearly defined purpose stating why people would want to join. Seed your community with appropriate content to encourage participation. Harvest and publicly recognize valuable contributions in order to reinforce behaviors and drive engagement.

Every online community benefits from people looking around, tending the soil, and clearing out the weeds. Those roles can be formal or informal, regular or periodic. They lend themselves to certain activities, too. Nancy White, co-author of *Digital Habitats: Stewarding Technology for Communities*, points out that online group interactions do not always happen spontaneously. They require care and nurturing: facilitation. The core of facilitation is to serve the group and assist it in reaching its goals or purpose. Some describe this role as a gardener, a conductor, the distributed leadership of jazz improvisers, a teacher, or an innkeeper. It can be this and more.[26]

Lee Levitt, Laird Popkin, and David Hatch write, "Communities are organic in nature and [you] can't make them successful or force them to grow. [You] can only provide the fertile ground on which a community may grow, and then provide some gentle guidance to help the group thrive."[27]

Community managers (often the formal title for facilitators) need to be genuine, authentic communicators, tending to their gardens no matter the weather or season. White adds, "Facilitation is a balance between functions that enhance the environment and content, create openness and opportunity, and protect members from harassment. It involves the sacred rituals around freedom of individual expression while preserving something of 'the common good.' It is juggling, tightrope walking, often without a net.

These multiple forms of media convergence are leading us toward a digital renaissance—a period of transition and transformation that will affect all aspects of our lives.
—Henry Jenkins

"Facilitators foster member interaction, provide stimulating material for conversations, keep the space cleaned up and help hold the members accountable to the stated community guidelines, rules, or norms. They pass on community history and rituals. They hold the space for the members. Perhaps more importantly, hosts often help community members do these things for themselves."

When members of a community begin taking on these roles themselves, they are gaining both the skills and experience to improve how they work and learn with people outside the community and their organizations.

Although many organizations begin by adopting outward-facing social media strategies, putting social capabilities on their externally facing websites, there are advantages to beginning inside first. While at EMC, prior to Akamai, Jamie Pappas helped to launch EMC|ONE with a key goal of driving employee proficiency with social media tools internally, without the added pressures and expectations that come with external collaboration. "It's much easier to develop the etiquette and best practices and course correct, if needed, when you're among respected colleagues. More people are willing to take a chance, take risks, and learn how to use the tools in an environment with supportive colleagues all learning at the same time," says Pappas.

To get as many people as possible ready for social tools, the consumer innovation team at Humana created a series of self-guided training modules for employees to learn about various social media tools without becoming overwhelmed. People can spend a little time each day to get up to speed and gain a sense of how these resources can help them. "LinkedIn in 15 Minutes a Day," for instance, gives employees a chance to learn enough to test it on their own. Other 15-minute courses introduce the basics of Twitter, YouTube, and Facebook. The team has also created modules on subjects such as RSS feeds and readers, blogging, search engine optimization, and social marketing campaigns. They post these modules in an online community-like space called the Social Media Commons, designed specifically as a place where people can practice and learn.

Make Connections

How is community created online? By connecting and creating a better world together. You're meeting someone in person for the first time and go visit their online profile so you get a sense of who they are. Viewing a person's profile should essentially provide the same feel as visiting his or her office—complete with pictures of the kids on the desk and certifications and awards on the walls.

CREATE AN ENVIRONMENT FOR KNOWLEDGE SHARING

Nancy White likens the spaces we create for community online to those we create outdoors in our communities. She suggests the following:

Create a simple environment using clean, well-drained soil. Make sure the technology you use is aligned to the core needs and tasks people need to do together. Other stuff can be added later, but if you start with a mess, you'll end with a mess.

Use a modular design to easily care for your garden. Can tools, processes, and content for, or developed by, the community be used easily in different ways? Can you repurpose something for another use if needs change or you need to expand or contract? Can you easily add and subtract activities and tools?

Notice all the creatures that contribute matter. Who is already doing something similar? Are there early joiners who have something to add to the initial start-up building and process? Use what is available. Be creative. Don't let things go to waste.

Use free stuff to build the soil. Look around and see what free things can support your community, just as leaves and grass clippings help the earth. Can you recycle existing resources? Can you put up with adware to get the tools you need to get started for free? If you have a budget, where is it best spent? On tools, or the rare chance for a face to face? On technology, or chocolate? Make recycled chic and focus your resources where they count—on people.

Cover unused beds. Empty spaces create empty feelings. Is some part of the community technology configuration unused? Are there lifeless forums? Pull out the good content and recycle it elsewhere; either archive or button up the empty spaces. Just be careful about what you delete.

Offer protection for early starts. Sometimes online communities need a smaller, protected space to germinate, build trust, and get strong to withstand some of the buffets of the open world. This may mean finding an existing set of core members and gradually growing, or creating a little hot house to get things going.

CREATE AN ENVIRONMENT FOR KNOWLEDGE SHARING (CONTINUED)

Raise the beds. Like higher planting boxes that reduce stooping, bring community close to where people are now rather than making them go further out of their way to participate. Can you integrate with their existing spaces rather than starting a new one? Are there some simple overlaps or complementarities that suggest some sort of cross-community collaboration?

Be intensive with your gardening. Good soil retains water and has greater yields. Good nurturing, leadership, stewardship, and followership make it easier for communities to focus on why they came together in the first place. This is not about control, rather creating space and conditions for success. So, a little extra work up front can go a long way (just don't get carried away). Like a garden, a community has its seasons, and it changes over time. Be as intensive as is right for the moment.

You're searching for who in your organization knows anything about gravity-feed drip irrigation. You search in the social network to find if anyone has talked about that in their profile or has posted something about it in a conversation thread. Profiles include the industry and sector each person focuses on; they provide a way for people to quickly find a French-speaking health specialist or a Spanish-speaking logistician. If people want to connect with parents of twins or a Hispanic employee network in the Midwest, they can do that with a few keystrokes.

In the middle of a conversation you realize that the person you're talking with really should know another of your colleagues. What better place to introduce them than online? Social spaces enable people to introduce colleagues to one another. When they meet there, they can also learn from their profiles what they've shared publicly and get a sense both of why you made the introduction and where to begin the conversation.

New hires can easily find five people who went to the same college they did, three who worked for the same company, and two who grew up in their small town. Whenever someone with a similar history joins the organization, he or she can get an alert. With the ability to make these kinds of connections, cold and impersonal quickly turns warm and welcoming.

Strategy 7. Work Out Loud

"We need to do better, not at documenting what people *do*, but how they *get things done*," says Jane Bozarth, author of *Show Your Work: The Payoffs and How-To's of Working Out Loud*. "People talk about their work all the time. How can we make that more visible?" People have a hard time

Knowing others is wisdom. Knowing self is enlightenment. But the good thing is one leads to the other.
—Lao Tzu

answering the question, "Can you tell me what you do?" All too often they end up just listing activities, for all the help that offers. Bozarth encourages people to instead ask (and answer), "What are you working on?" "What problems did you run into?" "What went easily? What turned out to be more difficult than you thought?" "Where did you have to stop to look for something, or someone?" She adds, "We could learn a lot if we did less telling everyone how to do their work and asking them to show us what they do. People talk about their work all the time. Supporting them as they show their work is a great way to help them keep talking."[28]

John Stepper, managing director at Deutsche Bank and author of *Working Out Loud: For a Better Career and Life*, says, "Working out loud is working in an open, generous, connected way so you can build a purposeful network, become more effective, and access more opportunities. Anyone can learn how to do it. Most people, though, find it difficult to get started or to develop new habits that will allow them to realize the benefits."[29]

Bryce Williams, social collaboration consultant at Eli Lilly, defines this practice with a simple formula:[30]

Working Out Loud = Observable Work + Narrating Your Work

Stepper describes WOL as having five dimensions:

1. Making your work visible

2. Making work better

3. Leading with generosity

4. Building a social network

5. Making it all purposeful.

"Because there is an infinite amount of contributing and connecting you can do, you need to make it purposeful in order to be effective," says Stepper. A goal might be as simple as, "I want more recognition in my firm" or "I'd like to explore opportunities in another location." With plenty of room for serendipity, this focuses your learning, your writing, your sharing, and your connections.

Sheila Babnis at Roche explains working out loud as a way of working that gives her better access to information. Along the way, she also gets a real feel for what's happening inside and outside of her organization so she can make better decisions and solve problems faster. She sees it as the "key to building and strengthening relationships, helping to identify the right connections, and having the right conversations that open the door to co-creation."

Part of her job is experimenting and exploring—and while the idea of working out loud was initially interesting, it was also a little uncomfortable. "How could I possibly find the time, with everything on my plate, to go to yet another online place and openly share my thoughts and what I am working about? I was a little more than skeptical at the outset," she says.

"But I decided to give it a trial run and see what happens. I blocked time on my calendar to share what I was working on with my community and also asked for feedback. I slowly found myself sharing work that was not yet complete. I started getting responses, which allowed me to take more risks. Now, the more I work out loud (and engage with what others are doing) the more fluent I am becoming.

"While at first I was uneasy posting everything that was going on in my head and recapping my meetings online, now it seems normal. Working in Pharma and making an impact in transforming drug development has made me realize that I would like to play a larger role in transforming healthcare. By working out loud, I am open to new exciting opportunities with a future-oriented leadership team changing the world."[31]

> *Observable Work + Narrating Your Work = Working Out Loud.*
> —Bryce Williams

If people are working and sharing out loud, you may discover that some people in your organization are ready for new roles, new responsibilities, and new job descriptions.

Rather than your talent development department employing trainers, why not community managers? Rather than hiring instructional designers, why not curators? Be open to radically altering the portfolio and attributes of your teams.

"Almost all the people I look up to and try to steal from today, regardless of their profession, have built sharing into their routine," says Austin Kleon, author of *Steal Like an Artist: 10 Things Nobody Told You About Being Creative* and *Show Your Work!: 10 Ways to Share Your Creativity and Get Discovered.* "These people aren't schmoozing at cocktail parties; they're too busy for that. They're cranking away in their studies, their laboratories, or their cubicles, but instead of maintaining absolute secrecy and hoarding their work, they're open about what they're working on, and they're consistently posting bits and pieces of their work, their ideas, and what they're learning online."[32]

Strategy 8. Earn and Build Trust

As organizations switch to a decentralized or distributed model, transparency from company leaders is a refreshing approach that builds trust and imparts critical insights. When employees are geographically dispersed and "walking the floor" isn't an option, companies use video to reach out in authentic ways.

Status updates and video allows leaders to connect more emotionally than through a memo or an email, and it's more personal. Videos can be documentary style, or they can be video blogs, town hall meetings, or even company newsreels that cut through corporate spin and deliver information without fluff. They can be quick talking points, questions and answers, or personal day-in-the-life narratives.

Employees often respond more favorably to a CEO's unscripted comments, filmed by a member of the communication team on a smartphone, than to a glitzy, professionally shot, heavily scripted video. The more authentic and unfiltered the message, the more credible it generally is.

When two of the world's largest steel manufacturers merged in 2006, Arcelor and Mittal used video to address employees' concerns about the new 320,000-person organization. Short documentaries addressed concerns about layoffs and the merger. The videos became a catalyst for conversations about the changes both inside and outside of the organizations, fostering additional support from the market, shareholders, and citizens. Over time, Arcelor-Mittal launched its own web TV network, loaded with videos and candid conversations with executives and the men and women at the heart of the company sharing their own experiences, challenges, and aspirations.

Face Naysayers

While at NASA, Kevin Jones once led a meeting of five people, one of whom didn't like that they were trying to use a collaborative tool. "I hate this," she said, "and you will never get me to use this! In fact, I dare you to convince me I should use this."

Near the end of the meeting, a big smile came across her face and she said, "Do you mean that I could . . ." and she described a solution to a business problem she was having. When she realized a major problem she had been facing could be resolved by using the online community, out of pure joy she clapped her hands, laughed, and said, "I get it! You convinced me! I love this!" And what did she do? She became an advocate and brought those around her along with her.

Build trust with critics by focusing attention on improving work. Help them overcome their fears. Work with them to understand working out loud isn't for sharing what you had for breakfast; rather it's actually being smarter when you work. Once you break through the emotional barrier, naysayers may

> *You don't really build trust; trust grows naturally based on a pattern of trustworthy interactions.*
> —David Kelly

first understand and then embrace this approach. Why embrace? Because you will have solved a business problem that particularly irritates them. Suddenly, it isn't such a bad thing.

Former critics may just turn around and bring other naysayers along. This happens over and over again. Whomever you talk to, don't overwhelm them. Don't tell them they need to start blogging and responding to all comments. Or that instead of taking notes on paper, as they have become accustomed to, they need to take notes inside of their social platform for everyone to see. Starting there might very well turn them off. Instead, give them the next step. It might be adding files to your collaborative tool rather than attaching them in an email. It might be starting a discussion rather than a mass email.

This is why taking a personal approach is so important. It is hard to give people the next step in a group, because they are all in different places. Plus, it is difficult to ask for commitment on a large level. One on one, you can ask for that commitment and get it. Work with individuals and let them help with the change.

Burst Forward

Aaron Silvers, a partner in MakingBetter, describes social networking as an act of sharing actions. He began using Twitter to connect with peers and industry leaders who could help solve his toughest on-the-job challenges. He was working at the industrial supply company Grainger and saw that short status updates could add value to Grainger's education initiatives and provide people across the organization new ways to engage. Says Silvers, "Once Twitter made sense to me, I saw its potential as a tool to connect employees to each other. Maybe not Twitter itself, but at least a tool like it. Something that could be secure yet accessible could kick start social networking in an organization."[33]

Then a senior executive at Grainger saw the media attention over Twitter and signed up for the grassroots enterprise community Silvers helped set up. Two hours later, the executive posted to his company blog that he had created an internal account and that he'd begun using it to talk with employees. By 8 a.m. the following day, the system had 306 users. Within a few weeks, more than a thousand people had joined in.

A year later, more than 3,000 people were sharing back and forth, many using the system for far more than learning what's on the leaders' minds. People shared stories and observations, what they'd learned with customers, and how they could improve their work. Social sharing has changed the company's culture dramatically. Silvers maintains that culture change was not the explicit goal; learning was. People at all levels share what they're working on and have conversations on topics they feel passionate about. This gives everyone an opportunity to learn from those who are willing to share their expertise.

Too frequently organizational knowledge sharing mirrors the news cycle society around us, in which we share the highs and lows, ignoring the ordinary stuff in the middle. It's in that middle ground that people make sense of the work going on around them, understand how to help fulfill the company vision, and know where to turn to find help.

These slender messages are interstitial; they inhabit and fill the seams of our organizations. Learning often entails asking people how to do things. The trouble is we customarily ask the person closest to us rather than someone known to have

> *Trust is the social lubricant that makes community possible.*
> —Cliff Figallo

the right answer. Social sharing helps us reach the right people without even knowing who they are. You can also enlist help en masse by asking large groups of people to focus on the same issue for a short burst of time to find a creative solution quickly.

The threads help us collectively construct understanding, foster new connections, and grow existing bonds, making for more agile perspectives, tighter teams, and resilient morale.

These tools work similarly to how we converse while passing one another in the hallway, representing a live ecosystem that shifts from moment to moment, where it is easier, faster, and more effective for us to brain dump as events happen.

Strategy 9. Use Rich Media to Look People in the Eye

According to Cisco research, by 2018 online video will be the most highly adopted form of media. No matter which industry you are in, and regardless of the use case, you most likely already use online video, or plan to start soon.

The Internet has enabled people to be just-in-time opportunists, getting information when they need it. Employees have that same expectation at work. Short clips that can be watched or listened to on a computer or mobile device are sometimes the best way to deliver that kind of experience fast.

Large organizations have been using audio and video for a long time in marketing and training. What sets the new social media-sharing solutions apart is that they can be fast, broad, and free.

"Once Twitter made sense to me, I saw its potential as a tool to connect employees to each other. Maybe not Twitter itself, but at least a tool like it. Something that could be secure yet accessible could kick start social networking in an organization."

—Aaron Silvers

Media sharing, especially video sharing, can provide a captivating way to convey a human voice, rich with emotion and expression, that people trust instinctively more than words on paper or still photos alone can accomplish. Following are some reasons organizations are turning to rich media.

Promote the Best Examples of Employee-Generated Video

When employees can create, comment on, and share video clips, the most effective content increases in value. At CENTURY 21 Real Estate, David Birnbaum's team had a hard time getting people to upload their own videos to the company's social portal. "Even though real-estate agents often use videos these days—for their local listings and to convey they are experts in certain neighborhoods—they weren't uploading videos in our internal system, showing best practices to other agents. We wondered if it was because they didn't want to give away their secrets to other agents; a competitive advantage. When we asked, the answer wasn't what we anticipated. We heard there was no incentive or reward for sharing the videos.

"So we turned their competitive nature into an advantage for all of us. Each month we featured one video in a prominently displayed blog post and named the agent who created the video 'contributor of the month.' Agents are proud of this and so they submitted more, then they ping one another asking, 'did you see me?' People wanted to be selected—and to share their best practices conveyed they are the best."

Many organizations jumpstart viral adoption of videos by giving certain clips prominence around the organization. They use tools that allow people to embed clips in email, on team pages, and in other parts of the social network. Some even ask for volunteers willing to spend off-hours finding the best videos on the internal site and rating them to give them more exposure.

Showcase Team Accomplishments

When the sales team has a big win or the development team passes an important milestone, someone inevitably captures the celebration through video and shares it far and wide. At large meetings, encourage people throughout the event to use their smartphones to videotape almost everything. Then show onstage how the event met the expectations and objectives set out at the beginning. This rallies the troops; shares lessons from those practicing their sales pitches, such as presenters in sessions talking about an important upcoming product release, and showcases a group of people deeply interested in helping their organization succeed.

Make Progress With Pictures

Sharing stories using visuals isn't new. Pictures on rocks and cave walls date as far back as 40,000 years. Even before our predecessors congregated in communities, they drew pictures to tell narratives that conveyed movement and meaning and passed on wisdom across space and time. These stories allowed us to evolve by communicating key details and messages not as easily passed on through other means.

HEALTHDOERS UNITED

The Collaborative Health Network is a social learning network designed to unite people taking action on improving health across program boundaries. "Health-doers" accelerate the pace of community health improvement independent of their funding, organizational affiliation, or program.

With support from the Robert Wood Johnson Foundation, and led by the Network for Regional Healthcare Improvement, the network builds on the strengths of a non-profit member organization with over 30 regional healthcare collaboratives across the United States. Their aspiration is to unite many more learning networks and the implementers who know firsthand what works.

Janhavi Kirtane Fritz, director of the network, sees social learning as "an exciting and pivotal opportunity to act and learn together to accelerate change." She says, "multi-stakeholder and multi-sector coalitions across the country are coming togeth-er to improve local health and healthcare." That benefits all of us in a time when healthcare can feel elusive despite so many people trying to make it a priority.

She says, "We have seen an explosion in the number of healthcare learning net-works recently, yet they are often fragmented and flourish alone without the capacity to extend their reach and their impact. With modern technology, hospitals, doctors, insurance companies, employers, and consumers shouldn't need to take on these challenges alone. The healthcare ecosystem is noisy, but we cannot afford to keep what we're learning to ourselves.

"When funding, public or private, for programs ends, many of these vibrant net-works fade, and people retreat back to their organizations. Without ready access to these resources and people, individuals and organizations start from scratch again and again. The shared learning cannot rest on a digital shelf gathering dust." The vibrant social learning can foster an ongoing and open dialog that can accelerate the pace of real change in community health.

With quality cameras dropping in price and video capabilities now built into more mobile devices, our ability to share still and moving images has expanded from down the path to around the world. We can now see faces and activities almost as easily as we can hear voices over the phone. Storytelling, which has always been central to the human condition, now travels across new forms of media to help us learn from, and connect to, one another.

Anything that can be digitized can be accessed and distributed on the Internet or an intranet. Videos, audio files, podcasts, slideshows, and digital pictures can all be used to improve business processes and collaboration. As bandwidth increases and compression algorithms improve, a migration from text-based content to full-motion video ensues. At the same time, more powerful, compact, and mobile access devices make it easier to find and learn from relevant content whenever it's needed.

Crowdsource how we learn: See one. Do one. Teach one. Share one. Social, relevant, meaningful learning.
—Cathy Davidson

In the past, only businesses with deep pockets and the right technology could bring corporate stories to life, broadcast time-sensitive news to all employees, reach people in far-flung locations, and generally increase the impact of what they convey.

Organizations of all sizes can now afford the technology to stream video directly to employees' desktops. No longer do they need to rely on business satellite networks or on distributing content on VHS tapes or DVDs in the vague hope employees will make the effort to watch them.

They can now provide rich stories and ad-hoc video clips from the field, or they can post short, online updates throughout the day—Headline News Network style—replacing a daily newsletter as stories are blogged, tweeted, and commented on online, by anyone.

Media sharing is more than a tool or a broadcast medium. It's more than the multimedia CD-ROMs of years past. It's a way to foster interaction and sociability, another way to cultivate community—a community that extends to co-workers, partners, suppliers, customers, and other people interacting in the workplace. Media capabilities open new opportunities to interact, share, produce, and collaborate.

Videos communicate in a powerful and succinct way. Images are far superior to print or digital text to convey the totality of a situation or effort. Watching a mechanic assemble an engine can be more valuable than reading 10 books on the topic. Video engages your eyes, ears, and imagination to help you picture yourself solving a problem.

People-powered content provides buzz and insight. As more people walk around with camera-enabled smartphones and install webcams and microphones, employee-generated content will offer greater insights to companies.

Phyllis Myers, producer of the NPR radio show *Fresh Air*, characterized viral video as a "sharing experience" instead of the old "shared experience" that broadcast networks and publishers typically offer. Rather than waiting for interesting content from media giants, people increasingly reach out to pull content they want.

They can find a broad assortment of free videos from commercial sites, including YouTube and Vimeo, as well as their organization's clips created with widely available, in-house-focused software.

If a single picture is worth a thousand words, widely available videos on an endless array of topics are priceless. A bottom-up approach to employee-generated video means just about anything related to your organization can and will be captured and shared. Furthermore, the YouTube factor, where people celebrate wacky and compelling stories, means as long as video is interesting and authentic, homegrown will often do. As many podcasters have already found out, content is more important than presentation. If you have something to say that is relevant and genuinely interesting, people will watch.

Eliminate Physical Boundaries

An internal survey at Marathon Oil, with operations spanning three continents, showed that communications from executives weren't delivering the personal impact desired to inspire and inform, and there were no effective ways to gather feedback.[34]

Marathon Oil also faced the challenge of effectively and affordably training dispersed workers on topics ranging from complicated IT issues to how to properly use a safety mask. For years, Marathon employees accessed documents and presentations over the company network.

Embrace good ideas and allow your people to experiment, which includes the possibility of failure.
—Steve LeBlanc

When Marathon wanted to ensure a high level of participation, a trainer went to visit employees on site. This was expensive and resource intensive.

To address this challenge, Marathon originally decided to deliver live video broadcasts over satellite. Several expensive broadcasts later, the company switched to affordable and far-reaching streaming media.

Using an in-house production studio, two dedicated streaming servers, and rich media creation software, Marathon was able to provide live daily streaming webcasts and a library of archived presentations available on demand. The presentations are scalable and can reach all employees at once. Typically, 1,200 to 1,400 employees participate in live broadcasts, and as many as 8,000 view on-demand content.

The technology is being used for training in business integrity, hardware operation, legal issues, records retention, wellness advice, health, driver safety, Sarbanes-Oxley compliance, and instruction on software updates. Video brings Marathon executives' personalities and inflections right to employees at their workstations, wherever that may be.

Recruit Talent

Prior to being acquired by Accenture, 300-person Gestalt LLC, a software developer in Camden, New Jersey, that serves the defense and energy markets, ran a video contest to spark interest in the company among highly skilled potential recruits.

The contest was open to all employees interested in creating a video and posting it on YouTube. A companywide vote determined the winner, who could opt for an Apple computer or $2,000 in cash. John Moffett won the contest with a 90-second video called *PatrolNET Woes* about a mission through the nearby countryside to "find people."

The video contest encouraged people to create messages that ultimately promoted the company and its culture and climate and was played for the world to see. In a company whose tag line is "value beyond the sum of its parts," this was pushing even its comfort zone. The CEO, Bill Loftus, who admits he was initially nervous about the video contest idea, said "Bigger companies might try to control the message, but I believe a company's true image comes from what people really are, not spin from the marketing department." In fact, Gestalt sent a link to the winning video to 16,000 people in its talent database and to various headhunting firms as well.

During the first weekend of sending out the links, the company received 4,000 hits from its candidate database and 750 people reintroduced themselves to the firm. The videos showed the employees' energy and excitement, which positioned the company well in a very competitive market.[35]

Cultivate Culture

A Silicon Valley startup uses video blogging on its intranet for employees and employees' friends and family members to post advice on everything from finding hotels to transforming their cubes into livable habitats. One video is a tour of local eateries, pointing out the specials and comparing how fast their service is.

The videos provide immediate, actionable solutions to common issues facing a young and lean team working around the clock. None of the videos took much time to make, and they were mostly created when someone thought, "I bet my co-workers would benefit from knowing this." The videos also give new employees a sense of the culture and challenges they'll face to show them how to solve problems on their own.

> *Many failed initiatives were explained as the result of "culture problems."*
> —Dave Gray

They have also captured their founders talking about how they came up with the idea for the organization and followed people around on their first few days of work as a way to connect people to people and ideas to their originators.

In less than a year, nearly 100 videos were created for fewer than 50 employees. As the startup gains momentum and additional staff, the company plans to incorporate instant video making into its training, human resources, and technical development functions, in the hope of ensuring that the vibrant social culture stays that way, no matter how large the company grows.

Capture Corporate Knowledge Through Expert Interviews

As some of the longtime gurus of a company head toward retirement, solving big problems and focusing on what they do best, newer employees have little opportunity to learn from them. When a senior developer gives notice, have a new member of the communications team trail her for a week, discovering everything she does, asking questions, and capturing for others to learn from in the years ahead. Through interviews or even simply capturing them in action, media sharing can transform people's experiences, stories, and living examples into easily consumable knowledge before it walks out the door.

If you do something very simple, such as implement a system in which your people know where to go to get the information they need to get their jobs done, you can save people a couple of minutes a day. You generate savings when your people don't need to search through their email because they can go to a community and search easily through media clips on topics that pertain to them. Right there they also find news about the organization and tips from their teammates, which save more time. You can calculate that a couple of minutes per person per day add up to 45 minutes per employee per month. That equals nine hours per year. These are very conservative estimates of the time saved. That little calculation does not even include the benefits you can realize from improved quality and customer service. It's just that simple.

> "Bigger companies might try to control the message, but I believe a company's true image comes from what people really are, not spin from the marketing department."
>
> —Bill Loftus

Strategy 10. Curate to Focus Attention

The networks we live in extend the reach of our learning communities. In the Village of Schaumburg, Illinois, the citizens expect 24/7 engagement with their local government. Hoping to make information more searchable and sharable for employees to service demand, the Village looked to the power of social media to create a one-stop shop for communication and productivity. "[Our portal] keeps all employees in the loop, while also giving our senior management an easy way to gauge progress," says Peter Schaak, Schaumburg's director of IT.

Schaak's team created curated posts, highlighting and packaging gems for the people in the Village from the flow of information as it passed through activity streams, wikis, blogs, articles, emails, periodicals, and videos. The direct connection of collaborative content with executable work requirements links information in a way that previously depended on each worker to match puzzle pieces needed to do a job—and in this case, to be a contributing citizen. Without people culling the "best of" together, websites can easily become ghost towns of information that are rarely visited. This approach continuously makes the ever-increasing knowledge stream relevant to people looking to others for guidance and care. Author and CEO of UK-based HT2, Ltd., Ben Betts succinctly describes such possibilities—where curation is a tool of work and where "we are all required to undertake continuous personal learning."

David Kelly, CPLP, vice president of program development at the eLearning Guild, points out that there are different types of curation. They include aggregation, filtering, elevation, mash or match-ups, and timelines. "In recent years, the definition of curation has expanded [beyond museums], as more information shifts to a digital format. The sheer volume of digital information that is available makes it increasingly challenging to find the information you are interested in. Curation in a digital world isn't a luxury; it's a necessity."[36]

Think big, start small and iterate.
—Sumeet Moghe

"Curation helps individuals to capture information that is important to them and to wrap it in a context that gives more meaning than the message alone would impart," Betts explains. "Typically, this is demonstrated with a by-line or a connection to 'how we do things around here.' Many of us do this in blogs, in tweets, and in other collections of knowledge that we share with the world. We take examples of methods, processes, or ideas and show the world how they worked out when we tried it for ourselves. We adapt theories and modify diagrams to show how we think things work out, or how we would do things differently. We build and critique to advance our understanding. We discuss and debate to defend our ideas or adapt them accordingly. We curate our understanding in public."

As we continue reassessing roles throughout the organization, curation can ensure that people in education-focused jobs transition into positions where they become filters and amplifiers. As Betts describes this new curated world: "Much of this is tied up in making the tacit more explicit. Codifying your thoughts, committing to publishing, practicing good personal knowledge management will not only make you better at your current job, it could also make sure you never need to look for a job ever again."[37]

Never Give Up

"The world isn't perfect, so you need to
believe in your team and believe in yourself."
—Michael Harth, Chief Culture Officer and
co-founder, LAZ Parking

WHEN WAS THE LAST TIME you experienced poor service from a company you were about to do business with—no acknowledgment, no help, no passion, just a blah presence without much personality? For most of us, that happens so often we've grown accustomed to it.

Now imagine someone greeting you with positive energy and enthusiasm—someone who genuinely seems to notice your needs, shows with their actions you are important, and gives you a boost from their vibe. That positive energy is usually the reflection of an amazing person who works for a terrific organization, with a strong service attitude that's unwilling to give up.

That positive, caring, service-oriented approach is at the heart of LAZ Parking's company culture. LAZ employees convey through their positive attitude and proactive approach that even if their clients have had a hard day, when nothing has gone right so far, they deserve to be treated with kindness and care. Hospitality goes a long way.

In 1981, LAZ Parking was founded by three childhood friends who had their share of car difficulties—and were tired of people treating cars and the people who drove them like problems, rather than as a source of hope, passion, and possibility.

Now, with hundreds of thousands of parking spaces and more than a dozen offices across the country, the LAZ culture is based on what they call their "Never Ever Give Up" philosophy, what their employees know as the "LAZ Way." On pace to grow considerably during the next five years, adding three to four new locations per week, there are nonstop challenges, including a shortage of managers to personally connect more than 7,800 workers in 250 cities and nearly 2,000 locations across the United States.

Andi Campell, CPLP, vice president of human resources, joined when the company had no training department, an almost-completely decentralized human resources function, and no consistent strategy for developing managers—a key business imperative given the company's rapid growth and commitment to promoting from within. People in different offices didn't have an easy way to share what was working for them so that their colleagues could learn from their experience.

Many employees at LAZ don't have corporate email accounts, although most have personal cell phones. Many work in relatively solitary environments, such as parking booths, and managers can often be miles from their closest peers.

Campbell knew lengthy courses and modules that make up "traditional" curricula were not going to be the right fit for this organization. She wanted a platform that enabled sharing, collaboration, and real conversations among a distributed workforce—something that would bring people together.

She put into place a social network, the LAZ Nation Online Tribe, where the company's entire workforce can connect to discuss problems and recognize and share ideas through mobile devices no matter their location. She also launched the LAZ Parking Manager Tribe, a social network for managers, LAZ executives, and those involved in leadership development programs to drive home caring ways to work with one another.

With a single sign-on from the LAZ University Learning Center, the company's learning management system, employees seamlessly connect into these online tribes. This approach makes it easy to navigate the portal full of mobile resources, including video, which are all part of how employees learn techniques for becoming more effective leaders and growing within the organization.

In the contours of the culture, follow the patterns.
—Karen Stephenson

Her team regularly seeks out podcasts, TED Talks, YouTube videos, and articles that demonstrate ideas and concepts that support the spirit that LAZ is working to create. These resources are complemented by internally created e-learning lessons on topics such as change management, leadership development, and business acumen. They also host monthly virtual, instructor-led classes on actionable topics, most of which are facilitated by company executives and managers.

The LAZ approach to learning goes far beyond the platform, though, as Campbell drives adoption through the use of positive language. She realizes that many of the words used to describe learning in other companies could potentially turn people off. She creates an appetite for more by using words that convey interactivity, such as saying "virtual classes," rather than "webinars," which can sound passive and uninteresting. Campbell says, "People have a desire to learn something new. Messages like 'Check out this article,' 'Watch this video,' or 'Let's interact' create interest and excitement. 'Watch these modules' sounded boring and long . . . and that wouldn't do."[1]

In the foundational leadership program, for instance, people are asked to search for and post in the Manager Tribe videos or online articles that are relevant to a particular topic. Participants in the track comment on the posts and engage in online discussions about the content. From these moments of talking about what resonated with them, they create a huge amount of coaching and development material, which leads to people finding and posting more relevant content, sharing what they've found, describing why they found it helpful, and beginning even more conversations. That can lead an up-and-comer to have a conversation with his manager about something he'd learned through a video a colleague had shared, which leads to more learning.

THE LAZ LEARNING RULES OF ENGAGEMENT

Five Great Minutes. All online learning lessons are less than five minutes, and if they're a full five minutes it's a brilliant five minutes. Most lessons are no more than three minutes long.

Experiences Over Classrooms. There are virtual classes in virtual meeting rooms, but never webinars or online lectures. Facilitators design for vibrant interaction as they would design for face-to-face, then think about how to create that same experience online.

Lessons, Not Modules. Online learning is referred to as lessons—conveying that they are quick, mobile, and actionable. Each lesson teaches one or two quick things. To convey something that takes longer than a lesson, a series of lessons would be created, each focusing on one key concept and no more than a couple of minutes here or there.

In two years since the launch of LAZ University, employee engagement has strengthened, manager collaboration has improved, and the company continues to build a pipeline of high-potential employees capable of helping to sustain the company's growth. Key to that was a set of hard-and-fast rules that asked people to stop thinking of learning like school.

The talent development team at LAZ includes everyone in the organization, not just the people who are officially part of the LAZ University team.

By engaging everyone in focusing on employee development, and never giving up on one another, the organization keeps pace with ever-evolving needs and business changes and offers relevant, personalized experiences for a diverse and distributed workforce.

The LAZ Nation Online Tribe has become "a lynchpin of our company culture," says Campbell. "It's a method that connects us all to each other, despite geographic and organizational barriers. Employees stay more engaged, and learning proliferates in a way that wouldn't otherwise be possible. Executives can connect directly to front-line employees; front-line employees can share ideas with executives. In fact, our executives are on Tribe all the time. It's one way that they can see what's happening around the country. Not to mention, it's also a lot of fun to use."

> *Passion is the gasoline of social media.*
> —Jay Baer

At Times, We All Make Mistakes

As you wade deeper into creating a culture where social learning is the norm, you might make mistakes and want to give up. This demonstrates you're pushing the limits and finding your boundaries, and that kind of change entails a range of movements both forward and back. The key is to create your own "never, ever give up" strategy and learn from your mistakes, so you can improve as you move ahead.

"Hi. I'm Kevin and I have failed: social mistakes, technology mistakes, human mistakes. At times, I want to give up." That's how Kevin Jones, CEO of viaPing, focused on employee engagement, begins his presentations at conferences and with his clients across the United States. He knows we've all felt this way, and will continue to, and figures it's best to get that on the table right away.[2]

What's key, though, is to never . . . ever . . . give up.

Jones points out, "Not all internal collaborative initiatives are successful. In fact, many fail. Yet no one talks about them. No one talks about how that feels. Why? No one wants to be labeled as the one who led to failure."

In the end, these experiences are swept under the rug with the hope they will be mercifully forgotten by companies and innocently left off of résumés. But if we were to lift up the carpet and pull out these experiences without defaming company or person, we would find valuable insights from their failures—from the people who didn't give up. Properly understood, these gems provide priceless clues to help us navigate the terrain of social learning while avoiding a fate similar to that suffered by those we're learning from.

> "Not all internal collaborative initiatives are successful. In fact, many fail. Yet no one talks about them. No one talks about how that feels."
>
> —Kevin Jones, CEO of viaPing

In this chapter, we have looked under those rugs, pulled some skeletons out of the closet, and looked at all that was allowed to bloom because people didn't give up. We have found what we believe to be the most common 10 reasons organizations fail or give up when trying to implement internal collaborative or social initiatives. These real-life examples are pulled from many different businesses and industries—yet to honor how far they've come we don't name them.

While listening to others' problems, learning when and where to find workarounds, can prevent some mistakes and outright failures, you will still face difficulties that are new and unavoidable. Such challenges can create paralyzing fear in some of us.

There's little progress to be made without looking at what's not working and finding ways to turn things around. Most errors are not catastrophic. Many are small and problematic in simple ways.

Researcher Brené Brown, author of *Daring Greatly: How the Courage to Be Vulnerable Transforms the Way We Live, Love, Parent, and Lead,* and whose TED

Talk "The Power of Vulnerability" is one of the most popular of all time, has made a career of pointing out it's when we understand we're not alone in our vulnerability that progress gets made, people make deep meaningful connections, and there is hope.[3]

This chapter is designed to serve as a reference to every problem we know of and to provide guidance on what you can do to overcome them when you face any in your work.

The challenge here is to look at failures and realize that one organization's flaming disaster may be another's glorious success. We frame failure in the language of discomfort because we're tired of the rah-rah "all-change-is-good" talk, knowing full well there are times when we feel the pain in our guts. We trust you'll find there are truly gems of joy in these descriptions, and will recognize them as the opportunities they can be. In this spirit, we offer our List of Don'ts:

Facing impossible odds often forges the best strategy. Win some and learn some.
—Nicole Lazzaro

Don't Underestimate the Power of Culture

The questions and comments continually came up in meetings: "Why don't we have this social stuff at our company?" "Is this play or real work?" "We are getting a lot of pressure to do something. So what's our move?" To figure it out, the company asked one person to look at what he might do.

A few weeks later a presentation was given on what they understood social might do for the company—charts and graphs, facts, figures, and definitions. The recommendation came at the end: Use a free version of enterprise social network software and test the waters. The risk seemed low, and the plan looked solid. Before expending any capital, the company would see if all of this was hype or serious business. The executives agreed.

Within a couple weeks they had an environment up and running, and they were promoting it in the weekly company email. The first few weekly statistical reports were impressive. Hundreds of employees joined right away. Discussions were started. Some interesting insights came out of the conversation.

After the fourth week, though, the buzz died down dramatically. It eventually slowed to a trickle. Although a thousand employees had accounts, only a small handful used the platform each day, and the conversations were not usually work related. The employees chatted about technology, the weekend, and the usual complaints about management. One particularly lively conversation had been about which was better, coffee or tea.

It was unanimous. The company's little experiment was successful . . . in showing that social technologies promoted time wasting and were only a fad. Although they didn't kill the program, no further efforts were made to increase collaboration through social technologies.

Unfortunately, what no one realized was that it wasn't a success. It was a complete failure. They threw something at the wall, and it didn't stick. The main reason for their failure? Culture.

Pit an internal project against the culture, and the culture will win every time, hands down. Culture is the steering wheel of the company. Culture is a powerful tide that is difficult, but not impossible, to change. You can come up with the best tool, process, or product that will save millions of dollars, but if it doesn't fit in with the values of the culture of the organization, there is a good chance it won't be adopted.

Questions to consider:

- What type of culture does my company have?
- Are there pockets of culture that will embrace social approaches?
- What specifically can we do to help our culture be more open and transparent?

- How can we create an environment (not just technically) that makes it easy for people to embrace working in new ways?

- Because making assumptions is so automatic, how do we remind ourselves to challenge our assumptions?

- What policies or company traditions are holding us back?

Don't Focus on the Tools

Too many times people begin their social journey by asking, "What tool should we use?" The answer should be, "To do what?" Usually, they don't have a clear answer. They cite being more collaborative, being social, making sure they are up on the technology. But, social learning is not about technology. Don't believe anyone who tells you it is.

Social tools are plentiful, making the landscape confusing. The shiny toys have a certain allure that calls to the IT manager, "Buy me!" "Wow!" they think. "Look at all it can do!" Then the natural next question is, "What product should we use?" But this sentence is fundamentally flawed.

Understanding technology comes from interaction through facilitation. Not through surfing and social media.
—Marc Prensky

"We want to learn more socially" is not solved by buying a tool. It can be aided, but the tool does not solve the issue. Although slight in semantics, the difference is huge in application. These organizations only want to see how they can be more social online.

Social technology can be selected when you have the other pieces in place. What business problem are you trying to solve? Remember step one in the implementation path? Revisit it now.

What are your purposes and goals? Who is asking? How are people working and learning now? What isn't working now, and where do you want to go? Why are you not there now? What's your culture like? What's your people strategy?

Once you have the answers in place, how to choose social tools will be so much clearer. Technology will be a side note as you work on the real issues of your business. This isn't about the tools.

If we forget that "social" and "collaboration" are 90 percent people and 10 percent technology, it's easy to focus on what we can control, at the cost of what we can't (and shouldn't try to), sidestepping those things we need to influence most: people, culture, communication patterns, and traditions.

Social learning is about people working and learning together. Figure out the goals and the people strategy first.

Questions to consider:

- Is our plan focusing on the tool to the exclusion of the people?
- What people strategy do we have in place?
- What business problems are we trying to solve?
- Are the people who are running this people or technology focused?

Don't Neglect to Get Leadership on Board

There are two major approaches you can use to get employees onboard. The first is to create demand from the front line. Many social-tool vendors use this tactic to their advantage. They allow employees to start an account with their company for free. The hope is that once it gains a following and enough usage, management will have no choice but to purchase an upgraded version. The second approach is introduce from the top.

Dell is a great example of this. Michael Dell, CEO and founder of the company, is an avid social-media tool user. Largely because of his example, the company is at the forefront of using social technologies to engage customers. They have an extensive training program to show their employees how to use the tool to be brand advocates. Once employees go through the needed training, they become certified to use these tools on behalf of Dell. It's an impressive program.

The best approach, however, is using both directions, from the top and bottom, at the same time. Some executives embrace it, giving the green light to employees and middle management to embrace it as well. Other executives are dismissive, almost antagonistic, toward the tool; out of fear of retribution, employees and middle management largely stay away from using the tools. Still others are in between the two extremes. They neither promote it nor discourage it.

In this scenario, only the brave employees adopt the technology. When you don't get management on board, you are fighting against the culture set by the executives. The more the executives advocate and use internal collaborative technology, the more it will be embraced and adopted by the employees. There is a high correlation.

> *21st century leaders are tasked with engineering an ecosystem of hope in the workplace and beyond.*
> —Salima Nathoo

In a 2012 study from IBM's Institute for Business Value, 1,709 CEOs and leaders were asked a series of questions about internal and external collaboration.[4] Just over half stated they were going to increase the use and promotion of internal social tools. What wasn't asked was how these CEOs and leaders were going to actually get their people to use the tools. Several years ago, the Gartner Group predicted that "through 2015, 80 percent of social business efforts will not achieve the intended benefits due to inadequate leadership and an overemphasis on technology."

When implementing social tools, senior leaders may require you do a return on investment analysis, but it won't convey why your organization should adopt these tools. What will? Stories and personal experiences. Stats don't move us to action—our emotions do. When we hear stories that resonate and when we have our own experiences, our emotions play a big part in how we will react. Shoot for the heart, not just the mind.

The transparent nature of social media makes it easier to measure what's going on because it can be observed and tracked. For instance, you can analyze what people are searching for and map what they find. You can analyze not only where people go with their social tools but also how they get there, how long they stay, and what they do when they are there. Although this does not verify the transfer of knowledge or skills, it is a pretty good indication.

Good measures look at functional outcomes rather than simply asking, "Did they learn?" There is little value to the organization if people don't apply what they take in. The best measures go the next step to connect using new skills and knowledge with how they affect measures such as the bottom line.

One approach to consider is appealing to people's interest in building a strong reputation. Research by Molly McLure Wasko and Samer Faraj states, "The results indicate that a significant predictor of individual knowledge contribution is the perception that participation enhances one's professional reputation." They go on to indicate that "cognitive social capital plays a vital role underlying knowledge contribution."[5]

Questions to consider:

- Who is not on board that should be?

- For those who are making the financial decisions, how can we help them understand and experience this new way of working?

- What are their apprehensions?

- How should they be involved to set an example for the workforce?

Don't Expect That Employees Will "Automagically" Engage

"Wow, this is powerful. I want my team to use this," the director said after being shown the tool's capabilities. "Great. One of the many things we will need to do is training around how to use the tool," the learning manager replied.

"What? This is a social thing, right? We don't need training. They are all on Facebook. Some of them have Twitter accounts. They'll get how to use it. It's simple."

"True, but they will still need training." "If they need training," the director said, "it isn't simple enough. And I don't want something complicated for my team. But after showing me this, trust me, it's simple enough."

We keep trying to employ the new tools and ideas in the same old ways.
—Dion Hinchcliffe

These assumptions prevail because these social tools look just like the social tools we use every day with our family and friends. So if it looks the same, people should get how it works. They understand how to share. They understand how to click the buttons and navigate around. So why aren't they using it? Once again, it's because we've asked the wrong questions.

We need to ask, "What should they 'get'?" The user experience (UX)? Sure, but that is secondary. The functionality? Yes, but again, that comes after. After what? After knowing why they should use it, and for what purpose. They may already understand the technical aspects, but they don't understand how to weave it into the way they work. And it is our job to help them do that. They understand they are using email too much, but they don't understand how to effectively replace it with something else. This may be the "something else" in many situations.

Remember, you are helping people change habits here, which is incredibly difficult—especially when everyone around you has the same habits. It is easy to transition to Facebook when your family has all gone there to communicate and post pictures and videos. It is much more difficult to change your habits in an organization when few are doing what you want to do, or there may be a fear of retaliation. Give them a purpose; help them find their "why."

They must have a cause. It can be a simple one and doesn't need to be a grandiose "change the company" purpose. It could be as simple as keeping others more informed of their project, or cutting back on email within a group. Try to be as specific as you can. Unless you are working toward specific business goals, you will not be successful. When a whole team is behind a purpose, they will support each other in the new habit.

When approaching the workforce from the standpoint of a business consultant, focus on integrating social technologies into their workflow, help them to transform the way they work, and when they see the benefits, it will be hard not to give it a try. This falls under what Kevin Jones calls the Umbrella Principle.

This principle states that when we focus on certain higher order things, the lower order things will take care of themselves. Social is a by-product of the work and the environment, not the product itself. Social is a lower-order principle. But if we focus on the higher order, the collaboration, and improving the way we work and communicate, the social will happen.

Here is an example of how to address a business "why." An aerospace engineering company had a long-cherished method they used to share their knowledge of rocket engine design and manufacture. Younger engineers would send email requests to their senior counterparts, requesting information on design intent, material properties, or manufacturing techniques. The senior colleague might spend days researching and crafting an answer, which would then be sent back to the requester in an email.

The problem was that access to all this wonderfully useful information was now confined to the few people engaged in the conversation. Within a short while the information and knowledge so thoroughly and carefully created was lost; frequently even to the original person asking the question. Email systems are often purged of old email, people leave the organization and their correspondence is destroyed, or the email titles that were once so useful, no longer provide any useful pointers at all. This is far less likely to happen with an even marginally functional enterprise social system.

Eugene Eric Kim, entrepreneur, author, and co-founder of two social change consultancies, points out that "people seem to get very caught up with getting *everyone* engaged. If you install a wiki in your organization of 100 people and only five are actively using it, some might see that as a failure. I have never seen a great social tool go from zero to everybody overnight. With large groups, you will always see a power law of participation, where only a small percentage of people are actively contributing. And there will be plenty to learn from that participation."[6]

Are you expecting a crowd or a community?
—Sandy Carter

Success should be measured not by how many people contribute but by a more discerning, finer outcome: developing something broader, deeper, or more innovative than any individual can create alone. Value grows from the ability to handle information and create knowledge that acts alive, continuously morphing over time to represent the current state of what's known and the status of a network of people's capability to identify and act on what's relevant.

Questions to consider:

- How are we approaching collaborative and social initiatives? Is it about getting work done or about being more social?

- Should we even use the word *social* at all?

- How should we approach this so that employees will understand this isn't a game?

- What type of in-person, brown bag-type meetings might be helpful?

Don't Make Social Learning an Extra Thing to Do

You're asked to create a blog for a sales group. The sales director wants more training for her team. You come up with a model you believe would work. She will post one situation per week on the blog, asking everyone to comment how they would handle the situation. They would then learn from each other's approaches, ask questions, and get answers. Then she would come in and comment on those approaches, giving pros and cons.

This worked. For week one. After that, participation tapered off very quickly. Not only did the sales team stop commenting, but the director often forgot to publish the initial post. After that, it was all over. It took a while to figure out why it didn't work. In the end, it came down to one small fact: It was an extra thing to do.

One more task to add to the sales team's already overloaded schedule. Plus, it was not directly related to selling more product, so it took a back seat. The number one key to implementing any internal social learning initiative is to integrate it into the workflow.

Laurie Buczek at Intel wrote on her blog, "Culture will change as a result of the pervasive use of social tools. Lack of cultural change is not social learning's biggest failure. The biggest failure is the lack of workflow integration to drive culture change."[7] Not only is her observation spot on, but her example is perfect. (Make sure you read the comments as well.) If you don't integrate social into the way you work, it won't become a part of the way you work, and it won't be used.

Dan Pontefract at TELUS points out, "We're all busy. The 1 percent of people who are power contributors on social platforms have already built the behavior of being social through the use of collaboration tools into their own workflow and time management plan. But, there are literally millions of employees who can't figure out how to be social, so perhaps the simple solution is to help them begin their transformation and development by a recommendation to allocate 30 minutes per day—booked in their calendar—to participate with the internal collaboration tools and communities that are at their fingertips. It's not a mandate, rather a recommended new habit or practice."

Questions to consider:

- What elements of your plan make this an extra task?

- How can this be integrated into their work?

- What processes or communications are broken or are severely crippled today?

- How can we use messaging to demonstrate this is not going to be an extra task?

Don't Be Mistrustful of Your People

The LAZ social platforms allow employees to post without receiving administrative approval. This initially raised some concerns with their executives. "What if employees post inappropriate content?" they asked.

As we pointed out earlier, Andi Campbell's response was simple, "If we don't trust our employees, we have a much larger issue here."

Not everyone must participate, but everyone must believe that if they participate it will be valued.
—Henry Jenkins

As a result, the engagement they're seeing on the Tribe is far greater than expected. In the Manager Tribe, participation was initially mandated as part of a curriculum; however, it has grown well beyond any required engagement. Since the Manager Tribe is accessible only by those who have been part of LAZ University's leadership development programs, managers feel safe to truly engage with one another. What follows is a real, genuine exchange of learning. It's part of what allows the LAZ culture to truly take root, and helps managers connect to tribal knowledge in a way that wouldn't otherwise be possible.

The LAZ Nation Tribe has become a big part of their company culture. Employees post pictures, share stories, share learning. The LAZ Nation Tribe allows employees to connect with other members of the LAZ Family in a way they simply wouldn't be able to otherwise. "If you're sitting alone in a parking booth, it's a way that you can still feel connected to other people who are doing similar work," says Campbell.

> "Lack of cultural change is not social learning's biggest failure. The biggest failure is the lack of workflow integration to drive culture change."
>
> —Laurie Buczek

People are social animals and they need and seek out connection with others. With the proliferation of smartphones and other devices that facilitate connection, they will form their own communities with or without organizational support. If you create a space for people to work in, learn from, and engage with, you provide them a viable way to work that doesn't involve going around the system.

Many organizational leaders we spoke with said their employees became more efficient and easier to monitor (and influence) when there was a private forum for sharing ideas, information, and work tasks. These spaces brought people together, and they began to work more as a unit without any suggestive pushing from management.

Most companies track how many people use the communities and how often and which sub-sites and topics get the most traffic. This allows site managers to make improvements based on real behavior. At the Intercontinental Hotel Group, for example, the Leaders Lounge is constantly fine tuned—based on actual usage—to replace content created by the learning team with content generated by the managers using the site.

In most social systems, all posts are attributed to the person who makes them. They are more discoverable than emails or a bulletin board where rumors or innuendo can circulate forever without attribution. This transparency makes it a lot easier to spot people who are posting things they shouldn't and address their comments or inappropriate behavior quickly.

Perhaps more important, contributors can actually build a reputation on the site. This becomes an incentive for some to adopt the tools, actively participate, and publish high-quality content, knowing they may gain the attention of leaders and others working in complementary roles throughout the organization.

Stories can affect change.
—Jeff Gomez

It was important at LAZ to also trust people as learners. If you create all learning content to first tell people what you're going to tell them, then tell them, and then tell them what you've told them, you likely lost them after the first telling. Modern media tools are faster and more to the point.

Step back from traditional instructional design rules to create fast and captivating lessons that will be remembered because they can be put into use. Try to mirror how people learn in real life now. Ask how would people learn this in real life and mirror that, because they already know how to work in that way.

Social media is generally self-policing. If someone posts something inappropriate, the next person to see it has something to say about it. Sharing is successful in part because of employee feedback and because so many other people will be watching. Trusting your people also means being open to whatever feedback they have to offer, whether it's good or bad. As Trisha Liu, former enterprise community manager at HP ArcSite points out, "Negative feedback is a gift. Don't put a muzzle on the gift horse."[8]

Organizations often want to offer their employees a community or social media toolset but don't want the conversations to wander off specific business themes. As social creatures, people thrive on meaningful connections with other people. Although most conversations should have a professional focus, connections across topics build relationships and trust sometimes more effectively than sticking solely to job-related areas.

Jamie Pappas from Akamai shares, "In my experience, the social conversations serve as excellent ice breakers and provide a way for people to connect on a topic that is not intimidating. Sharing ideas such as restaurant recommendations, or allowing employees to create book clubs, motorcycle clubs, and all sorts of other affinity groups allows people to begin their relationship with other colleagues sharing something that doesn't require expertise, just a common passion. It facilitates their ability to learn about other perspectives and talents across the organization, and it gives them common ground from which to build business relationships."

Although some organizations formally ban these tools, doing so leaves them out of an important loop encompassing customers, partner networks, and even families.

Time spent in online communities needs to be managed, but the same could be said about time on the telephone, using email, or in meetings. The challenge may be more about how to address some people's compulsion to constantly look busy rather than get their work done.

Although many enterprises today constrain employee access to social media on the Internet at work, there are few ways to block all social media use by employees, unless they are forbidden from using their personal smartphones entirely. Foster instead good practices and educated decision making for a longer-term solution.

The other side of the coin, however, just might be trusting a little too much. "Let's ask everybody what they think." That phrase is probably said somewhere in the world every second. Oftentimes, the people asking get perspective they wouldn't have heard without asking. But organizations can also easily fall into the trap of only hearing from the same people, not getting fresh perspectives, and believing that's good enough.

There are some added and unexpected powers of groups that aren't always used, though, and that should be factored in as well.

A group can help keep its members on track through constant reinforcement of good practices, building and communicating guidelines, removing inappropriate material, and having continual social dialogue about the right balance. On rare occasions, organizations need to take action, but those are few and far between and usually, in the end, reflect more positively than negatively because they demonstrate the power of peers managing one another.

Questions to consider:

- How trusting is your culture?

- If people aren't trusted is it because they aren't trustworthy or for some reason?

- Which policies and practices inhibit people wanting to work in trustworthy ways?

Don't Structure Information Flows to Model Your Org Chart

"This is going to change my organization? I didn't sign up for *that*!" The business unit manager who was enthusiastic about the social initiative is changing his tune.

It's not just that change can be hard; people taking control of their work lives by reaching around bureaucratic policies themselves can be scary to those who actually believe hierarchy charts represent how organizations function and whose perceived power is dependent on hierarchy. For many, the way things have always been has served them well. Why would they wish to see it change?

When you build your systems and practices to mirror your hierarchy, as if that's truly how information flows in your organization today, you miss the opportunity for people to make connections and learn from others they weren't learning from before. If, for instance, you provide social venues restricted to people at a certain level of the organization, allowing communities and groups to be started only by senior leaders, or create tools only for people on the front line with no channels of interchange from people at various levels, you are restricting the natural flow of information and knowledge that social technologies are designed to encourage and facilitate.

Joe Sullivan, an extreme problem solver in the corporate scientific community, finds that organizations lull themselves into a false sense of safety with their hierarchies, rather than recognize the danger of discouraging information flow, keeping data out of the minds of people who need it.[9] When information only flows in one direction, it can easily become diluted or ambiguous, filtered and repackaged or, in the worst case—much like the inevitable errors introduced in a childhood game of telephone—completely incorrect. It can be difficult to meet the fast-changing needs of the marketplace if you are hierarchically challenged because it takes precious time for critical information to move up and down the chain of command (if it's even possible). Lateral relations are needed to develop relevant relationships or access vital information. Many of the best ideas come through serendipitous interactions.[10]

Social tools present an opportunity to replace old, time-consuming processes with faster ones. You might believe you are too busy to learn a new tool or to deposit information in more than one place, but replacing your current processes with new, more efficient ones is not adding more duties.

When working in a collaborative system, people are encouraged to work with the broadest audience possible, which runs counter to many organizations' prevailing culture of specialization and the inevitable restrictions implied by need to know.

Without collaborative alternatives, people frequently duplicate work because information is lost in shared drives and old emails. It can be eye-opening to participate in a virtual community and realize you're not the only ones doing particular work or who have the information and insights others need.

The best way to support learning is from the demand side rather than the supply side.
—Jay Cross

In the CIA's Wikipedia-like *Intellipedia*, participants can create links among environments, creating breadcrumbs, leading from where you came to where you're going. The network can then control access. If people have access, they will be able to follow the link. If they don't, they at least know that more information exists, and they can begin following the breadcrumbs, seeking access if necessary and their need to know can be established.

Work to gain both grassroots and top-down sponsorship. Begin at whatever level works for your organization's culture. Some organizations respond best when people on the front line participate first. Others only get involved when they see senior leaders contributing. If you have early conversations with people from both groups, as well as those in the middle, you're more likely to garner the attention and participation of those who are curious, yet a little timid about jumping in.

Questions to consider:

- How hierarchical is your organization? Are people afraid to reach across lines on the organization chart?

- Where in the organization do people naturally work together across silos? Are there sports teams or a shared cafeteria? Are there challenges for people from various divisions to contribute to?

- What might you do in your online space to bring people together who wouldn't know one another otherwise? How can you do of that?

Don't Choose Just Any Tool

While this effort to implement social learning might not be all about the tools, it's still important to consider the tools that will be used. Too often we try to jump in with a tool first. Resist that temptation. But when it is time to choose a tool, it is a very important decision, one not to be taken lightly. Although social is not about the tool, the tool is a heavy component and careful scrutiny of its capabilities and workings should not be discounted.

For example, some of the features most often overlooked by a novice when choosing a tool are the number of clicks it takes to get information, the flow in which that happens, and the ways users are notified of new or changed content.

Many attributes have a hidden importance and, until you understand the social element, you very well may not uncover those needed features. So what to do? Make sure the person who evaluates potential tools has experience in this. (There are enough people out there, finding someone should not be a problem anymore.) Listen to them and weigh their advice. And then know this: No tool or set of tools will give you everything you need and want.

Companies are constantly looking to cut corners. When we choose cheap approaches to social tools, we might look for the cheapest, or even free, software. Maybe we don't put the technical resources behind it to make sure it runs well, or we fail to hire someone who knows how to help a company adopt it, hoping the "build it and they will come" strategy might work. If you decide to jump into social learning, do it right. Hire good people. Buy the right software. Put it on the right hardware. Give the team the time and resources they require. You don't have to be extravagant, but put in the commitment that will lead to success.

There is a tendency to go with the cheaper solution. Yet often that solution does not have what is needed. Although being social is not about the technology, the wrong technology will cripple any initiative.

There are gives and takes, many of which won't be discovered until you have purchased and implemented the tool in production. Just go with it and enjoy the journey! The tool should make your job easier. No tool is perfect, and you will never get 100 percent of what you think you need. At the same time, don't settle for just getting by. Make sure the tool works for you—not you for the tool.

Questions to consider:

- Will the tool we have chosen be able to give us 90 percent of what we need?

- As we look to contain costs, are we sacrificing needed functionality for cost savings?

- After this is launched, are we giving enough resources to build this initiative or only maintain?

- In what ways might we be trying to cut corners and can we justify those?

Don't Aim for Perfection

At EMC, work-in-progress content was viewed as more valuable than finished content because it showed how the organization had arrived at where it was— often a key element that employees, customers, partners, prospects, and even the media are keenly interested in.

There is a spectrum of knowledge that goes from the most nascent, early stages of information up to polished, presentable, deliverable content—in the form of reports, presentations, web pages, and more. If your organization relies on the sale or distribution of products that capture a situation on a certain date, consider the content created in a living tool such as a wiki as complementary rather than competing.

"Our works in progress also showed stakeholders that there was room for improvement and room for commentary, and, in fact, both were welcomed," says Jamie Pappas, who worked at EMC prior to joining Akamai. "This exposure makes the organization more vulnerable, yet also seem more human because not everything that comes out is polished and professional. It provides insight into the organization that might not have otherwise been gleaned and, in turn, offers stakeholders more reason to trust the organization because it has shown how it works."

FOLLOW THE HERD

Brent Schlenker, chief learning officer at litmos.com, has watched new technologies enter the workplace for over 20 years. He says, "Social learning has by far been the most disruptive force to those around me. I work with hundreds of trainers and thousands of learners each year, and they all seem to split into two distinct [and disruptive] camps."

He refers to them as "'A-players,' and 'Everyone else'—or 'B-players' for the sake of having a reference point.

"A-players are self-driven learners, self-motivated, and who embrace change quickly. The idea of connecting, collaborating, creating, and sharing were comfortable for them long before the rise of social networks. They appreciate and prefer to learn from anything and everything because they recognize the world is constantly changing and adapting to new approaches is vital to their success.

"B-players prefer to work from within their comfort zone, skeptical of change, and look to others to tell them what to learn next. Learning with social media is uncomfortable because there are not clearly defined objectives, outcomes, and paths determined for them by accredited experts. With each day, they are growing increasingly left out, unsure how to get back the confidence they once felt they could learn what they needed to in the formalized structure of training events."

He adds, "I'd prefer not to be the guy who has to break the news to the B-players that the world they remember isn't the world we'll live in ever again. The A-players are learning too much and having too much fun to ever agree to letting anti-social learning dominate again."[11]

Collaborative spaces are where people in your organization can synthesize issues, ideas, arguments, and actions into coherent, meaningful messages and learn from one another as they produce a product for a customer at a particular moment. These spaces become a venue for enhancing the thoroughness and comprehensiveness of the product.

Questions to consider:

- What are the advantages of working out loud, showing work in progress, and bringing people into the conversation before our ideas are fully baked?

- Who are the people already working in this way?

- How can you amplify their practices so others can learn from them?

Don't Be Too Timid

The aerospace industry is widely known for being cautious, conservative, and risk averse. Having joined the Space Shuttle Main Engine program shortly after the Challenger disaster, Rick Ladd was well aware of the reasons behind the caution. Regardless, he could see there was room for improvement in how information and knowl-

We need a "commons" where people who feel part of community can discuss and argue vexed issues in serious ways.
—Cathy Davidson

edge were created and shared. He also knew that NASA and the company he worked for, Rocketdyne, had engaged in many attempts to codify and preserve their hard-won knowledge of rocket engines and the technologies that went into successful launches.

As the lead for the Space Shuttle Main Engine team's knowledge management efforts, he'd heard all the arguments against what he was doing, which early on wasn't thought of as social learning. There was a well-worn saying offered as proof it was a waste of effort: "Every time we design a new engine, we have to blow it up at least once."

While it was true that rocket engine programs were long lived and, frequently, by the end of an engine's service life the people who had worked on its early design and seen its failures were frequently retired or had moved on, he was convinced there was a way to ensure that knowledge was passed down to the next generation of rocket scientists, engineers, mechanics, and everyone else responsible for those engines.

Shortly after the installation of a tool originally thought of as a knowledge management system—an expertise locator—Ladd realized they had actually brought in a social learning tool. The problem became, then, how to get people to use it the way it was intended. Although the company from which they purchased the tool had created a method for helping people complete their profiles, he found it was still difficult to get the engineers and scientists to pay much attention to it.

Although neither an engineer, nor a scientist by training, Ladd knew this was the right thing to do. Despite numerous objections, ranging from the fear that a janitor might hold himself out as a physicist, or that someone would unwittingly share sensitive information, he consistently pointed out the tool's superior features and continuously demonstrated to company executives how the system's benefits far outweighed the negatives some were so eager to point out. By sticking to his guns, Ladd was able to see the tool enjoy acceptance and growth.

Such is the job of the person who leads social initiatives. She or he must lead people into unfamiliar territory, frequently against their wishes. The challenge is to help people become comfortable when they're being asked to do something they resist.

Some people won't do the right thing because they fear personal backlash. Trust, openness, and transparency are bedrock ideals of social learning—yet too many company cultures avoid them. For organizations to enter into the next phase of economics and be successful, this must change.

We cannot expect to experience progress without change. What we need are those who will be bold; who are willing to take risks. Will there be times when they get slapped down? You bet. Times when the consequences will be unfair? Without a doubt. Times when they say what everyone else wanted to say, yet no one will back them up? Count on it. Stand strong. Be bold.

Questions to consider:

- Who are we scared to approach?

- What issues have been glossed over but should rather have been brought up?

- Who can we count on to be bold?

- Will they, at the same time, have the necessary tact and will they refrain from being overbearing? But if not you, who?

Don't Allow Failures to Define You and Your Work

We hope that you have learned from these 10 examples of how others have strayed from their path so you won't repeat the same mistakes. Never ever give up. With all this talk of failure, you may be apprehensive as you start out on your social learning journey. If so, good for you! You might not have a large, crashing failure, but you will fail in smaller ways. This is part of being social. There is not one right way to do this; if there was, we would all be doing it. Because every business culture is different, because each project has different needs, how we engage employees with collaborative technologies can be very different.

The best way to fail at social learning is to learn from it, and to allow others to learn from you. Failure will happen. Don't be afraid to show that you have failed. By showing your vulnerability, you also show your strength. At the same time, as others fail, cheer them on. Help them learn, learn from them, and do better next time.

One of the largest roadblocks to getting started on any new initiative is having the courage to face those who think what you're doing is dangerous or dumb—or who spend all their time picking at your failures. Maybe they have heard a story of someone doing something that scares them. Perhaps it's the unknown itself. That may be defining them, but it doesn't need to define you.

Now that you have learned, go and do your best. If it works, do it again and make it better. If it fails, don't do it, or do it differently. Set the expectation that you will experience failure. Then, when (not if) you do, you won't have to try to cover it up with obscure statistics. You can change on the fly and do better next time. The extent to which you fear failure is often the extent to which you inadvertently fear success. Learn from failure—even embrace it. Make it a strength instead of a weakness. By doing so, you will gain more trust from those you work with and who work around you. This leads to more chances to succeed. Study the failures of others, not to condemn, but to learn and grow.

Social learning is inherently innovative. The more innovation an initiative demands, the more tolerant of failure we will need to be. It comes with the territory. So our success depends not upon whether we only do things right, but rather how we handle failure when it happens.

Questions to consider:

- When failure happens, how will you deal with it and what attitude will you have?

- How can you help others to have a more iterative mindset?

- What's required for you to openly have a conversation about a project's faults?

- What steps can you take yourself to ask a question of anyone, showing you don't know all the answers (even when maybe you think you ought to)?

- How can you create an environment where people feel safe to bring up topics without fear of retribution?

- In your organization, what could be done so that anyone can point out a mistake another has made (with tact and in private), even if that person has more seniority?

- What mechanisms can you introduce to alert you to roadblocks, even if it might mean political backlash?

- How might you lead the way so that people can say what needs to be said, not only what others want to hear?

Analyze Insights
and Returns

"Prove that the risk is outweighed by the reward. Make
sure that the numerator is larger than the denominator."
—Ben Brooks

SIMON TERRY KNEW THAT as a banker, and in his role as CEO of HICAPS, a
healthcare-focused division of National Australian Bank (NAB), decisions
and investments were made on measurement, evaluation, and ensuring risks
were outweighed by returns. When a team member of NAB created a way for
people across the 40,000-person organization to work together more effectively, he knew he'd need to quantify this, too. The priority was to increase
collaboration, supporting the NAB transformational and cultural goals that
were already in place.

He admits now that he supported the project out of self-interest and knew
it would be easy enough to measure success. Many of his roles in NAB involved
collaboration across silos. The organization needed to be able to do that more
easily. As CEO, he spent part of his day answering emails from people across the
parent company's network. Most of these questions were fairly general, need-
ing answers that many different people could have answered, and the answers

to which should be easily found online if the right systems were in place. He wanted his time back and hoped the new tools would do just that.

At first he moved the inquiries from his inbox to the social network's update box so everyone could see his answers to the questions. Then he noticed people on his team began doing the same. Soon questions were being posted to the network, not sent to him directly, and people across the organization were answering them without him. His first goal had been achieved.

What had taken hours every week now took only minutes each day. Some days that time was then spent proactively answering questions people hadn't yet asked, but that he thought needed to be addressed. Other days, people who didn't even know one another were launching into broad and deep conversations that resulted in creating new services his division could offer and novel ways to work between teams that were making huge leaps in productivity.

Their initial system had not cost his department anything and was clearly delivering benefits to the whole organization. His getting peace of mind from the return of lost time had been enough justification for the investment of the people needed to set up the environment.

After two years into their journey, a general manager of the technology group socially shared that the system's license was up for renewal, but the institutional immune system didn't want to pay. Terry shared this news with the now-thriving online community and within days received 191 replies. People began adding into the system ways to measure and prove the value of how they were now working.

Another employee introduced the practice of tagging any business improvement posted in their network with the hashtag #wins. All the posts tagged that way were then curated so they could add up the money saved, the new business initiated, and the processes that could be measured, which Terry and the other sponsors of the collaboration could then share with the GM.

That led to adding additional hashtags for the four transformational goals of the larger organizations: #customerexperience, #increasemarketshare, #continuousimprovement, and #leadership. As people improved in any of these areas, they shared the wins and documented the successes. When it was time for the leaders of the community to report to the NAB leadership on how Terry's organization had made progress—and to make the case that the license fee was nominal in comparison to the organization's gains—the network compiled a report full of examples and real-time practices that could be used by other parts of the business.

> Social media is about time and value. Put in the time, see the value. See value, you put in the time.
> —Jane Hart

The group executive for people and communications surprised Terry by telling him the report was unnecessary, as he had followed the conversation as it unfolded and had a strong sense of the value the division was providing the organization overall. The social learning journey had brought everyone along.[1]

Look Back to Look Forward

Organizations invest time and money in the collaborative approaches that foster social learning for many reasons, as we've outlined in this book. The most common reasons we hear are related to addressing what's broken in the culture, namely stringent policies that restrict people from working across departments.

By adopting new practices, leaders hope to increase the amount and quality of knowledge sharing across the organization so that people can make better decisions, and to create an atmosphere where people build trust, increasing their desire to do good work. Everyone seems to believe that changing the fundamental conversation in the workplace helps employees find meaning in what they do and satisfaction in their time on the job.

Where does this fit with leaders who want to know if this engaged approach contributes to the bottom line? Where do we look to find new approaches that will make a bigger difference? How do we decide if and when one of the tools should be ditched altogether?

Do these changes somehow provide sustainable strategic advantage? If not, what can we do to the social tools or the organizational culture to make them effective? If so, how can we make sure we increase their benefit?

Specifically as it relates to learning, there are direct and indirect ways to gauge the amount, type, and quality of learning happening between people, especially using social software. The question becomes: Should that be your aim? Is that really what's important for you to understand? Is that the most useful thing for leaders in your organization to know?

Quantifying conversation can be equally misguided. Counting how much is said would be no more valuable than measuring how much students in a class weigh as a true signal of effectiveness.[2] Sure, it's evidence of something, but it doesn't provide value.

Too often, people are so fearful of assessment or so stuck in their ways they don't realize there are alternatives to the traditional metrics that have been used for eons in business and education. Many people still only know a few evaluation methods and choose which ones to use based on their convenience.[3] "I only have a few minutes at the end of this program to see if it was helpful so I'll pass out a simple form," is only effective if you're assessing people's interest in giving you feedback or capturing anecdotal evidence they may have remembered by the time it's over.

One human resources executive we spoke to while writing this book said that he doesn't want the rest of the organization to know all the workforce data and analytical tools he has access to, for fear people will task his department with doing even more than his meager staff can manage. He added that the vendors who give him access to this data assume he's going to do something useful with it, but his peers at the executive table give the impression it's the last thing on their minds.

KEY DEFINITIONS

Analysis is the process of pursuing to understand something puzzling.

Analytics are methods and tools to parse streams of digital bits into meaningful patterns for making more effective decisions.

Big data is more data than can be easily understood or analyzed without powerful processes. Its value is measured by its volume (amount), velocity (speed generated and available), variety (kinds), and veracity (accuracy).

Data are bits of information that come in all shapes, sizes, and kinds and are found everywhere.

Evaluation is traditionally a backwards-looking measure of how well something has been done.

Evidence is found in the signals along the path.

Measurement is a gauge of change.

Understanding and using analysis to make smart decisions requires focusing on what you aim to accomplish and the myriad factors that led to where you've arrived. Based on this leader, and the many others we spoke with, who either don't know how to quantify the people factor in their organization, or don't even believe it's possible, we realized there's a fundamental disconnect—perhaps several—between new social and collaborative practices, and the leaders who are interested in measuring their value.

People who tell us there is "no way to measure this stuff," because it seems too tacit and ephemeral, may not have taken the time or known where to look for ways to analyze this newly surfaced value in their organizations. For those at the beginning of the journey, we also want to remind them there are many ways to analyze what's ahead.

Most leaders are far more interested in understanding what elements are critical to deliver in line with their business strategy, as well as identifying their organization's largest challenges and risks. "The value an organization places on social initiatives will largely be based on its expectations," says Joel Postman, author of *SocialCorp: Social Media Goes Corporate*. Learning and talent management are factors, as is collaboration itself, yet those are means to a more critical end.

Look first at your goals, then look underneath them. As it relates to learning, is what people are learning reliably and sustainably advancing organizational goals, especially in economic terms? Are you more interested in changing opinions, behaviors, relationships, capabilities, or something else? Is what people are learning advancing the organization's position, long-term success, and the impact you can have on the world?

When an organization supports working in social ways, it is challenging old assumptions about how work gets done, how people work together, and how learning happens. It would seem incongruous not to also challenge staid practices in our search for understanding what worked, what didn't and, most importantly, what didn't work this time but could with a few changes along the way.

Almost everyone we spoke with about quantifying collaboration was adamant that we remind readers that correlation does not imply causation.

"Linear evaluation is focused on providing cause and effect for the sake of attribution—specifically showing when certain influencers cause specific outcomes—not to measure what we've done and how well we've done it," says Natalie S. Burke, CEO of CommonHealth ACTION. "Theories of change indicate that the purpose of evaluation is to show that people's lives or organizations have improved, that they are better than they were before, and that we know why.

"Too often people seek to evaluate if A leads to B, when in fact we should be evaluating the interaction of A, B, Q, R, and M. Understanding their interplay helps us to understand the role of each variable, in relation to others. If we don't approach evaluation like this, acknowledging complexity, we risk attributing change to all the wrong things or failing to give credit to the right things. [4]

"Think of it like this: I could say that the reason a duck can fly is that it flaps its wings. If it was really that simple, that linear, how can I explain the fact that a chicken can't when making the same motions? Clearly it takes more to fly than flapping wings," says Burke. "The same applies to change whether within a society or an organization. Evaluation and the analysis that goes along with it don't have to be complex, but they can't be overly simplistic either."

> *The best way to increase the likelihood of change in social groups is to increase the number of connections people have. That drives the speed at which new ideas can spread.*
> *—Stowe Boyd*

Rarely do people ask if the underlying purpose of evaluation is because the people funding the project want proof their contribution provided value or because they merely want the accompanying recognition.

"If that's the case we should just thank them rather than initiate a complicated and likely-not-very-accurate evaluation process," Burke says. "So much of bringing people to work together in new ways—the types of work that lead to significant change—requires many things to work well together and there need to be conscious efforts to remove constraints to collaboration, evaluation being one of them. The work of change is like soup, and you can't credit its flavor to one ingredient."

Attribution can be very powerful as it relates to getting funding and securing the support of leadership. Burke adds, "If you're being asked to evaluate your success you need to know what 'they' [the funders, the stakeholders, the decision-makers] really want to know. Is it about learning, understanding, impacting, and improving or is it about giving credit where they believe it is due."[5]

The simplest way to quantify your efforts is to position your costs against your savings, in a similar way to how Simon Terry did this at NAB. Terry calculated the cost savings from how he had adjusted his work, and deducted out the price of the technical systems. In addition to that, he worked with the people in the network themselves to capture the dollars saved and earned as a result of many people working and learning together.

"Too often people seek to evaluate if A leads to B, when in fact we should be evaluating the interaction of A, B, Q, R, and M."

—Natalie Burke

As Ben Brooks, business coach and former corporate senior vice president of human capital, says, "Make sure that the ratio works. Prove that the risk is greatly outweighed by the reward."[6]

If what gets measured gets done, as Peter Drucker is often quoted as saying, then we also need to be careful about focusing too much on the wrong things because we've decided to measure them.

Douglas Merrill, former CIO and vice president of engineering at Google, warns that while we should ask ourselves how to measure everything, we should also be careful about what we measure because people will work toward showing progress, regardless of whether or not it's productive. Measuring the wrong things can take away from focusing on what we really need and want from people.[7]

We also need to make sure what we choose to measure is grounded in sound and enduring principles. INSEAD associate professor of organizational behavior, Gianpiero Petriglieri, points out that while managers are inheriting scientists' love of data, "data without a good theory makes us more clueless."[8]

Andi Campbell at LAZ Parking says, "The more I coach, the less I need to provide structure because my team is motivated to perform at their best when they're responsible for, or at least participating in, setting the expectations. They're naturally aligning with the business, they're making good decisions, they're staying at our company, and the result of their work is a growing talent pipeline for our new locations."

It's taken me years to really understand but organizational culture is the output of a good system . . . not an input to change/manage.
—Rachel Happe

In other words, the real benefit of analysis comes from relating experiences to outcome— more sales, fewer complaints, stronger leaders, and happier employees.

"In some ways, our capitalistic system encourages decision because the forces applying pressures to achieve revenue and growth are rewarded more strongly than those encouraging ethical behavior. This may be a bit extreme, and your company is most likely a highly ethical one, but these pressures are very real, and even the most ethical people sometimes show very poor judgment when they are pushed hard to deliver difficult bottom-line results," says Joel Postman.[9]

"This is unfamiliar territory," some may protest as they do questionable things. "We're on the frontier of communications. The rules are being written as we speak." Nice try. Social approaches and new media do not require new morality. Most of us know right from wrong, and methods you haven't used within the workplace before don't release you from your responsibility for ethical behavior.

When metrics that are already used in the workplace link directly to your efforts, evaluation is easy. Revenue or time-to-quota clearly indicate the success of working in a social way. If you close a sale because of an exchange you have online or save a million dollars because a colleague suggests a simple hack that negates the need for even spending that money, few question the investment.

Unfortunately, not every program aligns easily with company metrics. Leaders may be skeptical when you claim business results amid many variables affecting success.

For these investments, you need to embrace a measurement toolbox that keeps pace with new approaches, one that looks beyond the business impact of past programs and can apply statistical certainty to the success of future programs.

> "Think of it like this: I could say that the reason a duck can fly is that it flaps its wings. If it was really that simple, that linear, how can I explain the fact that a chicken can't when making the same motions?"
>
> —Natalie Burke

Use Lightweight Analysis

Today, most large organizations rely on heavyweight applications, including enterprise resource planning (ERP) and customer relationship management (CRM), to collect and manage the critical business information that drives their daily operations.

As business evolves, organizations need to consider if lighter-weight approaches and applications might be used to get at the nature of change itself, and provide meaningful data to leaders more interested in in-the-moment insight than cumbersome, static reports.

Terri Griffith, management professor at Santa Clara University and author of *The Plugged-In Manager: Get in Tune with Your People, Technology, and*

Organization to Thrive, suggests organizations use lightweight experiments rather than all-or-nothing approaches to catalyze change in organizations.[10]

"Taking small steps is more important than ever, given the pace of the world around us. Find fast and inexpensive ways to test the leap-of-faith assumptions underlying the adjustments you want to make," Griffith says.

Have half of your teams try one form of flexible work scheduling and the other half another so you can learn from both. Use a crowdfunding campaign to test the market for a new product. Griffith cautions, "Steer clear of surveys, you don't want to base your change on someone giving you an answer they think you want to hear. Instead, measure behaviors like prepayments, performance, or repeat business."

There are many ways to measure changes that benefit you and your organization, both quantitatively and qualitatively, and within each of these the approach to gathering information varies, too. Just make sure first you know the real reason you're evaluating your work. What you are seeking to learn should dictate the type of measure you look for.

To help you quantify your work, we've created a compendium of approaches that get at the heart of people going further together.

Analysis 1: Perspective

What if you could get a sense of how the people in your organization felt about the company, each other, your customers and suppliers? What if you could better understand not merely what they felt, but how deeply they felt and how well they understood their perspective?

While employees and the press might like to believe that senior leaders of large organizations know all that's going on in their ranks, that's often far from reality. Spending time in meetings, focused on strategy and market share, leaves little time to get a read on what employees are thinking and feeling—about your organization and their work in general. For many years this disconnect was dismissed as the cost of doing business, yet we can all see the inherent risks. This may be acceptable for today's leaders, who don't understand the power of the tools available to them, but does anyone believe that will continue to be true in five years?

> "Taking small steps is more important than ever, given the pace of the world around us. Find fast and inexpensive ways to test the leap-of-faith assumptions underlying the adjustments you want to make."
>
> —Terri Griffith

Ronald Burt, University of Chicago sociologist and author of *Brokerage and Closure: An Introduction to Social Capital*, the seminal book on social capital, points out that people continue to work the way they learned in legacy organizations, in yesterday's organizational silos. He points out, "We are capable of coordinating across scattered markets of human endeavor. We are not yet competent in how to take advantage of the capability."

These are not new challenges, yet we have arrived at a time when they can be solved immediately. In many cases, the most senior leaders (as well as people in all levels and roles) can learn what their colleagues are doing and thinking with the click of a few buttons. This is now possible because people are sharing with the express hope they will be heard and understood by those who manage their organizations. Even when they're not sharing their views and experiences, they are frequently leaving behind breadcrumbs that can be decoded and acted on.

Analytics

While organizational functions including marketing, supply chain, and finance are becoming increasingly sophisticated in their use of analytics to inform decision making, and are seeing clear benefits in terms of business outcomes, many human resources organizations haven't been as proactive, even as the people side of business increases in importance each year.

Because human capital is the source of a company's intangibles, human capital management and analytics are essential competencies that all companies need. For instance, over the last 30 years, the role of intangibles, the source of creating organizational value, has increased sixfold.[11] Using analytics to extract and apply insights about the workforce is one of the biggest opportunities for any organization.

Marketing creates the brand, Support keeps the brand alive.
—Nenshad Bardoliwalla

There's already ample evidence that those organizations using analytics to understand and assist people in their work outperform organizations that don't. McBassi & Company has created a simple analysis to assess how your company stacks up in terms of your need to focus more on analytics.[12]

Priorities

When the CEO of a multinational company looked casually through several blog posts about a company event where he'd just spoken, one post about the lack of women on the stage caught his eye. He commented that other speakers had been invited, and that he appreciated the perspective. It was his first public comment, and he was surprised how easy it was to weigh in.

Within 24 hours, his comment had received dozens of additional responses, pointing out other incidents of easy-to-overlook sexism in public positions, and that the absence of women seems discontinuous with the organization's stated goals.

He'd asked repeatedly for feedback through the usual means for years, yet had never realized how important this was to his employees. Even if he had received considerable feedback through those channels, yet chose to ignore it as some believed, he now had firsthand stories and the voices of his employees—publicly stated and difficult to ignore—to consider as he made decisions going forward.

The data points he received were also quantifiable; within a week there were over 80 comments. Groups had begun to form that were curating lists of women within the company's ranks who would be great speakers, and who should be noticed not because of how loudly they'd been leading but because they were making a difference in their employees' lives.

Within just a week, this senior leader heard perspectives and priorities he hadn't for a long while, despite thinking he had been asking all along.

Attitude

For organizations looking for quantitative measures of the loyalty of their workforce, *sentiment analysis* measures how people feel about something: happy or disgruntled, committed or apathetic, trusting or not trusting. These emotions lead to the amount of time people are willing to devote to their jobs, their commitment to making good decisions on their employer's behalf, and the likelihood they'll stay or leave.

Sentiment analysis uses natural language processing to determine if people are communicating in either positive or negative ways related to a particular subject, person, organization, or brand. Lillian Lee, professor at Cornell, often credited with creating sentiment analysis, points out that when people are somehow connected, they may be more likely to hold similar opinions and attitudes, so there is value in looking at the sentiment held across groups.[13]

Also known as opinion mining, for years vendors have offered marketing organizations services that monitor public sources of opinion such as what is posted on Twitter, written in blogs, and commented in articles in order to provide insight on how public opinion is trending on a specific topic.

These same types of tools are available to assess sentiment inside organizations too, tracking what's termed *employee voice*. Rich textual data can be mined to better understand the opinions and sentiment of employees for the benefit of the organization. These tools are designed to understand employee chatter. They can aggregate and analyze data from internal and external social media sources, while respecting employee privacy.[14]

Should you be measuring people's attitudes about their jobs, your organization, its leaders, or even your competition? Only if you're going to do something about what you learn.[15] The larger question is whether you're looking for a change, presumably progress from negative to positive in what you're doing.

> *Most organizations still have an outdated and overly centralized model for working, and it's turned out to be a very difficult habit to break.*
> —Dion Hinchcliffe

With this information, you can systematically build and strengthen trust and foster an environment where people feel cared for and engage in reciprocity.

Empathy

At the 2014 World Economic Forum, a British bank CEO asked, "We all know it's important to be empathic, but how do I galvanize 48,000 people in my UK operations—most of whom think that empathy is for wimps?"[16]

As public calls for companies to engage in authentic dialogue grow louder, the desire to change is hampered by the fear of appearing weak and vulnerable, meaning most businesses still suffer from an empathy deficit. "Enlightened companies are increasingly aware that delivering empathy for their customers, employees, and the public is a powerful tool for improving profits, but attempts to implement empathy programs are frequently hamstrung by the common misconception of it as 'wishy-washy', 'touchy-feely', and overtly feminine," writes Belinda Parmar in the *Harvard Business Review*. "So empathy is de-prioritized, and relegated to the status of yet another HR initiative that looks good in the company newsletter. It is seen as a soft and frilly add-on rather than as a core tool."

Parmar, CEO of the consultancy Lady Geek, author of *The Empathy Era: Women, Business and the New Pathway to Profit*, and a 2014 Young Global Leader of the World Economic Forum, has created a way to measure an organization's empathy with the Empathy Quotient, inspired by Simon Baron-Cohen's Empathizing-Systemizing model.[17] The EQ combines customer, employee, and social media data streams to generate company ranking. Parmar is able to show with this methodology that empathy is a tangible quality that can be assessed, measuring how much empathy a company is delivering and where its greatest empathy deficits lie.

With this data, you can embed empathetic practices into the entire organization. Parmar notes, "There is nothing soft about it. It is a hard skill that should be required from the boardroom to the shop floor."[18] What if something similar were done inside your organization, looking at how internal messages are spread, demonstrating employee empathy?

Deb Schultz, Internet industry veteran and co-founder of YxYY, points out that if people talked to us in real life like marketers (or oftentimes our employers) do, we'd punch them in the face. Not much empathy there.

Emotional intelligence and empathy pay. L'Oréal sales people selected based upon their empathizing skills sold almost $100,000 more per year than colleagues hired based on the company's previous criteria, and had 6 percent less turnover during their first year.[19] Waiters who are better at showing empathy earn nearly 20 percent more in tips. Even debt collectors with empathy skills recovered twice as much debt.[20]

Paul Fabretti, global director of social media for Microsoft CAS, puts it this way, "Trust, empathy, and honesty are the keys to make social work."[21]

Simon Sinek, author of *Leaders Eat Last: Why Some Teams Pull Together and Others Don't* and *Start With Why: How Great Leaders Inspire Everyone to*

Take Action, says, "There is a pattern that exists in organizations that achieve the greatest success. . . . the ones with the highest loyalty and lowest churn and the ability to weather nearly every storm or challenge. These exceptional organizations all have cultures in which the leaders provide cover from above and the people on the ground look out for each other. This is the reason they are willing to push hard and take the kinds of risks they do. And the way any organization can achieve this is with empathy."[22]

René Schuster, former CEO of Telefónica Deutschland, implemented a Germany-wide empathy-training program to coincide with making their retail outlets more appealing. This led to an increase in customer satisfaction of 6 percent within six weeks among both men and women.[23]

Nike talks about "lessons shared" rather than "lessons learned."
—Larry Hawes

Rita Gunther McGrath, a professor at Columbia Business School and author of the book *The End of Competitive Advantage: How to Keep Your Strategy Moving as Fast as Your Business*, says organizations are becoming vehicles for creating complete and meaningful experiences.[24] This includes being able to listen and empathize. In this type of organization, building platforms for learning and creation will be particularly important.

Schultz says it's all about getting in touch with our humanness and remember the people behind the data we're collecting. "Why is it when we enter our cubes we forget how to be people? I blame the lighting!" The human factor, she points out, is what endures, while technological innovation is constantly shifting. "Technology changes, humans don't."[25]

Patterns

Social messages give the organization what data scientists call "unstructured data," meaning they travel with almost no metadata that relates them with other messages. Structured data is like data from a spreadsheet or from a database that allows it to be analyzed because of the additional detail it travels with.

Rachel Shadoan, data visualizer and design ethnographer at Akashic Labs, likens unstructured data to a pile of silverware at a flea market. If you to pull all of the salad forks from the pile, it would take a while because you need to pick up each piece of silverware to determine whether it's the type of fork you're looking for. If it's not, you need to place it in a different pile.[26]

"There is nothing soft about [empathy]. It is a hard skill that should be required from the boardroom to the shop floor."
—Belinda Parmar

New artificial intelligence technologies, including IBM Watson, are masterful at taking in both structured and unstructured data and delivering insights leaders had never even looked for—let alone seen—before.

For example, what would happen if organizations could identify their most valuable employees who were giving all the signals indicating they were about to leave? They could do whatever they could to retain those employees before it was too late. Organizations could use similar strategies with their employees that companies like your mobile carrier have been using for years, making changes in what they offer in order to keep from losing your business.

Universities, using the Predictive Analytics Reporting (PAR) Framework, an analytics collaborative taking the guesswork out of student success, have shown that even educational institutions, and the students they support, can benefit from looking at data patterns in new ways.[27] By analyzing both structured and unstructured data, organizational leaders now have the opportunity to understand patterns that would not have been visible or clear in years past.

Analysis 2: Engagement

How important is it to you to have a large majority of your organization fully engaged in the work they do, and keenly aware of your organization's vision and mission?

Employee engagement is the most widely evaluated human capital measure in most organizations. It analyzes the degree to which people participate in the organization and engage with one another. The results have been tied to performance outcomes for over a decade. The Gallup organization has shown organizational engagement is at an all-time low, and that the cost of a disengaged workforce can be catastrophic.[28] It's estimated that in the aggregate, disengagement at work costs U.S. businesses about $300 billion a year in lost productivity.[29]

TELUS credits their social initiatives with raising their engagement results from 56 percent engaged to 88 percent engaged over five years. Roche attributes their rising scores to an increased focus on both learning from one another and including patients and partners in their development process.

> *Keep moving by being open to new ideas and new paths for the community to take.*
> —Kelly Smith

A study of 65 firms in different industries found that the top 25 percent on an engagement index had greater profitability, and more than double the shareholder value compared to the bottom 25 percent.[30] Engaged employees are more likely to be productive,[31] associated with higher performance,[32] stay with their current employer,[33] and interact positively with clients.[34]

Rather than simply share high-level findings with colleagues, use the social network to share actual survey performance data, framed by the highest correlated drivers of colleague engagement. At one company, posting the engagement data resulted in over 33,000 visits to the site, with colleagues sharing ideas about how they could improve engagement, creating an appetite for more enterprise social media to enable collaboration.

Online Participation

Another way to gauge engagement, specifically as it relates to people partic-ipating in your social network, is through the dashboards most social tools offer to administrators that track online participation. It's fairly simple to ascertain things like number of visits to a site, growth in that number over time, and the number of people who subscribe to particular news feeds. You can also track the number of times a video has been viewed, the number of comments on a blog post, and the number of members and amount of discus-sion with the company's online communities. In many cases, there are dash-boards built into the administrative functions of each social application that will provide data in an aggregated form. It can be manually gathered as well.

While it's easy to dismiss this data as not useful in the big scheme of things, it can provide indicators to your vibrancy, adoption, and capacity to let people know what you're doing.

Some leaders are cautious not to report on these sorts of measures for fear the numbers may dip, but ebbs and flows should be expected. What's more useful is to notice if participation has dropped too soon to get traction or is changing for reasons that can be addressed and turned around.

What if a special committee of members of the community met periodi-cally to discuss how they would know if their network was "healthy," and the conditions they felt were essential for the network to achieve its long-term goals? They could identify several, all of them measurable:

- The number of participants is growing.

- An increasing proportion of members are actively involved.

- People are engaging in multiple kinds of activities.

- There are increasing levels of participation in the stewardship and management of the network.

- Membership is increasingly diverse.

- People are coming together in different combinations.

- People are making and taking advantage of both strong and weak ties.

Some of these indicators are about the network's connectivity, but others are about its usefulness to members and its attractiveness to nonmembers.

Generative Production

The word *generative* means to be capable of producing or creating. However, according to Jamie Notter and Maddie Grant, authors of the books *Humanize: How People-Centric Organizations Succeed in a Social World* and *When Millennials Take Over: Preparing for the Ridiculously Optimistic Future of Business*, "the word generative is not about a single act of production or the creation of a single thing. Being generative implies an *ongoing capacity* to generate and produce and create. Being generative is ultimately a sustainable capacity, not a one-off event. It is perpetual, like a species' ability to propagate and sustain life."

Once embraced, constraints are no longer constraints.
—Dibyendu De

As the self-centered and two-dimensional understanding of growth as "more of everything" embodying an eternal good starts to fail, organizations are looking at ways to measure their ability to generate, produce, and create value that can change along various dimensions over time. To be more generative is to be "more inclusive, valuing different voices, more internally and externally collaborative, with system and process and technologies that allow for ideas and innovation." When people in our organizations improve their relationship-building abilities and begin to bake in both inter- and intra-personal skills, accomplishing more—generating more—in better ways, generative becomes second nature.

Notter and Grant have created a series of worksheets leaders can use to analyze their generative capacity and the dimensions along which they ought to improve. The 20-question worksheet includes things like:

- Do you really see different people making decisions?

- Do people in your organization argue about which department owns certain processes?

- How much do you include people outside organizational lines in your process?

- How well do people build relationships, including their skill in doing that using social media tools?

These are the types of qualities to look for in cultures that value inclusion, whose processes involve collaboration, whose tools are humanizing, and who are increasing their capacity to generate more (not necessarily quantity, rather quality, "more and better").[35]

Breadth and Depth

David Birnbaum, vice president of learning at CENTURY 21 Real Estate, points out, "You can build it, but they may not come. For an organization made up primarily of independent contractors—in our case CENTURY 21 realtors—it's very important to know people are accessing and participating in our social portal. We can't mandate they come, yet we use the portal for key communication and training so it's important we provide reasons for them to want to come. There needs to be real business value."

In addition to measuring "adoption from all of our agents, we also measure by segment, subset, and target groups. That's so we can understand the needs and priorities of agents in the luxury market, for instance," says Birnbaum. "By being able to look at who is contributing, and what they are contributing, we know more about how broad and deep our reach is."

In addition to raw numbers, Birnbaum says, "We also track the amount of content shared. If we see a handful of regular contributors, but way more are logging in but not commenting, or rating other people's content, we can create approaches to incentivize more people to contribute their own self-generated content."

"Periodically we send out a survey asking the predicted value from participating in the portal," Birnbaum says. A recent survey showed a high correlation to both investments in time and job impact. When asked to

Social learning still often requires priming of pumps to get the collaboration/discussion going.
—Craig Wiggins

rate whether the time I spent using the portal was a worthwhile investment, 86 percent of respondents said yes. To answer the question, "I have applied knowledge acquired through the portal back on the job," 90 percent of participants said yes. Ninety-three percent also said they trusted the credibility of the shared content on the portal.[36]

Better Choices

Another measure is the opportunity cost of doing something that is no longer working or could have been stopped before it's started. For every program you create without gleaning useful insight from the people in your organization, there is an increasing likelihood their needs won't be met. Collaborative approaches provide a way to educate program development and can give you an indication of what people are neglecting as a result of being forced into outmoded and cumbersome ways to work.

Analysis 3: Connectedness

Do you want to be sure the people in your organization know each other or, at least, have a method by which they can know what skills and knowledge everyone brings to the table?

The connections people make across social networks and online communities seem important, but where's the proof? Some comes through the change that can span boundaries across those networks. Promising analysis approaches are illuminating the hidden social networks that existed even before organizations began adopting their online counterparts, giving leaders insight into how to accelerate change beyond formal vertical channels. The boxes and lines of organizational charts often mask how work actually gets done.

Information Flow

Organizational network analysis (ONA) is an analytical technique for mapping the relationships that run through all organizations. By investigating the structures and patterns associated with the flow of communications between people within organizations, ONA tools can show the informal connections within a traditional organizational structure that facilitate getting work done.

"These networks are often not part of the formal structure but grow out of the many collaborations and social interactions that occur daily within the organizational system and between members of the system and those outside it," says Rob Cross, associate professor at the McIntire School of Commerce at the University of Virginia.

"This method allows management to build upon, instead of ignore, the knowledge flows and exchanges that were already in place and growing," says Valdis Krebs, data scientist and software developer focused on social and organizational network analysis. ONA shows the "relationships, knowledge exchanges, and information flows that have already emerged around any capability, skill, interest, or process in an organization."[37]

Many different measures can be assessed on a network, including the strength of the relationship between individuals, the frequency or significance of formal and informal communications, or even the "energizing" or "de-energizing" influence one person has on another. A change in flows can also indicate if people are able to access the data they need to make informed decisions.

Cross, the researcher who formalized the term *ONA*, found that energizing relationships was the only consistent factor that determined who would connect to each other for the purpose of obtaining or sharing information.[38]

Energy, when examined on the backdrop of an organization's network of relationships, proved to be the most important factor for predicting information-seeking behavior. Evaluating how energy moves across an organization can show you how to enhance the information flow.[39]

> *Social learning is going on around us, all the time. It's like gravity, you only notice it when it's NOT there.*
> —Jane Bozarth

ONA data can be gathered from email, internal instant messaging applications, status updates, online forums, internal social networks, and blogs—any of the systems your organization has control over. If you use social tools across your larger enterprise ecosystem, with your partners, or even with your prospects and customers, you can track connections between people within and outside of the organization, too.

According to Patti Anklam, author of *Net Work: A Practical Guide to Creating and Sustaining Networks at Work and in the World*, organizational network analysis holds great potential in leadership development, innovation, knowledge management, organizational change and development, talent management, and organizational performance. It has been used to look at the flow of information for personal leadership, succession planning, expertise location, change management, mergers and acquisitions, positioning people in roles, professional network development, and team building.[40]

Pathfinders

In our online culture, the need for people to know everything is less and less important, yet they can provide extra value to the organization and their colleagues if they are able to quickly direct us to the right resource. Malcolm

Gladwell calls these people mavens. Libraries call them docents. Ronald Burt calls them brokers. Every one of us benefits from knowing one or several.

Pathfinders are people who are able to help us understand or identify an appropriate problem-solving approach and the information to back up our decisions. By using curation tools and attention analysis, we can ascertain how they are helping other people to learn.

You can look at the value of what you have learned from them by asking: Have my behaviors changed as a result of my interactions with this person? Have my behaviors changed with respect to other people as a result?

Pathfinders span boundaries and the gaps that exist between separate parts of any organization. "They are go-betweens, trusted negotiators, and guides for those who wish to collaborate with others outside their own function, geography, level, or group. They are the perfect people to engage in order to insure that issues of an interdependent nature are attended to and addressed," noted Rob Cross, Chris Ernst, and Bill Pasmore in research they did specifically on boundary spanning.[41]

Analysis 4: Fiscal Fitness

Do you fear that being social brings no real benefit to your organization? Are you afraid there's no way to measure the value many assure you is there?

Stuck in our number-driven organizations, the most commonly asked question we hear is whether there is a way to prove social networks result in net profits to the organization. There is.

Financial Gains

Surprising to many, it's easy to point out how these systems generate revenue. Adopt an organization-wide practice of using the hashtag #moneymade whenever someone posts to the network a company win as a result of a connection made or information shared that leads to a sale. Use a tag like #moneysaved for similar instances of company money not being spent because people were able to find alternative approaches.

At the end of the month, add up all of the instances in which these tags were used to easily show the socially created, bottom-line financial gains.

Here's how this has worked: A large travel company aimed to provide an internal tool for professional networking so that employees could connect quickly and easily. They had recently grown from a small U.S. operation into one with 10,000 employees in 59 countries, many tele-commuting and beginning to feel disconnected from colleagues and information.

. . . Not everything that can be counted counts, and not everything that counts can be counted.
—Albert Einstein

Employees complete a profile of their inter-ests and expertise. When someone posts a question to an online bulletin board, the system's predic-tive modeling software automatically sends it to the 15 people whose expertise is most relevant to the question. The more people who complete profiles, and the more questions that are asked and answered, the better the inference engine is able to assign questions appropriately.

"You have a greater chance of getting a useful answer if your question is directed not just to the people you already know, but to the people who have the most relevant knowledge," the manager of the network explained.

The online community is credited with substantial savings for the compa-ny. It identified $500,000 in direct savings the first year, but based on anec-dotal results, that figure doesn't come close to representing the total savings. They attribute the site's success partly to the fact that management ceded control over its use to line employees. The network is effectively creating a massive knowledge base that employees willingly populate with their own information.

ROI

Sanofi calculates the return on their investment regularly. Although they had almost no outlay of funds at the beginning (less than $2,000, mostly for giving out books—Simon Sinek's *Start with Why*), driven by a dogged pursuit of finding no-cost ways to collaborate, they show a return on investment regularly, far exceeding any costs incurred.

For instance, a new hire took the initiative to change her workflow at the call center (part of a six-month training before people are assigned to the field). The change doubled the number of calls she could make in a day with no loss of quality. Her new workflow approach is now the standard. No cost. No project team. The focus on new ways to work allows people to take initiative in their corner of the business.

Another example at Sanofi was to reduce the duration of the senior management team weekly meeting from two hours to one hour because people could update one another in the flow of work throughout the week. With 10 people in that group, the approximately 500 hours a year saved equaled approximately one-quarter of a full-time position. These are senior director- and vice president-level salaries.

All they had to do was offload most roundtable topics, information sharing, and nonurgent matters from the weekly meeting to Connect-M, their collaborative platform. These created more useful discussion during the meeting because simple updates were already done and people could focus on the topics themselves.

Benchmarking

As with almost any business processes, you can use various performance metrics to compare your work against industry practices from other companies. Many organizations provide resources to do this.

The Community Roundtable uses their Community Maturity Model (CMM) to help organizations understand, plan for, and assess the performance of community and social business initiatives. Their clients use the CMM both as a community management checklist and as an organizational road map. Internally, The Community Roundtable uses the model to organize their research, curated content, and training services so clients can easily connect the dots and implement the research and content in their strategic planning.

First published in 2009, the CMM is widely used to:

- evaluate and assess organizations' social and community efforts through gap analysis.

- understand the expertise and skill sets required for successful community development.

- develop a road map to advance community efforts in their organization.

- educate and manage expectations of executives, advocates, and colleagues.

- create training for those tasked with working on social strategy and community management.[42]

The Social Media in the Large Enterprise (SMiLE) index is a comprehensive and accurate analysis focused on the use of social tools within organizations.[43] Free to use, it is part of the Engage for Success movement, committed to the idea that there is a better way to work. Their Social Media and Digital Engagement Network is dedicated to applying new social enterprise tools in the quest for building employee engagement.[44]

As Clark Quinn, author of *Revolutionize Learning & Development*, points out, "We need to measure ourselves by our contributions to the organization and its endeavors. Benchmarking ourselves on efficiency makes sense after we have impact, but not before."[45]

With benchmarking models and indexes springing up regularly, you can find ones that suit your needs as you go further down the social path.

Opportunity

With help from Global Action Plan, British-based O2 determined the financial benefits of their Think Big program.[46] For every £1 that O2 invests in engaging their people in Think Big to deliver sustainability benefits, they deliver £1.40 back to the business.

Increased productivity reduced absenteeism, and decreased employee turnover delivered financial benefits for O2.[47] In addition, participation in the Think Big program was seen by both employees and managers as a significant development opportunity for employees, agreeing that Think Big offered a better development opportunity than traditional training options.

Of those people actively involved in Think Big: 64 percent of participants reported increased sense of motivation; 59 percent of participants reported increased confidence; 87 percent of participants reported being more positive about O2 as a brand, and; 60 percent of participants reported being more positive about O2 as an employer.

In addition: 88 percent of managers saw better team cohesion; 67 percent of managers saw higher productivity; 73 percent of managers stated their people were more motivated after being involved, and; 88 percent of managers said their people's confidence had risen.

They also calculated the direct business savings that resulted from employee engagement on sustainability. Financial savings included reducing waste to the landfill, which saved £6,400; water usage, which was reduced by 4 percent in 2012; and recycling 300,000 mobile phones, thanks to their call center and store staff, raising over £750,000.

To improve their model, Global Action Plan extends their research to other organizations. Developing the knowledge is the first step to improving the way that organizations engage with both their employees and sustainability.[48]

Reward-Risk Ratio

When we're embarking on something new, it's easy to think about why it won't work and what could go wrong. It's important to consider the risks, and assess their likelihood.

There's nothing wrong with risk management or attempting to mitigate unknowns. But nothing great was ever created without a degree of uncertainty. Venturing into new territory is worth the risk whenever the potential or upside is great, even if something does go wrong.

"If leaders in Silicon Valley had the risk appetite of your average HR or L&D professional," says Ben Brooks, "they would have never launched the iPhone, Instagram, or Uber. There were and still are many potential things that could go wrong with these innovations, but their upside potential has changed the way we work and live."

If you keep waiting until you're an expert to put things out, your inactivity will kill innovation.
—Justin Mezzell

It's easy for people to scrutinize what could go wrong, but difficult to reach for what will go right. "Like an effective lobbyist championing positive change," says Brooks, "you have to sell the upside potential."

In economic terms, consider applying dollars to both the cost of dealing with likely risks, should they manifest, and the impact of the rewards should they accrue. Let's say someone says something inflammatory on the network, even if it's by accident—but the cost is so great to your organization you choose to fire the employee (most don't). You could factor in the cost, including the price of severance, lost productivity, and training someone new. Those things can all be calculated.

"On the reward side," says Brooks, "if 5,000 sales people all knew about a high-margin capability that your organization was uniquely positioned to deliver, then calculate the economic value of that, too. Include the value of exposing employees to things they never knew existed and weren't even looking for.

"Using the same social network, where someone made a misstep, you have the potential to also generate returns. The upside potential eclipses the potential risk, and leading companies are running this calculation and moving forward."

The worry and fear of an employee saying something inaccurate is no greater in a social network than it is in an email, on the phone with a client, or at a bar or restaurant after work. If anything, because of social pressure, people are more careful about what they say online, knowing it is available for all to see. There's a far greater upside than there is the possibility of incurring costs. Yet seldom do we measure the benefit of clarifying misconceptions, and the value of making it possible for everyone to pay attention and be able to address them quickly and thoroughly.

Analysis 5: Impact

How do you know whether what you are doing is actually making an impact?

Many organizations view ROI as financial metrics. Amanda Slavin, CEO of CatalystCreativ, instead asks those she works with to consider a different ROI, what she calls "ripples of impact."

These layers of impact are best described through rich stories, integrating learning with new relationships, and integrating new opportunities for growth and development that were uncovered as a result of the experiences that created the ripples.

From Action to Expression

How do you gauge if people's opinions and attitudes are changing behaviors, creating these ripples?

British media critic Charlie Beckett writes, "It strikes me that social media embodies the connection between action and expression." Let's say you create a status update that announces you are changing the method used for reporting aggregate sales. "You can add a hashtag connecting you to others, and it acts as an expression of your opinion and call to action, and builds solidarity. It is democracy, efficient, and endlessly variable," adds Beckett. "It is personal but it increases social capital for the movement." It creates ripples of impact.

One's position within a community changes constantly: sometimes we make withdrawals, sometimes we deposit goodwill. We learn, we share, we inform.
—Julian Stodd

"One of the dangers of online conversation is if it remains conversation, never turning into action. Complaining is easy—much easier than getting out of your chair," notes Clive Thompson. "But it's always been this way." Long before the Internet, activists worried that young people were substituting T-shirts (pre-Internet hashtags) and political buttons for taking a serious stand in making change. "Mere conversation and sloganeering have always seemed like a potentially dangerous sap" to the energy of real activism, adds Thompson.[49] Online talk may be cheap but, because it's visible to other employees and linkable, it can catalyze multitudes.

In technology, the ripple effect metric shows what impact changes to software will likely have on the rest of the system. New research incorporates what is called ant colony optimization (ACO) and its prime artifact pheromone, which has been modified to minimize ripples when cross-coding. A standard benchmark data set has been taken to validate the performance of the proposed algorithm. This is promising for looking across organizations to measure their ripples of impact, too.[50]

Doing Well by Being Good

In 2011, economist Laurie Bassi, with coauthors Ed Frauenheim, Dan McMurrer, and Larry Costello, created the extensively researched Good Company Index (GCI) that ranked the Fortune 100 as employers, sellers, and stewards (of the community and environment).[51] Updated for 2014, the GCI now ranks almost 300 of the U.S.'s largest companies on these three criteria, with data from a wide variety of sources.

"One of the dangers of online conversation is if it remains conversation, never turning into action. Complaining is easy—much easier than getting out of your chair."

—Clive Thompson

Through this research they revealed that better-ranked companies in the same industry outperform their competitors. In other words, "in the new social marketplace, businesses that succeed will be those that prove themselves worthy of trust," says Daniel Pink. It shows that the convergence of social, economic, and political forces have ushered in a new era in business, in which good corporate behavior is no longer optional, but the key to success. The analysis shows that better-ranked companies in the same industry consistently outperform their competitors, sounding a warning that bad companies will wither while worthy ones will thrive.

Higher scores on the index predict better stock performance: companies with significantly better GCI grades than their competitors in the same industry outperformed their competitors by an average of 30 percentage points over the two-year period following the initial assignment of grades.[52]

In the years since, Bassi, McMurrer, and their team at McBassi & Company have launched a self-assessment that in just a few minutes can quickly assess your own organization (anonymously) and how well it meets Good Company standards.[53] At the end of the survey, you get a Quick Grade (from A to F) on how your company ranks as a Good Company, based on how you respond.

Analysis 6: Influence

Do you want to understand the ways collaboration and communication change measures of authority and the effect it has on who is seen to provide real value?

Jay Deragon, co-author of *The Emergence of the Relationship Economy: The New Order of Things to Come*, wrote on his blog, "People learn from people and subsequently are avoiding influence from institutions. . . . Conversations [between] people,

Small bits of learning happen ALL the time in tech.
—Gina Minks

one to one to millions, have become the power of influence." Ed Keller and Jon Berry's 2003 book conveyed the same with their title, *The Influentials: One American in Ten Tells the Other Nine How to Vote, Where to Eat, and What to Buy.*

One of the ways we see people analyze what's going on in their social networks is through who has and who builds influence in the organization.

Sway

A study from Deloitte Australia investigated the ways people derive influence from their position in the company hierarchy and their activity in D Street, their online social network.

They measured if people in higher positions in the hierarchy derived more influence from their position and if more active participants (measured by number of messages posted) derive more influence than those who were less active. Influence is measured as the average number of replies someone elicits for each message they post. The assumption is that it is a sign of influence when people are able to get more responses to their messages from the community.

They split the 110,000 messages in the dataset into three time periods with equal number of messages to capture any changes in the measurements and to see if influence in the network changes as the community emerges, grows, and matures.[54]

What they learned was that the formal influence people derive from their position in the organization is present only in the early stages of the organization's social shift. It disappears in later periods.

They also found the social approach afforded people an opportunity to move into positions of informal influence by way of their contributions to the network—more active people were more influential. This influence was strongest in the early stages, meaning that early adopters moved into influential positions initially. While still present in later stages, the influence diminishes.

They also learned the community became more egalitarian over time. Both forms of influence, formal and informal, diminish or disappear over time, which means that the social network produces more egalitarian and inclusive communication structures as the community matures.

While very imbalanced early, all hierarchical levels become more equally involved with the social network over time, and communication across hierarchical levels intensifies.[55]

As working socially becomes more commonplace, there is a growing network effect of staggering proportion that can be achieved through influence.

From this you can build simple models defining influencers, as people whose social messages are frequently repeated by others.

Today, the Social Business Index and similar services can track your brand's performance on the external web by scraping social sources, pulling in conversations and links, and analyzing the language of those tweets, posts, and comments.[56]

Organizations with wide social networks inside their walls can also measure social influence. The question then becomes, how is this information used? Said one manager we spoke with, "When can we know who influences whom, so we know how to persuade people to work longer hours next week? That's very different than a company I used to work for that wanted to influence its employees on who they vote for in the new political election." And then he reflected for a minute and said, "Or is that really not that different?"

Memes

Another measure of communication impact is messaging uptake, the degree to which an organization's messages reach people, are republished, and are evaluated. A "coverage report," like those typically generated in public relations, can be used to assess external message pickup. What about the messages spread within an organization, though? What parts of those messages have the most impact, and which take on a life of their own? A social media version of the coverage report could be the viral video.

Leadership should not be by title but by encouragement, feedback, motivation, and follow-up.
—Kelly Smith

A meme is an independently replicating "cultural unit" that emerges over time as it passes from one person to another. Ideas, words, images and styles are just some examples that spread voice to voice, through traditional media, and can go viral over social media.

The challenge with following memes is defining what it is you're trying to measure. Is it the cultural unit itself or how the idea that's spreading changes the environment around it?

Clive Thompson suggests that even more useful than tracking how ideas spread is to analyze what's not spreading. You have a big company announcement and none of your employees are talking about it through your social channels. A layoff is in the wind, and people have stopped chattering completely about new ideas and sales approaches for your upcoming products. In these cases, your social tools become instantly valuable; telling leaders there's a big problem with your messaging or that you're creating distractions that are negatively influencing productivity.

In what sociologists call *pluralistic ignorance*, whenever a small group of people underestimates how much others around them share their attitudes and beliefs, they impede social change. It's an information problem that happens because we don't know what's going on in other people's minds.

"Whenever we're faced with a socially dicey, delicate subject—Do other people notice that the company is in trouble? How much sex are other students having?—we're too squeamish to talk openly. Without correct information, we get it wrong. . . . But the converse is also true," writes Thompson. "It turns out that you can fight pluralistic ignorance by actively improving the flow of information—and letting people know the previously invisible views and thoughts of others."[57]

Social change can snowball when people make their thoughts visible. When members of society think in public and keep in ambient contact with one another, it creates a new environment—where we're increasingly aware of what changes might be possible.

"It turns out that you can fight pluralistic ignorance
by actively improving the flow of information."

—Clive Thompson

Analysis 7: Attention

Do you want to see how your employees can dramatically multiply the value of their own and their colleagues' knowledge? Are people paying more attention to the right things and less attention to distracting noise?

Attention is the scarcest resource in organizations. If social systems can hone people's attention on the most high-value information and experiences, these approaches will more than pay for their keep.[58]

Trends

Likes, +1, stars, and votes all provide ways that social systems themselves prompt people to analyze the value of content and sentiment. By deeming information useful in a public way, they draw attention to content and validate its fidelity. Those ratings also contribute to people's reputations. Sometimes they serve to elevate a person who isn't typically thought of as a resource in a particular area, while at other times they merely confirm the reputation of someone who is thought of as a valuable contributor.

We are in an age of collective learning, we co-create it. Always have, but now it flows much faster.
—Bernd Nurnberger

Nicole Radziwill, associate professor of integrated science and technology at James Madison University, points out that ratings "provide the currency of acknowledgement [helping to change people's state] or the currency of energy [helping to inspire people and build their confidence by using the information or pointers they provide]."[59]

While it's easy to misunderstand these ratings as the measure itself (after all, we can add them up and say, "therefore this content bit is more valuable than that one"), tracking the velocity with which they get attention is valuable and oftentimes is a better indicator of what's changing in an organization than watching what's been liked.

Detecting changes in velocity (accelerations) can help inform you that specific information or even a particular topic is becoming important—or that an individual's role as a resource for learning in this network is being enhanced.

When people aren't just reading and "liking" posts, they are also talking among themselves, sharing their own stories, and doing this with increased frequency. The organization's leaders can detect a change in behavior and shifting attention to a new area.

In what can be described as "eating their own dog food," the people in the world who consider themselves (or are considered by others) as gamification gurus have created a leaderboard to uprate and downrate their current achievements. The leaderboard "ranks players according to their digital impact around the topic of gamification each month."[60]

Avoid Distraction

Workday distractions consume more than two hours of the average employee's day, and focusing employee attention makes a big difference.[61] Multitasking as a route to productivity isn't as helpful as most people think. In fact, it can be an efficiency-killer, reducing productivity by up to 40 percent.[62]

Combine multitasking with a large, dispersed workforce and you've got a recipe for distraction. The good news is that you can rein in these diversions and help employees get down to business with social networks.

This may seem counterintuitive, but organizations that use these systems as their prime conduit of information pour resources through a single wide and deep channel.

Think about it. For many, the inability to hone in on what's important at work is driven by technology. In one recent study, nearly 45 percent of respondents cite interruptions like email and text messages as the culprit behind their distraction. Technology was second only to the 54 percent of respondents who indicated co-workers who want to socialize as the prime driver of their distraction. Others admitted the Internet often distracts them. Thirty-one percent of respondents said nonwork related online activities—like shopping, checking social media, and reading blogs or news articles—were responsible for their problems focusing.

When respondents knew they could find the content and the people they needed in one shared space, there was no barrier to reaching out, and that information would be available to others and the organization over time, they were far more apt to go there first, bypassing other distracting opportunities.

Likewise, they may pop over to Amazon to buy a book, but they were more likely to quickly return.

Although email is an important method for certain types of communication, it creates real limitations for social learning. In 2008, Luis Suarez, then an international community manager at IBM, began a journey he dubbed, "Life Without Email."

Social media is an ingredient, not an entree.
—Jay Baer

He argues that email is a conversation between a limited number of people; a conversation not searchable by others, and that frequently disappeared from the view of even the direct participants after a short time. Also, email between more than two people is susceptible to breaking the conversation thread when a participant fails to "reply all."

"[Life without email is] an opportunity to renegotiate how we collaborate with our peers, customers and business partners, helping everyone understand there are better and more effective ways of collaborating. A good number of use cases would be a good start [to] reducing incoming e-mail and instead rely more on social computing tools. And the journey begins."

Enterprise social networks, even something simple, is a better method for most internal business communication. Suarez adds, "Organizations are realizing that they can no longer ignore, nor neglect, the impact of becoming a successful social businesses . . . They know that to survive in the knowledge economy, they need to leap forward into the new reality of collaborating through networks, no longer the traditional top-down hierarchy."[63]

Focus

Another social approach to honing people's focus is to use specific tools and analysis to understand what people are focused on. Help employees curb the distractions and sharpen their focus so they can be their best, most focused, productive selves at work and beyond.

So, what's got employees' attention?

For some, there are simply other issues weighing on their minds, with 22 percent of respondents in one survey saying personal stress—like worries over relationships, family, or money—is a distractor at work up to five times a day. The workplace itself is distracting for some employees. "Other employees' conversations, outside noises, music etc. [distract me,]" said one respondent. "Cubicles are not very private, especially when they are only four feet high," said another. "[I work in an] open office, [and] can hear everything everyone is doing," a third said.

"[Life without email is] an opportunity to renegotiate how we collaborate with our peers, customers, and business partners, helping everyone understand there are better and more effective ways of collaborating."

—Luis Suarez

With an overwhelming list of to-dos and deadlines, it can be difficult for employees to feel like they're finishing meaningful projects. Support employees in tackling the top to-dos that matter each day. Not only will this facilitate productivity, but experiencing frequent feelings of daily progress in meaningful work boosts employees' emotions, motivations, and perceptions during the workday, and their creativity over the long-term. Even small daily wins make an impact and can enhance how employees feel and perform on the job. Help employees see daily success by encouraging them to identify the day's most important task—no matter how small—and seeing it through.[64]

One study showed that contextual factors in the workplace that lead to (or away from) focus include valence and mood, online activity, time of day, time during the week, and the role of breaks.

What is the best way to support employees' focus? Offer tools and resources that encourage all aspects of their well-being.

You'll help them manage their stress and make healthy habits a higher priority so they can feel their best and brightest, and get down to business on the job.

Movement

Today's employees are more productive than ever, yet between attempts to multitask, constant disruptions, technology alerts, and stress from all areas of life, they're also having a harder time honing in on their most important priorities. With distractions consuming nearly a quarter of the average workday, and multitasking being dubbed an efficiency-killer, supporting employees' focus is critical to driving companies forward.

In terms of doing work and in terms of learning and evolving as a person, you just grow more when you get more people's perspectives.
—Mark Zuckerberg

Research shows that moving around, literally shaking your arms, and walking increases your capacity to focus. If knowledge workers in the United States alone began moving more in their day, that could result in billions of dollars in increased productivity (not to even mention a decrease in the healthcare and workday absence costs). Social tools can be used to broadcast encouragement to get up and move, provide the impetus to do so—"We're all gathering in the courtyard to dance,"—and can give leaders the means to see that their employees have been at their desks for hours.[65]

Analysis 8: Capacity

Do you want to expand the methods you use to understand and maintain the critical skills needed for your workforce to support your current business, as well as pursue new and innovative services, products, or markets?

Key to workforce understanding is analyzing and coordinating your people's availability, their current knowledge, their interest in doing new things, and how they can improve their skills.

Worker Availability

Perhaps you're looking to staff a team for a new project your company was awarded. Maybe someone's sick the very day their presence is needed most of all. Deloitte uses D-Street, their social platform, as a means to both locate people with the set of skills someone needs, and a way for employees to switch organizations because they can look inside various departments, getting a sense of the pace and rhythm of their work.[66]

Because online community profiles include the industry and sector each person focuses on, they provide a way for others to quickly find a French-speaking health specialist or a Spanish-speaking logistician within moments.

Deloitte, IBM, TELUS, and practically every organization we spoke with talked of the ease with which people now join teams because they can create a baseline of comfort with other people on the team, through the social platform, before they begin their work. As experienced team members retire, there is a shortage of people with long-term institutional knowledge to replace them.

It means that as the next generation of workers is coming into the workforce, their networking, multiprocessing skills, and a global mindedness, serves them and the people they'll be working with well. Constant experience in the connected world has had a profound impact on their approach to problem solving, collaboration, and focusing together.

Kevyn Renner, retired technology executive at Chevron, uses the analogy of the kaleidoscope to describe the many perspectives that people experience when working in these new ways. It fits with organizations' mandate to have the right people in the right place with the right talent, so they can get work done in a timely and reliable way.[67]

Just realize that there's a downside of using social means to identify availability in that it can become a leash managers use to keep track of employees. While talking with people for this book, one senior manager confessed that she'd been considered unreliable because her director kept tabs on when people were active on their internal messaging platform. She kept being asked, "Are you there? Are you there?" during a conference call, only to learn that by setting her status to busy, she was being perceived as not being available for constant interaction. Not good.

Leadership

Valdis Krebs has been mapping employee networks for more than 20 years. One of the key outcomes of his process is revealing the actual leaders inside an organization and from that work he has learned there are many different kinds of leaders. He has heard descriptions including:

Social is how customers hear about you, search is how they find you, and content is how they remember you.
—Martin Jones

- I trust Luis to walk me through this career decision.
- I trust Karl's technical advice on this algorithm.
- I trust Anne's political take on this marketing decision.
- I trust Rita's grasp of what our key customer wants.
- I trust Pat to guide this organization through troubled times.[68]

Krebs points out that trust is key throughout. "We follow others for various reasons, some because of their knowledge, some because of their vision, some because of their personal appeal, and all for the confidence we place in them. Without confidence from others, a person cannot effectively lead."

How can you analyze (and foster) leadership with the assistance of social tools? Alongside formal measures of leadership readiness, a social approach to learning and work can inspire everyone to become inspiring leaders, teachers who share and grow with their colleagues. By focusing on facilitating knowledge sharing and relationship development, you can invite colleagues to share their expertise and learn from one another.

One person may prefer posting a video, another a blog, and another a file that others can use and adapt for their own work. Each of these builds trust because they show what people care about, what's on their minds, and that they are interested in helping others. By aiming for short, insight-rich content, alongside their own backgrounds and profiles, colleagues build strong internal relationships—across the world, across practices, and across business units, which demonstrate their leadership capacity and trustworthiness.

When Wendy Lamin, social media engagement strategist, was asked how many courses her social learning platform held, she said with enthusiasm, "None. Why would I bore my colleagues with courses? Our network is a vibrant source of insights from colleagues who have so much to teach one another." That's leadership.

> "Why would I bore my colleagues with courses?
> Our network is a vibrant source of insights from
> colleagues who have so much to teach one another."
>
> —Wendy Lamin

Interests

Chet Wood, chairman and CEO of Deloitte Tax LLP, says that through D Street, the organization's online community, "I am gaining a greater perspective on what's on the minds of our people. It's provided a unique platform to engage in very personal and candid dialogue."[69]

While walking the halls is no longer practical for many leaders, when people post to a collaborative space, they're letting their voices be heard and their perspectives speak. When a leader posts his or her insights, they can get immediate feedback when people comment in response or build on what's been said. That feedback can be invaluable and more useful than counting most anything.

Built into many systems, though, are also ways for people to quantify how many others share their interests and their perspectives. There are trending and rating measures, as well as grouping mecha-nisms that quantify how many people are interested in a specific topic or theme.

In 2021, informal learning and social learning will just be called learning.
—Koreen Olbrish

If, for instance, one of the purposes of your social efforts is to help your developers find one another and create a culture where technically oriented people can find others working on related topics, basic web analytics can make it simple to see how many people joined a group or clicked on a link to register as a developer. It's also easy to see how many people downloaded a particular piece of software or a whitepaper, or subscribed to receive status updates from the developer group.

These are just a few of the many situations in which your organiza-tion may already be automatically capturing simple information about the interests of people you work with, and those who visit online, and it can be expanded to include groups who want to work on new areas and share an interest in a topic or theme.

Blurring the boundaries of the silos people work in may seem scary to those who actually believe organization charts represent how organi-zations function, but most employees prefer more random and serendi-pitous interactions.[70]

Knowledge

Just as organizations keep track of an inventory of physical objects, everything from computers and paper to vehicles and chairs, many also keep an inventory of employees' knowledge and skills. In the past, the inventory might have been compiled from college transcripts and employee resumes. Add to that certifications and badges.

Organizations also often keep lists of who-knows-what so when the organization is running low on, say, people who know how to program in C++, the stock of C++ knowledge can be replenished by hiring new people or training current employees.

Profiles can catalog the skills within your organization and can be regularly updated by employees. Expose your job classifications and skills analysis to these systems and people can even tag for themselves their areas of expertise. If one week you have 34 people who know how to program in Ruby, and the following week you have 122, you haven't increased the size of your workforce, but you've been able to capture something you didn't know before, which can be put to use if your organization gets a big contract that requires that type of programming.

But here's the even bigger opportunity: New skills and knowledge must be applied regularly in order to add value to your organization. By knowing people's skills considered to be their most important, you can spend your time and money more wisely to help them stay current. There's also evidence of "forgetting curves" where cumulative operating experience actually leads to degraded performance.[71]

Increases in cumulative experience can have another detrimental effect. Old tacit and explicit knowledge can render an organization obsolete when it is not supplanted periodically, trapping an organization by the "innovator's dilemma." If all your organization knows is one way to work and has a limited breadth of skills, you're unlikely to discover the next big thing.

Content

Differing from what your organization knows because of the people inside it, social approaches can also identify and quantify the content—the reports, notes, charts, digital media, and so on—within your walls, either stored in content management repositories or available through media-sharing tools. This material doesn't walk out when an employee leaves but, through ratings and links, even reviews and curation, people can access that content far into the future.[72]

Geographic Distribution

As news of a crisis unfolds, organizations have an obligation to protect their people and their assets. Trouble is, oftentimes in the event of a physical calamity, people have to quickly evacuate buildings and can't easily work together to notify others about the situation.

> Organizations are slow to change, allow time for the company and team to adjust and find balance.
> —Megan Bowe

"Having a real-time map is almost as good as having your own helicopter. A live map provides immediate situational awareness, a third dimension, and additional perspective on events unfolding in time and space," writes Patrick Meier, former head of crisis mapping for Ushahidi, a global organization that uses open-source technologies to work through crises by leveraging the power of people on the ground to in effect crowd source geolocation, creating *crowdmaps*.

What makes these sorts of maps so powerful is that they easily allow for micro-contribution. Because it's easy for almost anyone to contribute a tiny bit of information, almost everyone does. In response to the 2010 earthquake in Haiti, Ushahidi's developers instantly set up a map so people in the region could scour blogs, social sites, and regular media looking for information useful to rescue crews—like locations of people in trouble or stations with fuel and medicine. Activity skyrocketed when they set up a mobile phone number where anyone, anywhere could text in news.[73]

Tools like this can also be used within organizations to look at what's happening on the ground during a major incident—as well as in roles where people are geographically dispersed, such as across mines or in a search and rescue. These maps are being augmented through head-mounted cameras and wearable computers that both show others a location and what's around them.

Analysis 9: Change

Do you want to understand your company's culture and how social approaches help transform what you can do?

When people get a sense of how others are working (through working out loud), the story behind why changes are being made (from leaders' videos and blog posts) along with progress (by way of status updates), behavior patterns of employees begin to change.[74]

Whether small changes like shifting locations for departments, or large changes because of mergers or acquisitions, change can be hard, but it happens. The myth that 70 percent of change efforts fail is not grounded in any substantive research, and we should all help reverse the tide of this myth, urges change agent Jennifer Frahm. [75] The numbers don't even align with most people's experiences or instincts. Who hasn't been part of big changes throughout their careers? Even if you've experienced a change initiative that didn't go smoothly, who among us can say most failed?

Jason Little, Agile coach, points out you cannot predict the outcome of change but you can reduce the threat response (also known as change resistance) by involving people ultimately affected by the change in the design of the change itself.[76]

"Rather than layer on new crosscutting structures or create ad hoc committees of people who may not be opinion leaders or have strong cross-boundary connections, change can be led by influential individuals who already occupy pivotal spots in the network," notes Rob Cross.[77] In this way, analyzing social networks can prove invaluable.

Culture Readiness

The learning culture audit, now used in organizations around the globe, was created in 2004 to give leaders an opportunity to assess their capacity to make meaningful change through learning and

Silos collaborate; they don't break down.
—Miko Matsumura

discovering together. The toolset can be used with teams, divisions, or entire companies before, after, or alongside introducing social approaches, gauging where you are today and setting your sites on the culture you aspire to create.

The audit process illuminates why most organizational cultures at first distrust anyone very social or relationship oriented—and provides a more interpersonal direction. Over time, based on the data, the organization can then evaluate how to interact in a healthy way to get work done and make informed decisions.

The audit asks leaders to assess where their organization is currently along a continuum. For instance, on one end of the spectrum, "Everyone creates, keeps, and propagates stories of colleagues who have improved their own processes. On the other, "Everyone believes they know what to do, and they proceed on that assumption."

Other behaviors range from whether, "Managers encourage continuous experimentation" or "Employees proceed with work only when they feel certain of the outcome." Also, "Leadership presumes that energy comes in large part from personal learning and growing," or "Leadership presumes that employee energy comes from corporate success and profits."

The core audit can be downloaded online for free. [78]

Transformation

It's one thing to track how many people saw your video online. It's another matter to look at the number and type of questions and comments prompted by each video, which may provide additional clues to how widely it was viewed and understood. The more interesting analysis is to look at what new ideas were introduced and then talked about. The conversations generated by a video are as valid a measurement of its appeal as the number of times it is viewed, and may even be more valid.

Should you create a communications plan for certain videos that includes a discussion of what viewers learned? Can you provide key messages and questions to help with the discussion? Consider soliciting feedback through a survey to gauge people's understanding and ask whether they found certain videos useful.

The idea here was stories of transformational science. The former National Science Foundation Office of Cyberinfrastructure (OCI) was having problems tracking the benefits of the learning that took place when people used their high-performance computing facilities. The solution was to craft rich stories and narratives around transformational science that occurred when someone had used those computing facilities and the science that could not have been done without those facilities. The impacts were primarily ideological. People's ingrained perceptions of scientific theories and approaches were changed by the new insights.

Analysis 10: Fill Holes

Would you like to help other people imagine the future and stimulate the exploration of topics and ideas that don't fit into existing structures? Would you like to understand the risk of not being able to fill in those missing holes?

Imagine if you could take an X-ray of your organization to identify employees who are opinion leaders. Then imagine you could see where direction, alignment, and commitment were breaking down and where more collaboration could knit together critical groups to implement a change.

Network analysis can provide this insight and accelerate change. "We have long known that informal networks exist, but we've understood them mostly through intuition, which is frighteningly inaccurate," write Rob Cross, Chris Ernst, and Bill Pasmore. "Leaders haven't thought much about leveraging networks to advance change or performance until fairly recently.

"It serves leaders well to identify the opinion leaders who can help engage others most effectively and efficiently in a change process. Equally important is to identify those who will likely resist the change and encourage others to follow suit."[79]

Personal Network Assessment

After years working with organizations to map their networks of relationships, Cross and a team of members from the Network Roundtable and Connected Commons Consortium created the Personal Network Assessment (PNA) Workbook.

Social learning did not wait for 2.0 to exist.
—Frédéric Domon

The self-guided PNA enables people to visualize their networks, and evaluate them against the network characteristics of high performers. It also offers a comprehensive overview of how to avoid career traps, decrease network overload, take specific actions to align your network with your professional objectives, and learn on how to be an energizing force in your network.

Over the past decade, Cross and those he works with have studied the networking approaches of high performers (those in the top 20 percent of their organization's annual performance ratings) across a wide range of companies and government agencies. This work contributes to debunking the "more-is-better theory of networking. Although hard-driving salespeople may thrive by building large, loosely connected networks, most high performers succeed by developing targeted networks that complement and extend their abilities," says Cross.[80]

A 10- to 15-minute web-based survey asks you (or those you work with) about key collaborators in individual networks and important dimensions of those relationships. For instance, are they important for information flow, decision making, best practice transfer, or career advice?

These individual networks can then be aggregated to reveal group-level collaboration patterns that show who plays highly influential roles in the inner workings of an organization—who can serve as a bridge across disparate groups, spanning boundaries. The people who often fill these roles may not be those who leaders would think to tap for facilitating change—but who should be.

Analyze Real-time Experience

The experience sampling method (ESM) was developed by social scientists in the late 1970s to capture data about people in the moment.[81] For example, one study used ESM to gain insight into "by whom" and "for what" people were willing to be interrupted by a text or a phone call.[82]

Because of the high cognitive cost of being interrupted, they wanted to be able to program a phone to ring or not based on who was calling. You're likely to feel differently about an interruption from a friend, your child, or a telemarketer—as well as by what each was calling about. People tend to be very unreliable when answering questions like this when they're not presented in the context in which the question is relevant.

With ESM, people are prompted at scheduled (or sometimes random) times throughout the day and asked to provide specific information about themselves right then. Though used in the past, the days of participants carrying around alarm clocks and recording their answers in notebooks are long behind us, and now ESM analysis can be conducted using apps built for mobile phones. In the interruption study, for example, participants were prompted to respond to a questionnaire every time they received a phone call and asked:

Who just called you?

Did you answer it?

Why or why not?

If it had been _____ (someone else), would you have handled this call differently?

Why?

Using automated ESM software, they were quickly able to gather over 1,200 responses in a format that was easy to analyze.

What if something like this were done in your organization every time people entered the elevator, at the end of a conference call, or at the start of a meeting?

Meetings at the WD-40 Company begin with the question, "What have I learned since I saw you last?" This practice provides participants an opportunity to consistently capture lessons learned and a simple way to observe progress.

> *The most important thing is a person. A person who incites your curiosity and feeds your curiosity, and machines cannot do that in the same way that people can.*
> —Steve Jobs

For a short period of time, so as not to give them "one more thing to do," consider setting your social tools to prompt participants after time online with questions, such as:

Why did you just use the system?

Were you successful?

How satisfied were you with your experience?

What did you learn?

This kind of data can be used to determine quickly why people are using the tools, if they are using the network for the reasons you deployed it, if they are having any sort of trouble, and what kind of changes could be made to improve the overall experience.

Questions Answered

Four years of double-digit growth has made training and retaining talent a priority in a mid-size investment management firm. It has also made their vice president of learning and organization development a very busy guy. Rather than create more traditional courses, he worked with the IT group to launch a company-wide, wiki-based, collaborative knowledge management tool that incorporates online forums, RSS feeds, bookmarking, tagging, and search.

With this platform, associates can ask difficult research questions and capture answers, creating new and emerging categories of relevant information. The program has increased the ability to publish and update information quickly. The robust search capabilities reduce the turnaround time for answers to research questions and leverage for future use all the information being submitted.

The system also serves as the infrastructure for one of the few new courses they've built, Building Change Capability, where associates can access a dedicated wiki site, blogs, and other social media tools to supplement the course materials, have ongoing conversations, and add to the course content so it gets better and more applicable over time.

Yet What About Learning?

Measuring learning, specifically, is really useful to understand what people need and are interested in across the organization. Doing so can provide an opportunity to add conversations and approaches to catalyze conversation and learning around topics that aren't getting noticed but should. We need to expand our repertoire of approaches.

Learning is a *change in state*, not the increase of a *stock of knowledge*. By changing states we're able to assume different roles, make different sorts of decisions, and do different work. This may or may not correspond to increasing our own internal stocks of knowledge. You could, for example, just have pointers to know where to find the information you'll need. Social systems help us better function as pointers and can connect us with people who help us become problem-solving pathfinders.

If we can think of learning not so much as increasing our knowledge, but rather as improving our understanding of the flow of information, it then makes sense to favor people as our pointers and pathfinders to increase the depth and breadth of that flow. Having accomplished that, we'll naturally be more open to devising metrics that recognize learning as an ever-changing

Vision is not enough; it must be combined with venture. It is not enough to stare up the steps; we must step up the stairs.
—Václav Havel

perception of self, as well as others' changing perceptions of our ability to participate in solving problems and making sense of that information.

With that approach, we are also more likely to acknowledge that we flow through the learning process itself. Likewise, there is information we added to our stock of knowledge years ago that is no longer part of the flow because we've forgotten how to use it or it's no longer relevant.

Using this new view, taking in more information is no longer as important as we thought it was in the past because we can all easily access it from others in the organization or the connected world around us. This has implications for whom you recruit and hire, too. Skills you didn't know your organization possesses in-house might have been there all along and can be accessed when you need them through people who have the aptitude and wherewithal to put them into practice.

Retention loss is also actually not as detrimental because you don't necessarily lose access to information if people aren't employed by your organization; if people are moving outside the organization, you still have access to their information.

The implication is that successful organizational learning produces these kinds of evidence, each with potential financial impacts.

In the end, while using analytical approaches is important, it will always be even more important to understand your organization as a system, and the people who make it tick as its heart.

In-Person Learning Reimagined

"An event should be a happening. If nothing happens then it's just boring. Change the energy. Demonstrate you're after something different. Create something for people to talk about and feel in their toes."
—Graham Brown-Martin, Founder, Learning Without Frontiers

IT'S 11:17 A.M. IN SÃO PAULO, Brazil. A stadium-sized room sports 4,500 pup tents, many settled by entrepreneurs and students, sleeping, finally, after another night innovating until dawn.

Campus Party organizers take over empty warehouses and even aircraft hangers, creating a giant petri dish where innovation thrives. The massive mashup includes fighting robots, beanbag chairs, leading-edge technology, big names in tech and science, and some of the youngest, brightest, most pioneering people in the world.

It's been described as "Woodstock for young geeks," focusing on technology, entrepreneurship, creativity, leisure, and the digital culture network.

Mix with that an Ivy-league level education and Outward Bound experience, rolled into one, and you'll see why tickets are the hottest on the planet. In Spain, Mexico, Peru, Colombia, Ecuador, El Salvador, London, Brazil. Annual and bi-annual events have both a larger-than-life energy and an intimate feel thanks to clusters of activities and widespread use of social media that connect people directly.

As far as the eye can see, future tech leaders—young people in emerging markets, eager to make a difference and a name for themselves along the way—experience collaboration's power firsthand. By uniting talent, they create the future.

They take learning very seriously, relevant not only to the future of the technology revolution, but also impacting on the future of the entire economy. They ask what new skills are needed and how this will be accomplished so passion can meet achievement. Together industrious people come up with solutions that can become products serving niches or whole industries.

Thanks to the arboretum-size pizza cafe and seemingly endless shower stalls, Campus Party smells sweeter than Woodstock would have on day four of a seven-day event. This is a new day and a new breed of party. Launched 20 years ago, having reached over 220,000 people, and still largely unknown in the English-speaking world, it's coming to a country near you.

Each event delivers a heady cocktail, frequently provocative, challenging, polarizing, exhilarating, thought provoking, and exhausting—everything that a good conference ought to be (yet few actually deliver). Participants frequently, and in most cases good naturedly, are drawn out of traditional comfort zones to confront the new.

While Campus Party's sheer size astounds, attitudes and vibrancy in the building take your breath away. In search of what is causing the buzz, you realize it's not one thing, rather many.

Intentional Encouragement

Imagine yourself standing in line at a busy supermarket, waiting to pay and finally go home. Your mobile phone rings and you confirm you're heading to Campus Party. You hang up, staring at the powerful device in your hand, wondering why you couldn't use this same phone to check out and leave.

When you arrive at the event you share this observation. A young woman you've never met says she wrote some code that could be used for something like this. An old friend searches the web for news of a similar system he's heard about. You calculate the percentage you would need to charge. Three more people begin writing other features, talking back and forth at their keyboards.

Within a few days you have a prototype. You pitch your idea to a roomful of leaders in various fields brought in by conference sponsors. They encourage your new team to consider where else this technology could help people get back to their lives. You're energized as you refine what a few days ago was only the question, "Why not?"

> We need to be more radical in asking how we would re-create companies today if we started from scratch, because I think we now have the social, cultural, and technological platforms on which to do a much better job.
> —Lee Bryant

Innovation is not something you can directly pursue. At Campus Party innovation rises out of the creative tension and electrified atmosphere that comes from asking "why not," followed by "how?" Trying, doing, mixing, fixing, then digging in again. It's born out of circumstance, intersections, and need.

In their book *Jugaad Innovation: Think Frugal, Be Flexible, Generate Breakthrough Growth*, Navi Radjou, Jaideep Prabhu, and Simone Ahuja introduced the colloquial Hindi word *jugaad*, which roughly translates to "an innovative fix." *Jugaad* is widely practiced in India, Brazil, China, and Kenya, anywhere entrepreneurs pursue growth in challenging climates. Brazilians call this approach *gambiarra*. The Chinese call it *zizhu chuangxin*. Kenyans refer to it as *jua kali*. It's a gutsy way to respond to adverse conditions, transforming insufficiency into opportunity.[1] Some of the most successful local innovations are simple solutions that address vexing problems fellow citizens face.

For example, as part of the Campus Labs Smart Society challenge, technology teams use the FI-WARE platform to develop projects that could improve agricultural yields and protect communities from natural disasters.

One of Campus Party's sponsors, Telefónica, awards a prize for the most commercially viable plan. The winning team gets a year-long contract with technical, marketing, and legal support so the ideas reach all the people who will benefit. Meeting with some of the teams, you discover each is authentically overjoyed at the opportunity to talk with people about their work. The prize was only a small part of what drove them.

Encouragement taps into an intrinsic well, filled as you turn a nascent idea into something valuable to the community around you. Encouragement amplifies as people celebrate with you because they know that what you can accomplish together is better than what any of you would do alone.

Inclusive Diversity

Campus Party, the brainchild of Belinda Galiano, Pablo Antón, and Paco Ragageles, was created to spur innovation in communities that have historically relied on the ideas of others. To generate energy and cross-pollinate thinking, they encourage something beyond working together with technology. They also focus on entertainment, geekdom, and #somethingbetter.

"It's wide and it's young," says Galiano. "We unite talent. They create the future." Young people want to put their creative skills to use for a larger cause. A report conducted by Euro RSCG showed 92 percent of millennials agree the world must change, and 84 percent consider it their duty to drive this change.

The same research showed a majority of millennials believes it is women, not men, who will lead change. Unlike some tech events we've all participated in, where men outnumber women five to one and everyone leaves their family back home, Campus Party nurtures a fusion of women, men, and children.

While the tented areas are for individuals, some families come for the day, imbuing an even-deeper sense of inspiration, creativity, and energy, grounded in the real world.

This ensures ideas flow in what Steven Johnson calls liquid networks, representing a free-flowing, high-contact medium. Campus Party provides an environment where an eclectic diversity of thoughts collide, people learn faster, and ideas spread widely.

Adapt what is useful,
reject what is useless,
add what is your own.
—Bruce Lee

Writes Ragageles, "The word impossible only lives in the minds of humans who have never loved. Campus Party is about people who, through their love for technology, are making the world a better place and for them nothing is impossible. Habito en el tercer planeta del sistema solar [I live on the third planet in the solar system]."

Impassioned Hearts

At the heart of Campus Party is the human factor. A banner reads, "The Internet is not a network of computers, it's a network of PEOPLE."

And they are happy people, participants and sponsors alike. Sponsors get access to a massive pool of tech talent and the vibrant energy that comes along with it. They often hire people from the event and provide yet another value, moving passion toward purpose.

Thought-provoking talks are given on the main stage from Stephen Hawking, physicist Michio Kaku, cyber peace specialist Camille François, writer Chris Anderson, and father of DSL John Cioffi. News zapped quickly around the twitterverse as participants tweeted insights gleaned in real time. The event began showing up in the list of Twitter's trending topics, and people worldwide joined the conversation. Everyone was using social media's powerfully magnetic method while asking themselves how their very tools could be made better, more effective so that their full potential is realized. They talked with those around them, onstage, and friends back home about how to blaze trails that will endure into the next generation, perhaps beyond.

Much of the event is captured by a small video crew and posted to the event's online community. People are connecting everywhere, blogging and typing, talking and reflecting, considering the implications of the experience on the work they do.

Radjou, Prabhu, and Ahuja found in their research that *jugaad* innovators rely more on heart and intuition than on analysis to successfully navigate a highly complex, uncertain, and unpredictable environment. "They use their gut intelligence and innate empathy for customer needs to innovate break-throughs that defy conventional wisdom. Their underlying passion acts as the fuel that sustains their efforts to make a difference in the lives of the community they serve." The fast-paced, volatile environment forces many to think on their feet all the time.

When Tim Berners-Lee set out to develop the web, he envisioned a technology that could serve as "a collaborative medium, a place where we can all play; a place where we can all meet, read, and write."

That vision plays out each day in unconference-style BarCamps, global online mega-events like IBM Jams, by offline and online hackathons focused by the Management Innovation eXchange on management and Facebook on code.

At Campus Party, where Berners-Lee has spoken several times, he explains that he now sees how the connections the Internet enables encourage people to foster change even when they aren't online. At this party, young entrepreneurs learn to be themselves, that they're not alone, and that ideas come in all shapes and sizes.

By finding encouragement, catalysts, and heart, young people locate a fountain they'll be able to learn from over a lifetime.

Brian Duperreault, president and CEO of the Marsh & McLennan Companies, has said, "There's now an equal, and maybe greater chance, that innovative ideas will come out of [emerging markets], where the action is, where the need to deliver more for less is even more heightened."

Campus Party is a global phenomenon leading the way; ensuring young entrepreneurs, women and men alike, are at the forefront of that action.

Growing Together

Coming together to talk, visit, and learn is as old as time. Using in-person opportunities to humanize learning that you've begun (and will continue) online adds a modern dimension.

Saul Kaplan of the Business Innovation Factory, which hosts communities and dialogues focused on what it takes to create transformative change, describes in-person events as a communal lab for growing connections and insights. "Incubation is spontaneous and palpable. It's as if there are luminescent tags networking us together. There is an electric feeling of potential and possibility."[2]

Why do so many people use the term "enterprise-wide" then? Why not "enterprise-deep"?
—Paula Thornton

At his two-day Business Innovation Factory Summit, held each year in the fall, unscheduled time is built into each day to facilitate what he calls, "Random Collisions of Unusual Suspects" (RCUS, for short). Attendees are encouraged to use the unplanned for serendipitous encounters where learning emerges in the moment.

"It is human nature," Kaplan says in *The Business Model Innovation Factory: How to Stay Relevant When the World Is Changing*, "to surround ourselves with people who are exactly like us. We connect and spend time with people who share a common worldview, look the same, enjoy the same activities, and speak the same language. The most valuable tribe is the tribe of unusual suspects who can challenge your worldview, expose you to new ideas, and teach you something new. A tribe of unusual suspects can change the world if it is connected in purposeful ways."[3]

Salima Nathoo, founder of RocktheGlow, says, "If you get a stage to share your knowledge, it is your duty to humankind to influence the way people think, live, believe, and behave—not just talk about yourself. Knowledge is power when it enables others to invite simplicity, ease, and greatness into their lives."

Every encounter, be it in a physical or virtual classroom, social media or in-person conversation, is a platform whose best use is to make someone's life and therefore universal existence, better. "It's what we all want at the end of the day—better sleep, better health, more influence, lower gas prices," says Nathoo. "We don't want to climb the hero soapbox and take the caped crusader's stance. We want to sit around the proverbial campfire to share stories . . . then take time to figure out what it all means. We don't want to *be like Mike*, we want to *be* Mike or Michaela 4.0."

Sociologist Ronald Burt has said that people who live in the intersection of social worlds "are at higher risk of having good ideas."[4] Ideas, like cold germs, diffuse through the relationships you have with people and the connections they have with others.

As Chris Anderson, who runs the talk-centered global nonprofit TED, points out, "You're part of the crowd that may be about to ignite the biggest learning cycle in human history."

By focusing on "ideas worth spreading," TED stimulates learning and networking through the creation of previously unimaginable physical and conceptual connections. Learning springs from the community, the speakers, the seemingly unrelated videos, and the entertainment at the events that sometimes seems random yet is designed to be provocative.

At its core, TED is an environment that transcends traditional boundaries of time and space, where words like *limit* and *impossible* are not even considered. There is a strong belief that sharing ideas globally will catalyze even greater ideas and action from the power of community and the learning that naturally springs from within it.

TED promotes ideas, but those ideas flow from the creative power of an open-minded community, willing to listen and support likeminded thinkers whose collective clarity defines the problems they aim to solve. Anything is possible, and often becomes likely, through the power of collaboration.

To extend and deepen collective and individual opportunity to grow in the connected world, we've introduced you to social learning approaches you can use in your organization. People in physical proximity to one another can also use each approach we've covered up to this point.

Formal education will make you a living; self-education will make you a fortune.
—John Rohn

In this final chapter, we meld the in-person practices we all know with technologies that can enhance the experience in fresh ways. As Soren Kaplan, author of *Leapfrogging: Harness the Power of Surprise for Business Breakthroughs*, says, "Go outside to stretch the inside." Although our focus is mostly on conferences, many of these practices can be applied to classes and small ad-hoc and informal gatherings. We will show how the use of social tools can increase their value, making them remarkable and exhilarating.

Events can mash up the physical and the online worlds. Social networks you already belong to can connect you to people at the event who have interests similar to yours.

This chapter assumes you wear many hats. Sometimes you're a speaker, playing a part akin to a teacher in a classroom, often on a bigger stage. Other times you're an event attendee, a student of sorts, interested in learning all you can. Occasionally, you're an event organizer or meeting facilitator, and sometimes you pay the registration fees for your employees, wanting the greatest value for your dollars and their time spent. These events can be conferences put on by professional event producers, corporate events, or gatherings of association members.

"The most valuable tribe is the tribe of unusual suspects who can challenge your worldview, expose you to new ideas, and teach you something new. A tribe of unusual suspects can change the world if it is connected in purposeful ways."

—Saul Kaplan

In today's connected world, you are probably also an influencer of the work done by those putting on events and who want your business or seek your counsel. Each role provides opportunities to make informed decisions and offer sound advice.

We address how you can take action in each role and then offer a glimpse of some alternative event formats that are beginning to catch on.

Speaker, Teacher, Audience, Student

If you speak often at events, meetings, or classes, you know firsthand that audiences no longer sit quietly absorbing your words and the images you show, waiting to ask a question or make a comment. Technology-enabled societal shifts have started moving the ground under your feet, says Joel Foner, a project manager, process consultant, and blogger, who has engaged large hyperconnected audiences for years.[5]

The new social learning, with its emphasis on people learning from one another, plays up the fact that both speakers and attendees have something valuable to share.

"What if you forked out thousands of dollars to attend an industry event—flight, hotel, Town Car, expensive sushi, fancy socks, designer suit to sit in the front row in a middle seat, listening to a person who enjoys the sound of their own voice and took pride in the chaos of mismatched colors and the unskillfully animated collision of Comic Sans, Calibri, and Times New Roman Bold fonts in the name of learning?" asks Salima Nathoo.

The benefits of collaboration are many and have not changed over the last 20 years.
—David Coleman

More importantly, what if this is a key part of "your own hustle for happiness. What makes you different, lining up with your branded boxed lunch and vendor swag, than the assembly line workers with their faded jumpsuits, hair nets, and lunch pails? What makes you different is capacity to engage. What really makes you different: Nothing, until you consciously click."[6]

Olivia Mitchell, a presentation trainer who writes the Speaking About Presenting Blog and is considered the leader in tackling thorny issues about presenting in the digital age, says, "There has been a shift in power from the speaker to the audience. The best speakers don't care about themselves, they care about their audience, and they care passionately, working hard to ensure everyone is getting value from their time together."[7]

Through global communication technologies, people now have so much access to each other and to information that they've "grown accustomed to the idea that they can and should be able to discuss, rate, rank, prioritize, link, and converse in text with anyone, at any time," says Foner. "They comment on and rate websites, blog posts, music, videos, books, vendors, manufacturers—and you and me. Social media everywhere has made this hyper connectedness part of everyday life."

Robert Scoble, a technology evangelist, author, and popular blogger, reminds us that, "We're used to living a two-way life online and expect it with an audience, too. Our expectations of speakers and people on stage have changed, for better or for worse."[8]

Instead of looking across a sea of faces, you may be speaking to an ocean of heads looking down at their laptops and smartphones, or watching you from behind smartphones with video connected to people in other rooms and around the world.

When audience members using Twitter add an event hashtag (#) to their tweets, they open the conversation to anyone on Twitter who's interested in the event, including those in the room specifically following that tag. For example, #SXSW is the hashtag used each year for the South by Southwest conferences, #CES is used for the Consumer Electronics Show, and #ATDyyyy is for the ATD International Conference & Exposition. Anyone can run a Twitter search to find all the backchannel tweets (which will likely include links, photos, and videos) related to that event.

Tools like Storify allow people to assemble related elements from various social media platforms, creating a coherent and annotated "story" from those elements. You can search on a particular hashtag and pick out the most relevant posts, all while eliminating duplications, which happen frequently when people are tweeting at conferences.

The back channel is increasingly a factor in any type of education where Wi-Fi connections allow people to chitchat, check facts, rate sessions, and evaluate their experiences. Continuous improvement in smartphones has also increased the number of pictures and videos that are becoming part of the backchannel.

Presenting while people are talking about you can be disconcerting and distracting. In the past, you may have used eye contact with your audience to measure their engagement. Now when you say something brilliant, instead of nods of appreciation, there may be a flurry of thumb tapping. This kind of communication can be terrifying to a speaker because everybody in the room and around the globe participating virtually can now rate you, share their thoughts, comment on your work for better or worse, and point out mistakes—or what they think are mistakes—in the middle of your sentences. For some people, that is "scary beyond measure," adds Foner.

Mitchell says, "To balance that shift, there are huge benefits to individual members of the audience and to the overall output of a conference or meeting. Most of all, it shows people are interested in what you're saying—so interested they want to capture it and share it with others."

REDEFINE YOUR EVENT

What should your focus be at in-person events? How about answering these questions:

- As we continue to have unprecedented access to a growing reservoir of knowledge while being inundated with the noise of useless information, how do we create lean learning opportunities in the workplace?

- Who are the disruptors designing and facilitating the types of exchanges and encounters that create best places to work, while pioneering the new frontier for employee engagement and getting sh!t done?

- Which platforms are fundamentally changing the way we cultivate lasting relationships with the art and science of knowledge acquisition—creating love affairs with micro-learning?

Then, show up. Be curious. Raise the game.

—Salima Nathoo

In-the-Flow Participation

The backchannel blurs the line between the presenter and the audience and even between those physically in attendance and those participating from afar. Now everyone can participate and share information.

Gary Koelling, founder of Best Buy's BlueShirt Nation, said of a Twitter-fueled meeting, "What struck me was the dynamic of this meeting. It was participatory. No one was talking out loud except the guy presenting. But the conversation was roaring through the room via Twitter. It was exploding. People were asking questions. Pointing out problems. Replying to each other all while the PowerPoint was progressing along its unwaveringly linear path. The contrast couldn't have been more striking. Here are two tools that couldn't be more at odds with each other; the linear, planned, predictable progression of slides versus the raucous, organic free-for-all of Twitter. I wanted the Twitterfeed to actually change the presentation—to update it, edit it, extend it, pull it into areas it wasn't exploring."[9]

Graham Brown-Martin, author of *Learning {Re}imagined* and founder of Learning Without Frontiers, is passionate about learning, innovation, technology, music, and people. His greatest skill, however, has been in spotting trends early and connecting the dots. Although he's put on dozens of events across the world, he doesn't consider himself an event organizer as much as someone who brings together "happenings" that he would like to attend on topics he is passionate about and believes in. He brings about change by using social media to create a platform to see, hear, and engage with those doing remarkable work. He says, "It's the only way to do it. Social media is the perfect way to connect with the right people, almost like osmosis, creating a venue—and opportunity—where we each can be more."

In-the-Flow Focus

"Prior to the technology advancements, I backchanneled with myself," notes Dean Shareski, a digital learning consultant. "That is, I processed by thinking or taking notes. I would ask questions and answer them myself. The more engaging a speaker, the less I backchannel. That said, some less engaging speakers who understand and permit back channeling can create as powerful a learning experience as the most dynamic speaker. The more the presentation relies on the backchannel, the more I focus. Knowing that my comments are going to be seen by the presenter or live participants seems to make me pay more attention. The more I'm allowed to interact and play with the content, the more I'm engaged and ultimately the more I learn."[10]

People collaborate only when there's a need to. The problems need to be complex enough to demand more than one head.
—Sumeet Moghe

Online community maven Rachel Happe likes that Twitter enables her to participate in presentations without disrupting them. Happe says, "Twitter allows me to add my perspective to what is being presented and that keeps me more engaged than just sitting and listening—even if no one reads it."

THE BACKCHANNEL

Real-time text communications among audience members using something like Twitter or a local chat room during a live event is often referred to as "the backchannel." *Backchannel* is a term coined in 1970 by linguist Victor Yngve to describe listeners' behaviors during verbal communication. Today the new backchannel represents an audience who is now networked—connected in real time, learning with each other and the world all the time. The backchannel doesn't have a limited number of chairs—anyone can join—and this changes the game for presenters, the audience, and the rest of the world outside the room.

Brown-Martin tells a story of being focused on real-time like no other. His youngest daughter, lovingly referred to as "Handheld Learning Girl," was born several days before he was scheduled to launch an inaugural conference in 2005 on mobile learning. He delivered his daughter himself, at home with the aid of instructions on his smartphone because the midwife had not yet arrived. His daughter's development as a person and the technology advancements in those same years offer a timely glimpse of social tool evolution.

In-the-Flow Innovation

As your presentation sparks ideas, audience members can tweet them and build on one another's thoughts. They can build and share their own insight into what's being discussed.

As a speaker, if you monitor the backchannel, you can innovate along with the audience. Jeffrey Veen, designer, author, and entrepreneur, was moderating a panel at a conference and monitoring the backchannel through his smartphone. "As the conversation on stage continued, the stream of questions and comments from the audience intensified. I changed my tactics based on what I saw. I asked questions the audience was asking, and I immediately felt the tenor of the room shift in my favor. It felt a bit like cheating on an exam."[11]

In-the-Flow Contribution

People tweeting during presentations add explanations, elaborations, and useful links related to the content. "My 'take-away content' from the backchannel equaled or surpassed what I got from presentations directly," said Liz Lawley, professor, interactive games and media at the Rochester Institute of Technology. "I can already see that there's more I want to go back to and digest, discuss, and extend."[12]

Instead of asking your neighbor, "What did she mean by that?" you can post your question to the group, and someone will respond. Social media maven Laura Fitton recounts a time when some of her colleagues, who'd helped with the presentation, were following the event virtually and were answering questions asked by those in the audience as she gave her talk.[13]

Remote or on stage, Bryan Mason, co-founder of Typekit, calls this person an "ombudsman for the audience." At an event he and Jeff Veen hosted, they put a desk on stage and had a friend sit right there keeping tabs on Twitter, an instant message tool, and email, listening to what people were talking about. She synthesized the questions and sprinkled them into the conversation in real time.[14]

William Deyamport III, district instructional technologist for Hattiesburg Mississippi Public School District, focused his doctoral degree in social learning because he could see there was no excuse for teachers, administrators, or schools—like a job site or a concert—to be disconnected. He taught teachers how to develop a personal learning network through Twitter, a bookmarking site, where teachers themselves can pick what they wanted to learn, and who they want to learn from.

> Social learning has proved to be the most powerful pedagogical tool we have.
> —Henry Mintzberg

A private community was created for the district, designed to serve as a hub for teachers to post lesson plans, resources, and insights, providing them a space to ask one another, "Have you seen this video," or "what do you think about this program?" This allows educators from across the district to pull and learn from each other's talents and insights, even though they rarely have time to come together to collaborate face-to-face.

One posts a comment, another responds, and yet another adds their understanding. Together they're learning in real time.

With this sort of approach, bringing in-person delivery and online connection, they can also be learning though their mobile phone under a dryer at the hair salon, at the dentist, or in line at Costco. Wherever people are, thinking "I'm going to be here for a while," they can now also recognize, "Let me see what I can learn." No matter where they are, they can tap into their local district's brain share and the global community that surrounds us. Now there's no limit to what you learn and how you learn. Deyamport adds, "For me, it's everything."[15]

In-the-Flow Connections

Being at a conference where you don't know anyone can be intimidating. People who know each other cluster together, and you can feel out of the action. But if you participate in the backchannel, you get to know people virtually and can then introduce yourself in person at the next break.

Because of Twitter and Google+, Deyamport has had people at conferences engage with him for the first time as if they've met in person before. Those tools change the barriers people have between them in a way that makes them feel safe and invited to learn together right way.

He also knows firsthand that educators and leaders, even those responsible for large groups of students, feel isolated when they're not connected with their peers. It's harder for them to learn or network, or go beyond what their organizations give them.

He used to have to wait for leaders in his school district to formally request training. Then a colleague added a simple reservation system where teachers and administrators can request what Deyamport calls "personalized social trainings," so he can stop by their classroom and show them more about Google apps, for instance. During a planning period or after school, teachers can get individualized instruction rather than "drive by training," the old norm.

Other times, someone sees the requests of a colleague and asks if they can join in or, he says with some thrill in his voice, "they ask one another to teach something" without getting him involved. They form relationships around learning.

Moving to a connected model, they've transformed learning to a coaching process, where people think to themselves, "Where do I want to be in six weeks and nine weeks." My job, says Deyamport is to "get educators excited again about what they're doing. I'm there to support them, either by fixing a problem or helping them work together, reimagine their classrooms, connected."

In-the-Flow Evaluation

With a backchannel you get immediate feedback when you search the event's #hashtag and the speaker's name and presentation keywords.

Paul Gillin, author of *Secrets of Social Media Marketing: How to Use Online Conversations and Customer Communities to Turbo-Charge Your Business!* and *The New Influencers: A Marketer's Guide to the New Social Media*, still can recall years ago waiting six months to get audience evaluations, so the immediacy of tweeted feedback has been wonderful for him. He's also used it to get a quick read on the tech savviness of his audience and adjusted accordingly.[16]

When reflecting on all the events he's run in his career, Graham Brown-Martin recalls how he would know an event was working well when he received ample feedback, even when people sniped about the coffee or the price of London beer. He reposted all comments to an online community. It was part of the personality of his organization to encourage and publish commen-

> *The ability to build virtual relations and work with a myriad range of individuals from different cultures and countries will be increasingly critical in the coming years.*
> —Sahana Chattopadhyay

tary, even if it was outrageously negative. Asked why, he responds, "Because they can be so funny!" He adds that feedback can be helpful in seeing situations from others' vantage points.[17]

In-the-Flow Burning

Nicole Radziwill and Morgan Benton, associate professors at James Madison University, began thinking differently about in-person events after they were inspired by the culture and ethos of Burning Man, an annual gathering of approximately 70,000 people in the desert of northwestern Nevada.

Participants create anew each year Black Rock City, dedicated to community, art, and self-expression, based on 10 principles underlying the culture's value system:

1. radical inclusion

2. gifting

3. decommodification

4. radical self-reliance

5. radical self-expression

6. communal effort

7. civic responsibility

8. leaving no trace

9. participation

10. immediacy.

With these values come a "rich, naturally social learning environment," says Radziwill. No one is obligated to conform to the identities they have in the rest of the world. Benton adds, "The culture natively seeks to drive out the fear associated with new experiences and taking on new perspectives. Learning becomes more like breathing: everyone is doing it all the time, but no one really notices." That's how they both wanted their classes to be—and that's what they are working toward creating in all of their work, their research, and the community.

The culture and community that have emerged around the Burning Man model create a "hyper-socialized" experience based on co-creating value across boundaries: the usual boundaries of experts and novices, the boundaries of time, and those of space. If everyone shows up with their best ideas and the openness to listen to the spirit of what others are saying, they can generate together new and stronger ideas that can spur on real change.

Events can provide a microcosm for studying idea generation, team formation, emergent leadership, new product development, and the full product development cycle compressed into a short time span. Gatherings organized in the spirit of Burning Man have a history spanning almost 30 years, involving groups ranging in size from just a few participants to tens of thousands, providing proof this sort of culture can work on many different scales.

What surprises newcomers to Burning Man, who have only learned about it online, is that there's very little cell service in the dusty dessert. The digerati must use their authentic social skills to interact with one another . . . and only occasionally send pictures back home.

Takeaway

We've all been to events where good ideas are hatched and projects are planned, but often, despite the best intentions, things lose steam after the event is over and nothing much gets done. Can we—should we—really rely on just our brains and notes to gain value from events?

Twitter drags you out of your own head.
—Laura Fitton

Even the best presentations have limited value if you can't revisit their best content as you reflect on what you experienced. New digital tools can support such access.

These include just-in-time book publishing, live blogging, and live video blogging.

Publish a Book

Just-in-time book publishing is a way for anyone to create and publish a book. Event organizers can produce such books compiled from content created by speakers and attendees. Pepper the book with observations from people walking the event, doing interviews, taking polls, and snapping photos.

The books can be sold online and delivered in hard copy. Events including PopTech, Maker Faire, and Web 2.0 Conference create their own books, sometimes from the main stage, giving participants a different medium to learn from over time.

Live Blogging

Live bloggers transcribe or create commentary about an event as it unfolds. The blogs (sometimes just a sharable document) capture the essence of the event and quote speakers taking the stage. These shared online spaces unite the offline and online character of events and bridge the voices of people in various places around topics that matter to them. Other participants in the room, people who are at the event but in another room, or people participating virtually can dialogue together around the blog, spurring on conversation, which can be brought back into the event to build even more ideas and perspectives.

Bloggers use conventional blog tools, shared document apps, wikis, or, for large-scale events involving many writers, may opt for tools specifically designed for live blogging so that it's easy to cross reference between posts. Some of these tools even provide the ability to integrate images, audio files, video clips, presentation slide decks, and other multimedia content, enabling feedback and participation with the blog stream.

Noah Flower, strategy consultant and director of Knowledge Management at Monitor Institute, finds himself live blogging the events he attends as a way to reinforce for himself what he's learning and also to provide careful notes for colleagues around the globe.

Live Video Blogging

Taking live blogging a step further, live video blogging enables bloggers to send real-time video streams to the web during events. With live video blogging, web viewers can see and hear the event as it happens, and those at the event can have a record of everything that happened.

Today, a handheld video camera, a webcam attached to a notebook computer connected to an application such as Google Hangouts on Air, or even just a smartphone that supports live video streaming can show thousands of people across the world the event as it happens and go viral with the event's tweets and blog posts.

Because the stream can be recorded, after the event it can also be indexed and made part of a media-sharing site or online community along with videos captured but not streamed by event participants. Together these videos can convey a message and generate conversation that can lead to more learning and change.

Respond to Critics

As with all new and atypical ideas, there will be resisters. Here are the most common objections we hear and ways we believe you can address them.

Social learning needs community, blogging encourages it.
—Megan Bowe

People Aren't Paying Attention

People who appear to be fully engaged with their smartphones and laptops may still be paying attention to you—even more so than if they are looking at you. But if you think you'll do a better job if people are looking at you, consider opening your presentation this way: "I notice many of you are using your phones and laptops. I'm absolutely fine with that. But I also know that I can do a better job if you are engaging with me and looking at me. So when you're not using your phones and laptops I'd love it if you can look up."

Scott Berkun in his book, *Confessions of a Public Speaker*, describes an approach he's taken. He says to his audience, "Here's a deal. I'd like you to give me your undivided attention for five minutes. If after five minutes you're bored, you think I'm an idiot, or you'd rather browse the web than listen, you're free to do so. In fact, I won't mind if you get up and leave after five minutes. But for the first 300 seconds, please give me your undivided attention."[18] Most people close their laptops and put their smartphones away.

Another approach is to put your Twitter ID on your first slide and then ask who in the room is currently on Twitter, a social networking site, or is live blogging. When you see their hands you know who is probably writing about you and not ignoring you.

People Cannot Learn From Me and Social Media Simultaneously

Many people still assume that someone who appears to be doing something other than listening to a presenter cannot be learning what the presenter is covering. This assumption, however, is not supported by evidence.

Many people use secondary tasks to help them stay engaged and focused. In an experiment reported in *Applied Cognitive Psychology*, doodlers were able to recall 29 percent more details from a phone conversation than non-doodlers, for instance.[19]

Researchers believe that by using slightly more mental resources, doodling helps prevent the mind from wandering. This study is part of an emerging recognition in psychology that secondary tasks aren't always a distraction from primary tasks but can sometimes actually be beneficial.

Edie Eckman, fiber arts educator, author of *How to Knit Socks: Three Methods Made Easy* and *The Crochet Answer Book: Solutions to Every Problem You'll Ever Face; Answers to Every Question You'll Ever Ask* points out that when she speaks to people who are comfortable crocheting and knitting while listening, she sees laser-like focus. It's as if the handwork allows them to connect with other people far better than if they were empty-handed.[20]

The secondary tasks we use to stay focused are now often high tech. People can take notes on their smartphones and laptops, or they may have a game on their phone equivalent to doodling. Seeing a tweet can reinforce what's going on in the session or introduce peripheral topics that will expand the attendees' thinking. Taking notes in an online community can offer useful detail to others back at the office and provide a springboard for further conversation when returning to work.

TIPS FOR GREAT CONFERENCE WEBSITES

Encourage conference producers to include the following on their event websites, all updated frequently:

- Attendee list, with links to participants' websites and Twitter feeds

- Schedule, updated regularly, with changes noted

- Twitter posts from the event, organized by RSS feed from the #hashtag, can also have a stream of tweets from the official event Twitter account

- Facebook fan box linking to the event's Facebook page

- Flickr or Instagram badge and links to tagged photos and videos; flipcharts and graphs can be scanned or photographed throughout the event, then posted to the photo sharing site and to the website

- Video feed of sessions fed live into the site, then archived

- YouTube search results tagged with the event's hashtag

- A place where an audio feed can be added in real time and where podcasts of sessions can be made available later

- Links to blogs of those attendees writing about the event

- A wiki, online community, or content management system where delegates can post notes from event sessions

- An RSS feed for tracking changes to all of the above

- Speaker biographies with links to their websites and Twitter feeds

- Local information for parking, mass transit, local restaurants, hospitals, and museums.

Recommendations

We opened the chapter with a quote from Graham Brown-Martin because he has created dozens of events across the globe, combining the benefits of technology and the joy we get from connecting with people in person in real time.

As we spoke with Brown-Martin and others who are spurring on the new social learning at in-person events, we found the following themes.

Don't Go Unless There's Time to Share a Meal

People may open up more when sharing a good meal. If you only have time for one short day of people talking at you, consider ways you can learn from them online instead. So far, there's no way to duplicate online that emotional connection—the joie de vivre, the juice—we share in person.

Trust One Another

To attend an event involves sacrifice. People come together because they are committed to getting something valuable from the event. When organizers trust attendees and speakers to determine for themselves what patterns are relevant, what connections are valuable, and which stories are most energizing, events are more likely to be memorable. Although it seems basic, our nature is to be prescriptive, to tell people what they are supposed to get out of an event, what conclusions they are supposed to reach, with whom they should collaborate, and what they should work on. If you trust the audience to create the insights and connections that make sense to them and you provide an environment that is conducive to connecting, the magic will happen.

Prepare Yourself

If you choose to go to an in-person event, prepare yourself beforehand by learning as much as you can about what the event offers. Kaliya Hamlin, at the forefront of the unconference movement, encourages people to identify questions you want to ask and topics you want to learn more about.[21] Here are more suggestions for preparing:

- To prepare to visit trade show booths, type keywords about your industry niche into your favorite search engine and see what suppliers come up. Visit the websites of the companies that will be demonstrating their wares. Figure out which suppliers you want to meet and talk with.

- To prepare for the content of the event, read papers and articles posted to the event's website before you go. See if speakers have posted slide decks from previous conferences and look through them.

- To get a sense of speakers' styles, whenever you can, see if you can find videos they've shared and watch them.

- Get a sense of who will be there by reading the blogs and viewing different social streams of speakers and anyone you know will be attending.

Face time with other people is valuable, rare, and expensive. Have meaningful conversations, get advice from peers, and tackle challenging issues in ways that you don't feel you could do online.

Get Twitter-Ready

If the conference doesn't provide it, give your presentation a Twitter hashtag. Make it as short as possible so people can include it on every tweet. Make it unique so people outside your audience don't accidentally use it. Consider firing up an app like Storify to collect, aggregate, and show the story that those tweets tell.

Encourage people to get the conversation going ahead of time by using the hashtag that you developed. Their questions may reveal themes you will want to cover in the presentation.

Stream and display the Twitter backchannel on a screen behind you that everyone (including you) can see and ask people to tweet their questions and comments. Spend time at the beginning of your presentation explaining how you will respond to the Twitter stream, and you'll find audience members will be more likely to use it responsibly rather than tweet things like "Hi Mom."

Ask a colleague or a volunteer from the audience to monitor the feed and interrupt you if any questions or comments need to be addressed right away. If you can't find someone to take on this role, take regular breaks to check Twitter. You can combine this with asking the audience for "out-loud" questions, too.

Invite people to use the hashtag after the session, posing additional questions and tapping into the collective experience of others who participated in person or virtually.

Set a Mood

Consider all of the conditions that enhance a social atmosphere: time to talk with people, comfortable seating and lighting, and even good music. People tweeted, downloaded files from the website, ordered CDs, and talked to those around them while they listened. This created an energetic vibe that said, "Get ready for something great." As a speaker, consider adding music to your presentation, providing time for people to talk with one another, and thinking about the environment you're creating where people are excited to learn.

Appendix: Social Media Governance

ORGANIZATIONS CONSIDERING DEPLOYING SOCIAL software for communication and learning are often concerned with how to govern its use. Should they be highly directive in their policies or trust people to use common sense? The most effective policies we've seen fall somewhere in between: comprehensive and educational, using the guidelines to coach employees through how they are expected to behave online and treating people as trustworthy.

> Chris Boudreaux, a digital strategist and technologist, created SocialMediaGovernance .com, a site full of tools and resources to help managers and leaders with social applications. The policies page on this site provides examples of social media guidelines from organizations of all sizes in the public and private sectors.

IBM

An exemplar in social media governance is IBM, whose official guidelines aim to provide helpful, practical advice—and also to protect both IBM employees and IBM itself, as the company embraces social computing. The guidelines were created in 2005 by IBMers collaborating with one another using an internal wiki. In 2008 and 2010, IBM employees revised the guidelines in light of evolving technologies and online social tools. These efforts broadened the scope of the existing guidelines to include all forms of social computing.

They begin with a request to those reading the guidelines: "Have you seen social computing behavior or content that is not in keeping with these guidelines? Report inappropriate content via email" (which is sent to a content administrator who looks into the report).

IBM Social Computing Guidelines: Blogs, Wikis, Social Networks, Virtual Worlds, and Social Media

Responsible Engagement in Innovation and Dialogue

Online collaboration platforms are fundamentally changing the way IBMers work and engage with each other, clients, and partners.

IBM is increasingly exploring how online discourse through social computing can empower IBMers as global professionals, innovators, and citizens. These individual interactions represent a new model: not mass communications, but masses of communicators. Through these interactions, IBM's greatest asset—the expertise of its employees—can be shared with clients, shareholders, and the communities in which it operates.

Therefore, it is very much in IBM's interest—and, we believe, in each IBMer's own—to be aware of and participate in this sphere of information, interaction, and idea exchange:

To learn: As an innovation-based company, we believe in the importance of open exchange—between IBM and its clients and among the many constituents of our emerging business and societal ecosystem—for learning. Social computing is an important arena for organizational and individual development.

To contribute: IBM—as a business, as an innovator, and as a corporate citizen—makes important contributions to the world, to the future of business and technology, and to public dialogue on a broad range of societal issues. Because our business activities provide transformational insight and high-value innovation for business, government, education, healthcare, and nongovernmental organizations, it is important for IBM and IBMers to share with the world the exciting things we're learning and doing.

In 1997, IBM actively recommended that its employees use the Internet—at a time when many companies were seeking to restrict their employees' Internet access. In 2003, the company made a strategic decision to embrace the blogosphere and to encourage IBMers to participate. We continue to advocate IBMers' responsible involvement today in this rapidly growing environment of relationship, learning, and collaboration.[1]

Nordstrom

The retail giant Nordstrom provides social media guidelines for its employees to help them connect with customers and others during working hours. The company explains that these guidelines are intended to help employees understand how to represent Nordstrom in the virtual world. The guidelines encourage employees to do the following:

- Use good judgment
- Be respectful
- Be responsible and ethical
- Be humble
- Be a good listener
- Avoid conflicts of interest.

In addition, the company asks employees not to share confidential information or private and personal information—"yours, customers' and co-workers'." And they ask employees to be cautious with respect to images, other sites, and endorsements.[2]

Mayo Clinic

The Mayo Clinic operates a blog where patients, family, friends, and clinic staff may share stories. Comments are reviewed before they're posted, and those that are off-topic or clearly promoting a commercial product are blocked. The guidelines encourage civility and mutual respect.

The Mayo Clinic also has a set of guidelines for employees and students who use social media of all types. These guidelines apply whether employees and students are posting to their own sites or commenting on other sites.

Here are some of the guidelines:

- Follow Mayo Clinic guidelines regarding confidential and proprietary information, including patient confidentiality.

- Write in the first person and make it clear you are writing on your own behalf, not that of the Mayo Clinic.

- If you comment about Mayo on public internets, identify your connection to Mayo Clinic and your role.

- Be professional, use good judgment, and be accurate and honest in your communications.

- Ensure that your social media activity does not interfere with your work commitments.

- Mayo Clinic strongly discourages "friending" of patients on social media websites.

- Mayo Clinic does not endorse people, products, services, and organizations.[3]

Notes

1. Introduction to IBM Social Computing Guidelines:
   www.ibm.com/blogs/zz/en/guidelines.html;
   see also: www.socialmediagovernance.com/policies/.

2. From the Nordstrom social networking guidelines:
   www.shop.nordstrom.com/c/social-networking-guidelines;
   see also: www.socialmediagovernance.com/policies/.

3. From the Mayo Clinic employee guidelines:
   www.sharing.mayoclinic.org/guidelines/for-mayo-clinic-employees/;
   see also: www.socialmediagovernance.com/policies/.

Notes

Chapter 1

1. Many of the OPENPediatrics videos are also available for the public on YouTube, https://www.youtube.com/user/OPENPediatrics/.

2. C. Shirky, Web 2.0 Expo NY, blip.tv/web2expo/web-2-0-expo-ny-clay-shirky-shirky-com-it-s-not-information-overload-it-s-filter-failure-1283699.

3. The British government first sponsored a Longitude Prize in 1714.

4. M. Conner and S. LeBlanc, "Where Social Learning Thrives," *Fast Company*, February 11, 2010, http://www.fastcompany.com/1546824/where -social-learning-thrives.

5. Jane Bozarth's book *Social Learning for Trainers* offers specific approaches to facilitate social learning by educators. For self-organizing approaches, find a friend or colleague and talk about what you're curious about right now.

6. D. Lavoy, "Social Business Doesn't Mean What You Think It Does, Neither Does Enterprise 2.0," *CMS Wire*, September 2011. http://www .cmswire.com/cms/social-business/social-business-doesnt-mean-what -you-think-it-does-neither-does-enterprise-20-012620.php. Also see https://productfour.wordpress.com/.

7. C. Shirky, http://www.shirky.com/writings/group_enemy.html.

8. S. Jones, ed., *Encyclopedia of New Media: An Essential Reference to Communication and Technology* (Thousand Oaks, CA: Sage Publications). The WELL is still a vibrant online community with die-hard fans who have participated since its inception and newcomers curious what makes it so captivating after all of these years. See for yourself at http://well.com.

9. From http://marciaconner.com/blog/defining-social-learning/.

10. S. Boyd, Interview with authors.

11. For more on social learning theory, see B. Elkjaer, "Social Learning Theory: Learning as Participation in Social Processes," in *The Blackwell Handbook for Organizational Learning and Knowledge Management*, eds. M. Easterby-Smith and M.A. Lyles (Malden, MA: Wiley-Blackwell, 2003).

12. A. Bandura, *Social Learning Theory* (Upper Saddle River, NJ: Prentice Hall, 1977), 173.

13. J. Piaget, *Psychology of Intelligence, Routledge Classics*, trans. M. Piercy and D.E. Berlyne (London: Routledge, 2001).

14. This set the stage for Peter Berger and Thomas Luckman's social construction of reality, which led to the prominence of social constructivism. See P. Berger and T. Luckman, *The Social Construction of Reality: The Treatise in the Sociology of Knowledge* (London: Penguin, 1967).

15. In addition to these widely accepted theories and practices is Connectivism, "a learning theory for the connected age" put forth by George Semens and Stephen Downs. Holocracy, similar to Wirearchy, is the organization model espoused by Zappos founder Tony Hsieh, http://holacracy .org/how-it-works.

16. A. Weber, http://www.fastcompany.com/36819/learning-change.

17. P. Senge, *The Dance of Change: The Challenges to Sustaining Momentum in a Learning Organization* (New York: Doubleday, 1999).

18. More on Getzendanner's website at http://joelgetz.com.

19. K. Stephenson, "What Knowledge Tears Apart, Networks Make Whole," Internal Communication Focus, no. 36. 1998, http://www.netform .com/html/icf.pdf. There's also an excellent video of Stephenson on the Rotterdam School of Management website: http://bit.ly/1aHpqfr.

20. For some terrific insights on lean and agile, see http://www .hackerchick.com.

21. S. Nathoo, Interview with authors. For more, see http://salimanathoo .com/lean-learning/.

22. C. Quinn, "Making 'Sense,'" February 24, 2015, Learnlets: Clark Quinn's Learnings About Learning Blog, http://blog.learnlets.com/?p=4220.

23. "Broadcast: Heidi Forbes Öste, PhD Research on Wearable Technologies and Presence of Mind," http://startupproduct.com/broadcast-heidi-forbes -oste-phd-researcher-wearable-technologies-presence-mind/.

24. B. Ives, Interview with authors.

25. G. Bradt, "The Mantle of Leadership Is Passing to Millennials—Get Ready." *Forbes* online, http://www.forbes.com/sites/georgebradt/2014/11/12 /the-mantle-of-leadership-is-passing-to-millennials-get-ready/.

26. W.S. Smith, *Decoding Generational Differences: Fact, Fiction . . . Or Should We Just Get Back to Work?* Deloitte Development LLC, 2008, https://www.insala.com/whitepapers/decoding-generational-differences.pdf.

27. 2012 Sitel Study, http://www.prweb.com/releases/2012/10 /prweb9962757.htm and Kimberlee Morrison, "Millennials Are Hugely Influential Among Peers on Social Media, "*SocialTimes*, September 26, 2014, http://www.adweek.com/socialtimes/millennials-hugely-influential -among-peers-social-media/205293.

28. Although Baby Boomers are retiring in droves, according to labor force predictions, more of them will be staying in the workforce for longer than the generations before them due to economic conditions and an interest in staying active. http://www.bls.gov/emp/ep_pub_labor_force.htm.

29. *The Rise of Social Media: Enhancing Collaboration and Productivity Across Generations* (Alexandria, VA: ASTD Press, 2010).

30. Learn more about PG&E's Power Pathways program: http://careers .pge.com/career-training-development/ and their labor shortage: http://www .marketplace.org/topics/economy/clocked/utility-tries-head-silver-tsunami.

31. J. Notter and M. Grant, *When Millennials Take Over: Preparing for the Ridiculously Optimistic Future of Business* (IdeaPress, 2015).

32. For more on IBM's millennial study, "Myths, Exaggerations and Uncomfortable Truths: The Real Story Behind Millennials in the Workplace," download an executive summary or the entire report from http://ibm.biz /MillennialMyths.

33. M. Winograd and M.D. Hais, *Millennial Momentum: How a New Generation Is Remaking America* (New Brunswick, NJ: Rutgers University Press, 2011) and "The Republican Party Ignores Young Millennials at Its Peril," *Los Angeles Times*, May 10, 2009.

34. T. Koulopoulos and D. Keldsen, *The Gen Z Effect: The Six Forces Shaping the Future of Business* (Brookline, MA: Bibliomotion, 2014). More information at http://www.thegenzeffect.com/.

35. For more on women's use of social media, see She's Connected Multimedia Corporation, "The Power of Social Networking for Women: A Compilation of Primary and Secondary Research," 2009, http://shesconnectedmultimedia.com/pdf/report.pdf.

36. Pew Research Center: Social Networking Fact Sheet, http://www .pewinternet.org/fact-sheets/social-networking-fact-sheet/.

37. G. Pellegrino, S. D'Amato, and A. Weisberg, *The Gender Dividend: Making the Business Case for Investing in Women* (Deloitte Report, 2011), http://www.deloitte.com/genderdividend. Also see "A Guide to Womenomics," *The Economist*, April 12, 2006 and S. Lawson and D. Gilman, "The Power of the Purse: Global Equality and Middle Class Spending," Goldman Sachs Global Research Institute, August 5, 2009.

38. "Families and Living Arrangements in 2005," http://www.census.gov /population/pop profile/dynamic/FamiliesLA.pdf.

39. M. Gordon, *The Roots of Empathy: Changing the World Child by Child*, (New York: The Experiment, 2009). Also see: http://www .rootsofempathy.org.

40. M. Szalavitz and B.D. Perry, *Born for Love: Why Empathy Is Essential— and Endangered* (New York: William Morrow, 2010).

41. Y. Wang, "More People Have Cell Phones Than Toilets, U.N. Study Shows," March 25, 2013, *Time*, http://newsfeed.time.com/2013/03/25/more -people-have-cell-phones-than-toilets-u-n-study-shows.

42. "Global Shoppers Consider Ethics and Environment," November 21, 2008, http://www.nielsen.com/us/en/insights/news/2008/global-shoppers -consider-ethics-and-environment.html.

43. M.J. Berland, "What America Cares About: Compassion Counts More Than Ever," *Parade*, March 7, 2010.

44. "Despite Economic Crisis, Consumers Value Brands' Commitment to Social Purpose, Global Study Finds," Edelman, November 17, 2008, http://www.edelman.co.uk/2008/11/despite-economic-crisis-consumers -value-brands-commitment-to-social-purpose-global-study-finds/ and http://www.edelman.com/practice/business-social-purpose/.

45. The Cassandra Report: http://www.cassandra.co/report/.

46. Mind the Gaps: The 2015 Deloitte Millennials survey (executive summary), http://www2.deloitte.com/content/dam/Deloitte /global/Documents/About-Deloitte/gx-wef-2015-millennial-survey -executivesummary.pdf.

47. V. Landau, E. Clegg, and D. Engelbart, *The Engelbart Hypothesis: Dialogs with Douglas Engelbart*, 2d ed. (Berkeley, CA: Next Press, 2009).

48. H. Cleveland, "Learning and Learning with Nobody in Charge," in M. Conner and J. Clawson (eds.), *Creating a Learning Culture: Strategy, Technology, and Practice* (Cambridge University Press, 2004).

49. P. A. Moss, "Reconceptualizing Validity for Classroom Assessment," *Educational Measurement: Issues and Practice*, 22(4), 2003, 13-25, http://deepblue.lib.umich.edu/bitstream/handle/2027.42/72390 /j.1745-3992.2003.tb00140.x.pdf.

50. É. Wenger, http://wenger-trayner.com/introduction-to-communities -of-practice/.

51. É. Wenger, *Communities of Practice: Learning, Meaning, and Identity* (Cambridge: Cambridge University Press, 1998).

52. Studies include "Unlocking the Value of On-the-Job Learning," Learning and Development Roundtable, Corporate Executive Board, 2009, http://ldr .executiveboard.com.

53. C. Malamed, "Informal Learning: An Interview with Jay Cross," The eLearning Coach, http://theelearningcoach.com/elearning2-0/informal -learning-an-interview-with-jay-cross/.

54. More from LeBlanc on https://sleve.wordpress.com/everything/.

55. J. Hart, "It's Not About Adding Technology to Training but About Changing Training," Learning in the Social Workplace Blog, December 6, 2014, http://www.c4lpt.co.uk/blog/2014/12/06/its-not-about-technology -to-training-but-changing-training/.

56. H. Jarche, "Work Is Learning, and Learning Is the Work," Harold Jarche Blog, June 2012, http://jarche.com/2012/06/work-is-learning-and-learning -is-the-work/.

57. H. Rheingold, *The Virtual Community: Homesteading on the Electronic Frontier*, rev. ed. (Cambridge, MA: MIT Press, 2000). http://www.rheingold .com/vc/book/.

58. D. W. Hock, *Birth of the Chaordic Age* (San Francisco: Berrett-Koehler, 1999).

59. While it used to be widely quoted that 70 percent of change efforts fail, research touting that number has come under scrutiny. Given that most people in the corporate sector have personally experienced more failed changes than successes, we can at least say with confidence "many fail." http://conversationsofchange.com.au/2013/09/02/70-of-change-projects -fail-bollocks1/.

60. B. Brooks, Interview with authors. More on Brooks at http://benbrooksny.com and https://www.youtube.com/user/BenBrooksNY.

61. E. Wagner, Interview with authors. Also see http://elearningroadtrip .typepad.com and http://parframework.org.

62. A. Rossett, Interview with authors. See http://allisonrossett.com for more.

63. J. Hart, *The Social Learning Handbook* (United Kingdom: Centre for Learning & Performance Technologies, 2014) and http://www.c4lpt.co.uk /blog/2011/09/12/social-learning-doesnt-mean-what-you-think-it-does/.

64. L. Bassi and D. McMurrer, "Does Engagement Really Drive Results?" *Talent Management Magazine*, March 2010, http://www.mcbassi.com /email_pdfs/DebunkingEmployee%20EngagementMyths.pdf, with more at http://mcbassi.com.

65. G. Fowler, Interview with authors.

Chapter 2

1. From an interview of Edgar Schein posted to YouTube on March 3, 2014, http://youtu.be/4Fw5H7GWz0g.

2. E. Semple, *Organizations Don't Tweet, People Do: A Manager's Guide to the Social Web* (Chichester, UK: Wiley, 2012), 69. For more from Semple, see http://euansemple.com.

3. The Community Roundtable has created a Community Maturity Model that provides far more dimensions and can be used to benchmark your organization against other organizations. Learn more at http://www .communityroundtable.com/research/community-maturity-model/.

4. https://www.jobvite.com/wp-content/uploads/2014/10/Jobvite _SocialRecruiting_Survey2014.pdf.

5. A. Baron, Interview with authors. Learn more at http://ayeletbaron .com.

6. S. Scrupski, Interview with authors. More on Scrupski at http://susanscrupski.com/.

7. T. Liu, Correspondence with authors. More on Liu at http://mortrisha.com/.

8. K. Rollag, S. Parise, and R. Cross, "Getting New Hires Up to Speed Quickly," *MIT Sloan Management Review*, Winter 2005, 35-41, http://www .robcross.org/Documents/Publications/SMR_Promoting_Rapid _Onboarding_with_Networks.pdf.

9. C. Crummey, Conversation with authors.

10. J. Bughin, M. Chui, and J. Manyika, "Capturing Business Value With Social Technologies," *The McKinsey Quarterly*, November 2012, http://www .mckinsey.com/insights/high_tech_telecoms_internet/capturing_business _value_with_social_technologies; see also McKinsey's Social Economy report: http://www.mckinsey.com/insights/high_tech_telecoms_internet/the_social _economy and S. Billett, "Learning Through Work: Workplace Affordances and Individual Engagement," *Journal of Workplace Learning*, 2001, 13:5, 209-214, http://www.emeraldinsight.com/doi/abs/10.1108 /EUM0000000005548.

11. Society for New Communications Research, Beeline Labs, and Deloitte, "The Tribalization of Business," 2008, http://www.tribalizationofbusiness .com.

12. C.N. Quinn, *Revolutionize Learning and Development: Performance & Innovation Strategy for the Information Age* (San Francisco: Wiley, 2014).

13. More on Ledford's hands-on approach in this YouTube video: https://www.youtube.com/watch?v=mgXPDJEOyNM.

14. http://www.robcross.org/consortia_network_alignment.htm.

Chapter 3

1. T. Vander Wal, Folksonomy. http://vanderwal.net/folksonomy.html.

2. D. Pontefract, Interview with authors. Also see http://danpontefract .com and *Flat Army: Creating a Connected and Engaged Organization* (Wiley, 2013).

3. E. Brill, Interview with authors. Also see http://www.edbrill.com.

4. E. Duval, K. Verbert, X. Ochoa, and W. Hodgins, "The Snowflake Number" *WebScience Journal*, 2009, http://journal.webscience.org/203/2 /websci09_submission_108.pdf.

5. M. Conner, "Data on Big Data," marciaconner.com http://marciaconner .com/blog/data-on-big-data/, M. Conner, "Time to Build Your Big Data Muscles," *Fast Company*, July 2012, http://www.fastcompany.com/1842928 /time-to-build-your-big-data-muscles/, and M. Hilbert, "How Much Information Is in the Information Society?" *Significance*, Special Issue on Big Data, August 2012, http://onlinelibrary.wiley.com/doi/10.1111/j.1740 -9713.2012.00584.x/abstract.

6. Interview with authors.

7. K. Kruse, "What Is Employee Engagement?" *Forbes*, June 22, 2012, http://www.forbes.com/sites/kevinkruse/2012/06/22/employee -engagement-what-and-why/.

8. T. Davenport and J. Beck, *The Attention Economy: Understanding the New Currency of Business* (Boston: Harvard Business School Press, 2001).

9. D. Cohen and L. Prusak, *In Good Company: How Social Capital Makes Organizations Work* (Boston: Harvard Business Press, 1991).

10. J. Lave and É. Wenger, *Situated Learning: Legitimate Peripheral Participation* (Cambridge: Cambridge University Press, 1991) (First published in 1990 as Institute for Research on Learning Report 90-0013).

11. R. Cross, T. Laseter, A. Parker, and G. Velasquez, "Using Social Network Analysis to Improve Communities of Practice," *California Management Review*, 49:1 (Nov 2006), 32, http://connection.ebscohost.com/c/articles/23160322/using-social-network-analysis-improve-communities-practice.

12. R. Cross, A. Cowen, L. Vertucci, and R.J. Thomas, "Leading in a Connected World: How Effective Leaders Drive Results Through Networks," *Organizational Dynamics*, October 2009, 93-105, http://doi:10.1016/j.orgdyn.2009.02.006 and http://www.robcross.org/pdf/research/leading_in_connected_world.pdf; additional information on the Connected Commons at http://www.robcross.org/consortia.htm.

13. R. Happe, Interview with authors.

14. R.J. Light, *Making the Most of College: Students Speak Their Minds* (Cambridge: Harvard University Press, 2001).

15. W.S. Smith, *Decoding Generational Differences: Fact, Fiction . . . Or Should We Just Get Back to Work?* Deloitte Development LLC, 2008, https://www.insala.com/whitepapers/decoding-generational-differences.pdf.

16. C. Thompson, "Brave New World of Digital Intimacy," *New York Times*, September 5, 2008.

17. C. Shirky, "A Speculative Post on the Idea of Algorithmic Authority," 2009, http://www.shirky.com/weblog/2009/11/a-speculative-post-on-the-idea-of-algorithmic-authority/.

18. P. Thornton, Interview with authors.

19. B. Kaliski, Interview with authors.

20. M. Flinsch, Interview with authors.

21. J. Roush, Interview with authors.

22. "Jacksonville Sheriff's Office on the Cutting Edge," *Law Officer*, August 9, 2008, http://www.lawofficer.com/articles/2008/08/jacksonville-sheriffs-office-c.html.

23. A. Levin, "BookBlog," 2009, http://www.alevin.com/?m=200909.

24. V. Landau, E. Clegg, and D. Engelbart, *The Engelbart Hypothesis: Dialogs With Douglas Engelbart*, 2d ed. (Berkeley, CA: Next Press, 2009).

25. L. Fitton, Interview with authors.

26. "N. White, "An Overview of Online Facilitation," http://www.fullcirc.com/resources/facilitation-resources/an-overview-of-online-facilitation/. Also see É. Wenger, N. White, and J. Smith, *Digital Habitats: Stewarding Technology for Communities* (Portland, OR: CPsquare, 2009), http://technologyforcommunities.com/.

27. L. Levitt, L. Popkin, and D. Hatch, "Building Online Communities for High-Profile Internet Sites," 1999, News Internet Services, USA, https://www.isoc.org/inet98/proceedings/1b/1b_3.htm.

28. J. Bozarth, *Show Your Work: The Payoffs and How-To's of Working Out Loud* (San Francisco: Wiley, 2014).

29. J. Stepper, *Working Out Loud: For a Better Career and Life*, http://workingoutloud.com/.

30. http://thebryceswrite.com/2010/11/29/when-will-we-work-out -loud-soon/.

31. More on Babnis from a series of articles on WOL, https://www.linkedin.com/pulse/working-out-loud-21st-century-way -collaborating-sheila-babnis.

32. A. Kleon, *Show Your Work!: 10 Ways to Share Your Creativity and Get Discovered* (New York: Workman Publishing, 2014)

33. A. Silvers, Interview with authors. More at http://MakingBetter.us.

34. Accordent, "Marathon Oil Corporation Taps Rich Vein of Streaming Media Content for Educating and Communicating with Its Global Workforce," Case Study.

35. T. Starner, "Video Nation," *Human Resource Executive Online*, October 2, 2007, http://www.hreonline.com/HRE/story.jsp?storyId=33267457.

36. D. Kelly, "Is Content Curation in Your Skill Set? It Should Be," *Learning Solutions Magazine*, October 2012, http://www.learningsolutionsmag.com /articles/1037/is-content-curation-in-your-skill-set-it-should-be.

37. A. Anderson and B. Betts, eds. *Curation in Learning* (Alexandria, VA: ATD Press, forthcoming).

Chapter 4

1. A. Campbell, Interview with authors; more at http://LAZparking.com.

2. K. Jones, Interview with authors; more at http://vinjones.com and https://www.youtube.com/user/vinjonesvids.

3. B. Brown, "On Vulnerability," TED Talk, 2010, http://www.ted.com /talks/brene_brown_on_vulnerability.

4. IBM Institute for Business Value, "2012 CEO Study: Leading Through Connections," http://www-935.ibm.com/services/us/en/c-suite /ceostudy2012/ (a listing of all C-Suite studies is available on the IBM website: http://www-935.ibm.com/services/c-suite/ceo/).

5. M. McLure Wasko and S. Faraj, "Why Should I Share? Examining Social Capital and Knowledge Contribution in Electronic Networks of Practice," *MIS Quarterly*, 29(1), 2005, 35-57, Special Issue on Information Technologies and Knowledge Management.

6. Conversation with authors.

7. From L. Buczek, "The Big Failure of Enterprise 2.0 Social Business," Blog post, Beyond the Cube Blog, http://www.lauriebuczek.com/2011/08/23/the-big-failure-of-enterprise-2-0-social-business/.

8. The Jive Community Social Business Blog, https://community.jivesoftware.com/community/socbiz/blog/2012/02/08/community-management-101-no-censorship.

9. J. Sullivan, Interview with authors.

10. C. Brown, C. Efstratiou, I. Leontiadis, D. Quercia, and C. Mascolo, "Tracking Serendipitous Interactions: How Individual Cultures Shape the Office," *ACM Proceedings of the 17th ACM Conference on Computer-Supported Cooperative Work & Social Computing*, 2014, 1072-1081.

11. Interview with authors.

Chapter 5

1. S. Terry, Interview with the authors. More at http://simonterry.tumblr.com.

2. In 1995, Gloria Gery put forth the idea that counting the number of people that were trained was no more useful than their aggregate weight. Attendance was being counted because it could be and people didn't know what else to measure. G. Gery, *Electronic Performance Support Systems* (Tolland, MA: Gery Performance Press, 1995).

3. N.M. Radziwill, *Statistics (The Easier Way) With R: An Informal Text on Applied Statistics* (Lapis Lucera, 2015).

4. More about the Theory of Change at http://www.theoryofchange.org/.

5. N. Burke, Interview with authors. More on Burke's work at http://www.commonhealthaction.org/message.html and https://www.youtube.com/watch?v=FY4miyfd7ms.

6. B. Brooks, Interview with authors.

7. A. Bryant, "Douglas Merrill of ZestFinance: Steer Clear of What You Can't Measure," *New York Times*, March 20, 2014, http://www.nytimes.com/2014/03/21/business/douglas-merrill-of-zestfinance-steer-clear-of-what-you-cant-measure.html.

8. More from Gianpiero Petriglieri at http://petriglieri.com.

9. J. Postman, *SocialCorp: Social Media Goes Corporate* (Berkeley, CA: New Riders), 114.

10. T. Griffith, Interview with authors; see also http://www.terrigriffith .com/.

11. Aberdeen Group, 2009, and others.

12. Assess Your Organization's Need for HR Analytics, http://gca.mcbassi .com/s3/AnalyticsAssess?srp=mcbt.

13. http://www.cs.cornell.edu/home/llee/papers.html.

14. N. Sadat Shami, J.Yang, L. Panc, C. Dugan, T. Ratchford, J. Rasmussen, Y. Assogba, T. Steier, T. Soule, S. Lupushor, W. Geyer, I. Guy, and J. Ferrar, "Understanding Employee Social Media Chatter with Enterprise Social Pulse," *ACM Proceedings of the 17th ACM Conference on Computer-Supported Cooperative Work & Social Computing* (New York: ACM Press, 2014), 379-392, http://dx.doi.org/10.1145/2531602.2531650.

15. P. Lilienthal, "If You Give Your Employees a Voice, Do You Listen?" *The Journal for Quality and Participation* 25(3), 2002, 38-40.

16. World Economic Forum, 2014, Forum for Young Global Leaders, http://www.weforum.org/community/forum-young-global-leaders.

17. S. Baron-Cohen, *The Essential Difference: Male and Female Brains and the Truth About Autism* (New York: Basic Books, 2003).

18. B. Parmar, "Corporate Empathy Is not an Oxymoron," *Harvard Business Review*, January 2015, https://hbr.org/2015/01/corporate-empathy-is-not -an-oxymoron.

19. C. Cherniss, "The Business Case for Emotional Intelligence," http://www.eiconsortium.org/reports/business_case_for_ei.html, citing L.M. Spencer, Jr. and S.M. Spencer, *Competence at Work: Models for Superior Performance* (New York: Wiley, 1993) and L.M.J. Spencer, D.C. McClelland, and S. Kelner, *Competency Assessment Methods: History and State of the Art* (Boston: Hay/McBer, 1997).

20. B. Parmer, "Can Empathy Really Work in a Business World Dominated by Testosterone?" *The Guardian*, June 2014, http://www.theguardian.com /women-in-leadership/2014/jun/18/empathy-secret-revolutionise-business.

21. I. Macleod, "Trust, Empathy and Honesty the Keys to Make Social Work—Telefonica Europe's Digital and Social Lead," *The Drum*, June 2014, http://www.thedrum.com/news/2014/06/25/trust-empathy-and-honesty -keys-make-social-work-telefonica-europe-s-digital-and.

22. S. Sinek, *Leaders Eat Last: Why Some Teams Pull Together and Others Don't* (New York: Portfolio, 2014); more from Sinek at https://www.startwithwhy.com/.

23. http://www.cmo.com/articles/2015/4/7/quick-chat-lucie-sarif-head-of-strategy-and-planning-lady-geek.html.

24. R. G. McGrath, "Management's Three Eras: A Brief History," *Harvard Business Review*, July 30, 2014, https://hbr.org/2014/07/managements-three-eras-a-brief-history/.

25. S. Taplinger, "Mar-Tech Future Merges Data and Humanity," http://thedma.org/news/mar-tech-future-merges-data-and-humanity/.

26. R. Shadoan, "Structure: A Better Way of Thinking about Data," Akashic Labs, March 6, 2015, http://www.akashiclabs.com/structure-a-useful-way-of-thinking-about-data/.

27. The PAR Framework team uses new data-focused technologies to share their big data journey with others and to collaborate across organizations with similar goals. For an example, see https://community.datacookbook.com/institutions/par.

28. The 2012 142-country study, *State of the Global Workplace*, showed only 13 percent of employees worldwide are engaged at work. http://www.gallup.com/services/178517/state-global-workplace.aspx.

29. G. Johnson, "Otherwise Engaged," *Training*, 41(10), 2004, 4.

30. W.H. Macey, B. Schneider, K.M. Barbera, and S.A. Young, *Employee Engagement: Tools for Analysis, Practice, and Competitive Advantage* (Chichester, UK: Wiley-Blackwell, 2009).

31. A.M. Saks, "Antecedents and Consequences of Employee Engagement," *Journal of Managerial Psychology* 21(7) 2006, 600-619.

32. B.L. Rich, J.A. Lepine, and E.R. Crawford, "Job Engagement: Antecedents and Effects on Job Performance," *Academy of Management Journal* 53(3) 2010, 617-635.

33. J.K. Harter, F.L. Schmidt, and T.L. Hayes, "Business Unit-Level Relationship Between Employee Satisfaction, Employee Engagement, and Business Outcomes: A Meta-Analysis," *Journal of Applied Psychology* 87(2), 2002, 268-279.

34. N.E. Chalofsky, *Meaningful Workplaces: Reframing How and Where We Work* (San Francisco: Jossey-Bass, 2010).

35. J. Notter and M. Grant, *Humanize: How People-Centric Organizations Succeed in a Social World* (Indianapolis: Que, 2012). For the "How to Be Generative Worksheet," see http://www.scribd.com/doc/65255892 /Humanize-Worksheet-Generative.

36. D. Birnbaum, Interview with authors.

37. V. Krebs, "Discovering Emergent Communities of Knowledge in Your Organization," TNT: The Network Thinkers Blog, March 2015, http://www .thenetworkthinkers.com/2015/03/discovering-emergent-communities-of -.html.

38. http://robcross.org/pdf/roundtable/energy_and_innovation.pdf.

39. R. Cross, W. Baker, and A. Parker, "What Creates Energy in Organizations?" *MIT Sloan Management Review* (2003) 44(4), 51-57, http://sloanreview.mit.edu/article/what-creates-energy-in-organizations/.

40. P. Anklam, *Net Work: A Practical Guide to Creating and Sustaining Networks at Work and in the World* (London: Routledge, 2011); for more information, see http://www.pattianklam.com/blog/.

41. R. Cross, C. Ernst, and B. Pasmore, "A Bridge Too Far? How Boundary Spanning Networks Drive Organizational Change and Effectiveness," *Organizational Dynamics* (2013) 42, 81-91, http://dx.doi.org/10.1016/j .orgdyn.2013.03.001.

42. To learn more about the CMM and find free resources, see their website: http://www.communityroundtable.com/research/community -maturity-model/.

43. Find more on SMILE at http://www.simply-goodadvice.com/smile-sub /index.htm.

44. Learn more at http://www.engageforsuccess.org/sub-groups/social -media-digital-engagement-subgroup/.

45. C.N. Quinn, *Revolutionize Learning & Development: Performance and Innovation Strategy for the Information Age* (San Francisco: Wiley/ATD, 2014), 167. For those wondering why we haven't addressed the training department stalwart, the Kirkpatrick four levels of evaluation, Quinn does a masterful job explaining how the model has been misused in organizations, almost always done in the reverse of how it was intended and having none of the effect it was designed to achieve. See Quinn's book for how to approach learning and development measurement in a meaningful way.

46. More on Think Big at http://www.o2.co.uk/thinkbig.

47. To quantify the financial benefit, they looked at employee engagement scores (from their annual Reflect survey), at annual appraisal scores, sickness days, and on-boarding costs. They also asked people and their managers about the skills they developed when getting involved and then cross-referenced everything with the literature available to determine its strength.

48. http://www.globalactionplan.org.uk/News/starting-at-square-one.

49. C. Thompson, *Smarter Than You Think: How Technology Is Changing Our Minds for the Better* (New York: Penguin, 2013).

50. Minimizing the ripple effect of web-centric software by using the pheromone extension, http://dl.acm.org/citation.cfm?id=2160227.

51. http://www.goodcompanyindex.com.

52. The explanation is simple. Worthy firms enjoy the benefits of energized employees, enthusiastic customers, and empathetic communities. These features not only help boost the bottom line, but also create a virtuous cycle. Workers, customers, and investors will be drawn to companies that do right by their stakeholders.

53. http://www.goodcompanyindex.com/good-company/self-assessment/.

54. Due to the large scale and quantitative nature of the analysis, they only used structural data (metadata), e.g., who responds to whom, but did not take into account the actual message content. In the study they also point out that Deloitte is ideally suited to study influence because, 1. As a professional service firm, hierarchy and formal influence is an important mechanism for work allocation; 2. Much of their work is knowledge work, which means the collaborative space plays an active part in informal influence as people search and seek additional knowledge; and 3. Deloitte social network, D Street, is highly successful and widely adopted across the organization, which makes it a good candidate to study community emergence.

55. K. Riemer, S. Stieglitz, and C. Meske, "From Top to Bottom: Investigating the Changing Role of Hierarchy and Influence in Enterprise Social Networks," *Business & Information Systems Engineering* (DOI 10.1007/s12599-015-0375-3) and "Or: How Influence in ESN Changes Over Time," bbr [backed by research], Kai Riemer's blog, https://byresearch.wordpress.com/2015/03/05/esn-community/.

56. http://socialbusinessindex.com.

57. Clive Thompson was introduced to this concept by legal scholar Andrew K. Woods, He writes about this in *Smarter Than You Think*, 254.

58. G. Mark, S.T. Iqbal, M. Czerwinski, and P. Johns, "Bored Mondays and Focused Afternoons: The Rhythm of Attention and Online Activity in the Workplace," *Proceedings of the SIGCHI Conference on Human Factors in Computing Systems* (New York: ACM Press, 2014), 3025-3034, http://research.microsoft.com/apps/pubs/default.aspx?id=241877.

59. Conversation with authors and from M.C. Benton and N.M. Radziwill, "A Framework for Assessment of Social Learning in Organizations (Manuscript in preparation, 2015).

60. https://www.leaderboarded.com/gurus.

61. C. Wallis et al., "Help! I've Lost My Focus," *Time*, January 9, 2006.

62. "Multitasking: Switching Costs," American Psychological Association, http://www.apa.org/research/action/multitask.aspx.

63. Visionary Marketing: The Blog, http://visionarymarketing.com /en/blog.

64. M.E. Weksler and B.B. Weksler, "The Epidemic of Distraction," *Gerentology*, 2012; 58(5), 385-390, http://www.ncbi.nlm.nih.gov /pubmed/22572729; D.M. Sanbonmatsu, D.L. Strayer, N. Medeiros-Ward, et. al., "Who Multi-Tasks and Why? Multi-Tasking Ability, Perceived Multi-Tasking Ability, Impulsivity, and Sensation Seeking," *PLoS One*, 2013, 8(1): e54402, Epub 2013 Jan 23, http://www.ncbi.nlm.nih.gov/ pubmed/23372720; and T.M. Amabile and S.J. Kramer, "The Power of Small Wins," *Harvard Business Review*, May 2011, http://hbr.org/2011/05/the-power-of-small-wins/.

65. M. Conner, "Minds at Work: Achieving Transformation Beyond Wellness, Social, and Even Culture," May 2015 http://marciaconner.com /minds-at-work/.

66. M. Conner, "Turning Social Capital Into Financial Capital," *Change This*, November 2010, http://changethis.com/manifesto/show/76.03. NewSocialLearning.pdf; M. Mazmanian and I. Erickson, "The Product of Availability: Understanding the Economic Underpinnings of Constant Connectivity," *Proceedings of the SIGCHI Conference on Human Factors in Computing Systems* (New York: ACM Press, 2014), 763-772; and R. Teodoro, P. Ozturk, M. Naaman, W. Mason, and J. Lindqvist, "The Motivations and Experiences of the On-Demand Mobile Workforce," *Proceedings of the 17th ACM Conference on Computer-Supported Cooperative Work and Social Computing 2014* (CSCW)(New York: ACM Press, 2014).

67. K. Renner, Interview with authors.

68. V. Krebs, TNT: The Network Thinkers Blog, http://www .thenetworkthinkers.com/.

69. Quote from blog on Chet Wood's D Street profile.

70. C. Brown, C. Efstratiou, I. Leontiadis, D. Quercia, and C. Mascolo, "Tracking Serendipitous Interactions: How Individual Cultures Shape the Office," *Proceedings of the 17th ACM Conference on Computer-Supported Cooperative Work and Social Computing* (New York: ACM Press, 2014), 1072-1081.

71. The "Forgetting Curve" was first hypothesized by Hermann Ebbinghaus in 1885—http://en.wikipedia.org/wiki/Forgetting_curve.

72. K.A. Neuendorf, *The Content Analysis Guidebook* (Thousand Oaks, CA: Sage Publications, 2002), http://academic.csuohio.edu/kneuendorf /content/ and P.J. Stone, "Thematic Text Analysis: New Agendas for Analyzing Text Content," chapter 2 in *Text Analysis for the Social Sciences*, ed. C. Roberts (Mahwah, NJ: Lawrence Erlbaum Associates, 1997), http://academic .csuohio.edu/kneuendorf/content/cpuca/ccap.htm.

73. http://www.ushahidi.com/.

74. "Making Change Work Study," IBM Global Services, http://www-935 .ibm.com/services/us/gbs/bus/pdf/gbe03100-usen-03-making-change-work .pdf.

75. J. Frahm, "70% of Change Projects Fail: Bollocks!" Conversations of Change, September 2013, http://conversationsofchange.com .au/2013/09/02/70-of-change-projects-fail-bollocks1/.

76. J. Little, "Is the 70% Failure Rate a Myth?" Agile Blog, September 2013, http://www.agilecoach.ca/2013/08/23/70-failure-rate-myth/.

77. R. Cross, C. Ernst, and B. Pasmore, op. cit.

78. M. Conner, Learning Culture Audit, marciaconner.com, http://marciaconner.com/assess/learning-culture/.

79. R. Cross, C. Ernst, and B. Pasmore, op. cit.

80. R. Cross, et. al. "Personal Network Analysis Workbook," http://www .robcross.org/Documents/Personal_Network_Analysis_Workbook_Final.pdf; the PNA Workbook can be downloaded.

81. R. Larson and M. Csikszentmihalyi, "The Experience Sampling Method," *New Directions for Methodology of Social and Behavioral Science*, 15, 41-56 (San Francisco: Jossey-Bass).

82. S.A. Grandhi, N. Laws, B. Amento, and Q. Jones, "The Importance of 'Who' and 'What' in Interruption Management: Empirical Evidence from a Cell Phone Use Study," *AMCIS 2008 Proceedings*, http://aisel.aisnet.org /amcis2008/79.

Chapter 6

1. N. Radjou, J. Prabhu, and S. Ahuja, *Jugaad Innovation: Think Frugal, Be Flexible, Generate Breakthrough Growth* (San Francisco: Jossey-Bass, 2012), http://jugaadinnovation.com; see also N. Radjou and J. Prabhu, *Frugal Innovation: How To Do More With Less* (New York: *The Economist*, 2015).

2. S. Kaplan, Interview with authors. Learn more at http://www.businessinnovationfactory.com/.

3. S. Kaplan, *The Business Model Innovation Factory* (San Francisco: Wiley, 2012).

4. Michael Erand, "Think Tank: Where to Get a Good Idea: Steal It Outside Your Group," *New York Times*, May 22, 2004. http://www.nytimes.com/2004/05/22/arts/think-tank-where-to-get-a-good-idea-steal-it-outside-your-group.html.

5. J. Foner, Interview with authors.

6. S. Nathoo, "Death by Conference: When Smart People Use Comic Sans," http://salimanathoo.com/2013/10/death-by-conference/.

7. O. Mitchell, Interview with authors. More at http://www.speakingaboutpresenting.com/.

8. R. Scoble, "Twitter and the Mark Zuckerberg Interview," *WebProNews*, March 11, 2008, http://www.webpronews.com/blogtalk/2008/03/11/twitter-and-the-mark-zuckerberg-interview.

9. G. Koelling, Interview with authors.

10. D. Sharesky, Interview with authors, also see more at http://ideasandthoughts.org/.

11. J. Veen, Interview with authors. https://about.me/veen.

12. L. Lawley, "Confessions of a Backchannel Queen," Mamamusings blog post, March 30, 2004, http://mamamusings.net/archives/2004/03/30/confessions_of_a_backchannel_queen.php.

13. L. Fitton, Interview with authors. Also see https://about.me/pistachio.

14. J. Veen, Interview with authors.

15. W. Deyamport III, Interview with authors; more about Deyamport at http://www.iamdrwill.com.

16. P. Gillin, "While I Talked, People Twittered," Blog post, September 11, 2008, Social Media and the Open Enterprise, http://gillin.com/blog/page/36/.

17. G. Brown-Martin, Interview with authors. More at http://www.grahambrownmartin.com and http://learning-reimagined.com/.

18. S. Berkun, *Confessions of a Public Speaker* (Sebastopol, CA: O'Reilly Media, 2009).

19. J. Andrade, "What Does Doodling Do?" *Applied Cognitive Psychology* 24(1): 100-106.

20. E. Eckman, Interview with authors.

21. K. Hamlin, Interview with authors. More at http://www .identitywoman.net/.

Further Reading

Analyzing Social Media Networks with NodeXL: Insights From a Connected World, Derek Hansen, Ben Shneiderman, Marc A. Smith (Burlington, MA: Morgan Kaufmann, 2010).

Changing the World of Work. One Human at a Time: Twenty-One Essays on How Companies Can Overcome Organizational Inertia and Forge a Connected Workforce Founded on Trust. (Change Agents Worldwide, 2014), http://changeagentsworldwide.com/book/1.

The Cluetrain Manifesto: 10th Anniversary Edition, Rick Levine, Christopher Locke, Doc Searls, and David Weinberger (New York: Basic Books, 2011).

Cognitive Surplus: Creativity and Generosity in a Connected Age, Clay Shirky (New York: Penguin, 2010).

The Collaborative Organization: A Strategic Guide to Solving Your Internal Business Challenges Using Emerging Social & Collaborative Tools, Jacob Morgan. (New York: McGraw-Hill, 2012).

Communities of Practice: Learning, Meaning, and Identity, Étienne Wenger (Cambridge, UK: Cambridge University Press, 1999).

The Connected Company, Dave Gray (Sebastopol, CA: O'Reilly Media, 2012).

The Corporate Blogging Book: Absolutely Everything You Need to Know to Get It Right, 2nd ed., Debbie Weil (London: Piatkus, 2009).

Creativity, Inc.: Overcoming the Unseen Forces That Stand in the Way of True Inspiration, Ed Catmull and Amy Wallace (New York: Random House, 2014).

Daring Greatly: How the Courage to Be Vulnerable Transforms the Way We Live, Love, Parent, and Lead, Brené Brown (New York: Gotham, 2012).

"The Deloitte Millennial Survey 2015: Mind the Gaps," http://www.deloitte
.com/MillennialSurvey.

Design for How People Learn, Julie Dirksen (Berkeley, CA: New Rider, 2012).

Digital Habitats: Stewarding Technology for Communities, Étienne Wenger,
Nancy White, and John D. Smith (Portland, OR: CPsquare, 2009).

The DNA of Collaboration: Unlocking the Potential of 21st Century Teams, Chris
Jones (Charlotte, NC: Amberwood Media Group, 2012).

Doug Engelbart Institute, http://dougengelbart.org/.

Drive: The Surprising Truth About What Motivates Us, Daniel H. Pink (New
York: Riverhead, 2009).

The Engaged Leader: A Strategy for Your Digital Transformation, Charlene Li
(Philadelphia: Wharton Digital Press, 2015).

Everybody Writes: Your Go-To Guide to Creating Ridiculously Good Content, Ann
Handley (Hoboken, NJ: Wiley, 2014).

Flat Army: Creating a Connected and Engaged Organization, Dan Pontefract
(Hoboken, NJ: Wiley, 2013).

*From Digital Natives to Digital Wisdom: Hopeful Essays for 21st Century
Learning*, Marc Prensky (Thousand Oaks, CA: Sage, 2012).

The Gen Z Effect: The Six Forces Shaping the Future of Business, Tom
Koulopoulos and Dan Keldsen (Brookline, MA: Bibliomotion, 2014).

Get Bold: Using Social Media to Create a New Type of Social Business, Sandy
Carter (Indianapolis: IBM Press, 2012).

Good Company: Business Success in the Worthiness Era, Laurie Bassi, Ed
Frauenheim, and Dan McMurrer (San Francisco: Berrett-Koehler, 2011).

Groundswell: Winning in a World Transformed by Social Technologies, 2nd ed.,
Charlene Li and Josh Bernoff (Boston: Harvard Business Review Press,
2011).

Here Comes Everybody: The Power of Organizing Without Organizations, Clay
Shirky (New York: Penguin, 2008).

How to Shoot Video That Doesn't Suck: Advice to Make Any Amateur Look Like a Pro, Steve Stockman (New York: Workman, 2011).

HR Analytics Handbook, Laurie Bassi, Rob Carpenter, and Dan McMurrer (McBassi & Company, 2012).

Humanize: How People-Centric Organizations Succeed in a Social World, Jamie Notter and Maddie Grant (Indianapolis: Que, 2011).

Informal Learning: Rediscovering the Natural Pathways That Inspire Innovation and Performance, Jay Cross (San Francisco: Pfeiffer, 2006).

Learning Reimagined, Graham Brown-Martin (New York: Bloomsbury, 2014).

Net Smart: How to Thrive Online, Howard Rheingold (Cambridge, MA: MIT Press, 2012).

Never Eat Alone and Other Secrets to Success, One Relationship at a Time, 2nd ed., Keith Ferrazzi (New York: Crown Business, 2014).

A New Culture of Learning: Cultivating the Imagination for a World of Constant Change, Douglas Thomas and John Seely Brown (CreateSpace, 2011).

New Media Literacies Project at USC, http://www.newmedialiteracies.org/.

Next Learning, Unwrapped, Nick van Dam (Lulu, 2011).

Open: How We'll Work, Live and Learn in the Future, David Price (Crux Publishing, 2013).

Opting in: Lessons in Social Business from a Fortune 500 Product Manager, Ed Brill (Indianapolis: IBM Press, 2013).

Organizations Don't Tweet, People Do: A Manager's Guide to the Social Web, Euan Semple (Chichester, UK: Wiley, 2012).

Out of Our Minds: Learning to Be Creative, Ken Robinson (Chichester, UK: Capstone, 2011).

The Pursuit of Social Business Excellence, Vala Afshar and Brad Martin (San Rafael, CA: Charles Pinot, 2012).

Quiet: The Power of Introverts in a World That Can't Stop Talking, Susan Cain (New York: Random House, 2013).

Rebels at Work: A Handbook for Leading Change From Within, Lois Kelly and Carmen Medina (San Francisco: O'Reilly, 2014).

Reinventing Organizations, Frederic Laloux (Brussels, Belgium: Nelson Parker, 2014).

Revolutionize Learning & Development: Performance and Innovation Strategy for the Information Age, Clark N. Quinn (San Francisco: Wiley, 2014).

Show Your Work: The Payoffs and How-To's of Working Out Loud, Jane Bozarth (San Francisco: Wiley, 2014).

Situated Learning: Legitimate Peripheral Participation, Jean Lave and Étienne Wenger (Cambridge, UK: Cambridge University Press, 1991).

Smarter Innovation: Using Interactive Processes to Drive Better Business Results, Katrina Pugh, ed. (London: Ark Group, 2014).

Social Business by Design: Transformative Social Media Strategies for the Connected Company, Dion Hinchcliffe, Peter Kim, and Jeff Dachis (San Francisco: Jossey-Bass, 2012).

The Social Employee: How Great Companies Make Social Media Work, Cheryl Burgess and Mark Burgess (New York: McGraw-Hill, 2013).

Social Intelligence: The New Science of Human Relationships, Daniel Goleman (New York: Bantam, 2006).

Social Learning Handbook 2014, Jane Hart (Bath, UK: Centre for Learning & Performance Technologies, 2014).

The Social Life of Information, John Seely Brown and Paul Duguid (Boston: Harvard Business School Publishing, 2000).

Social Media for Trainers: Techniques for Enhancing and Extending Learning, Jane Bozarth (San Francisco: Pfeiffer, 2010).

The Social Organization: How to Use Social Media to Tap the Collective Genius of Your Customers and Employees, Anthony J. Bradley and Mark P. McDonald (Boston: Harvard Business Review Press, 2011).

Socialized!: How the Most Successful Businesses Harness the Power of Social, Mark Fidelman (Brookline, MA: Bibliomotion, 2012).

Spreadable Media: Creating Value and Meaning in a Networked Culture, Joshua Green, Henry Jenkins, and Sam Ford (New York: NYU Press, 2013).

Swarm Stupidity: We Can Only Be This Stupid if We All Work Together, Gunter Dueck (Frankfurt, Germany: Campus, 2015).

"Telefónica Global Millennial Survey," 2014, http://survey.telefonica.com/.

To Sell Is Human: The Surprising Truth About Moving Others, Daniel H. Pink (New York: Riverhead, 2013).

Too Big to Know: Rethinking Knowledge Now That the Facts Aren't the Facts, Experts Are Everywhere, and the Smartest Person in the Room Is the Room, David Weinberger (New York: Basic Books, 2012).

When Millennials Take Over: Preparing for the Ridiculously Optimistic Future of Business, Jamie Notter and Maddie Grant (Ideapress Publishing, 2015).

Wired for Culture: Origins of the Human Social Mind, Mark Pagel (New York: Norton, 2013).

Working Out Loud: For a Better Career and Life, John Stepper (Ikigai Press, 2015).

Working Smarter: Informal Learning in the Cloud, Jay Cross, Charles Jennings, Jane Hart, and Clarke Quinn (Berkeley, CA: Internet Time Alliance, 2010).

Glossary of Social Learning Lingo

"Prior to the Internet, the last technology that had any real effect on the way people sat down and talked together was the table."
—Clay Shirky

Activity Feed: The rolling list of status updates and recent additions to a social network conveying what people are doing or feeling in real time.

Astroturfing: The formation of citizen groups or coalitions that appear to be grassroots based but are primarily conceived, created, and/or funded by corporations, industry trade associations, political interests, or public relations firms.

Backchannel: Real-time text communications among audience members using something like Twitter or a local chat room during a live event. Coined in 1970 to describe listeners' behaviors during verbal communication, today backchannel represents an audience who is now connected in real time, learning with each other and the world all the time.

Blog: An online journal (web log) that usually provides information or commentary on a particular issue, event, person, or topic.

Blog Posts: Primarily text, yet can contain photos, illustrations, videos, and links to other websites.

Bloggers: Writers of blogs, they typically welcome comments and interaction by and among readers and themselves, all of which can be as interesting as the original post.

Brandscraping: When someone mentions a brand (or even an associated hashtag) prominently in social media to draw attention to themselves rather than for the intended purposes of the brand.

Cloud: The phenomenon of storing data and locating services and infrastructure on a remote server accessible by the data owner from any device with an Internet connection. Social media data live in the cloud.

Collaboration: Enhancing the exchange of insights and expanding ideas on-demand and in real time; also defined in practical terms as solving problems in teams.

Collective Intelligence: Wisdom that emerges from the collaboration, collective efforts, and/or competition of many individuals. Collective IQ is a measure of collective intelligence, although the two are often used interchangeably.

Communities of Practice: Groups of people who share a concern or a passion for something they do and learn how to do it better as they interact regularly.

Community Manager: An online conversation facilitator who builds, grows, and manages online communities, often around a company, a brand, or a cause.

Crowdfunding: The practice of funding a project or venture by raising numerous small amounts of money from a large number of people, typically via the Internet.

Crowdsourcing: Soliciting content, ideas, and skills via the Internet from people who are passionate about a topic and who are willing to contribute their resources to further the work.

Curation: The careful selection of items for collection and sharing; once used mostly in art museums (exhibits) and radio stations (play lists), today, curated collections of great online resources help people learn quickly through social media.

Derp: Internet slang signifying stupidity or acting foolishly. It's used as a label, an epithet, as in, "He's a derp."

Enterprise Social Network (ESN): A social network designed specifically for people within a business enterprise, with enhanced security and department or role-specific forums. Many such systems are available and the market for them is growing and competitive.

Geofence: A virtual barrier representing a real geographic area through a software program. Dynamically generated around a specific location or predefined by physical boundaries, it can send trigger notifications when a device enters or exits the boundaries defined by the geofencing administrator.

Geotagging: Adding location-based data to media such as photos, video, or online maps that can help people find services based on locale.

Hashtag: The # symbol preceding a word or run-on phrase within social media to bring attention to a topic or emotion that can be indexed, searched on, and followed by anyone, even those who don't follow the people using the tag.

Influencer: Subject matter expert respected for his or her opinion, with the capacity to shape the opinions of others.

Keyword: A subject or descriptive term that identifies the topic of text, used to index documents for retrieval by search engines or other aggregators. A keyword can appear in the body of the text, subject heading, or pay-per-click advertising.

Link Shortening: Converting a long web address to a short link, which can more easily be shared across social media and can be tracked to see how many people clicked it.

Mashup: Assembling unique items to create something new. Producing new results from pre-existing bits and pieces can result in new songs, new software, new courses, and new job roles.

Meme: A cultural theme that emerges over time as it's passed from one person to another. Memes generally circulate through graphics or photos and their accompanying explanatory or declarative texts that are shared repeatedly on social media. One popular and unexpected one is Rickrolling, the practice of misdirecting a link to a video of a Rick Astley song from 1987. Internet memes relevant to business include "Ain't nobody got time for that" and "Too soon?"

Metadata: Frequently referred to as "data about data," there are structural metadata and descriptive metadata. Both are used to describe the content and the context of files and objects such as web pages, blog posts, and photographs. Metadata are used primarily to facilitate search and discovery of relevant information.

Microsharing: Short bursts of text shared across social network activity feeds. They are usually limited to a finite number of characters—often 140 because, along with a 20-character header, they fit the 160-character limit of SMS (TXT) messages; also referred to as microblogging.

Online Community: A virtual, online space where people can share content and engage around specific topics with colleagues, business partners, customers, and subject matters experts—anyone with the permission and interest in building on what they know, as well as discovering new perspectives. Often used synonymously with social network, online communities allow anyone within the space access to anyone else in the space.

Open Source: A software production and development methodology that allows unrestricted access to the end product, including its source code; in contrast to proprietary software, which requires ownership or a structured relationship with the owner, such as a license, in order to access the end product.

Photosharing: A type of social network where people can upload, manage, and share photos publicly or with their networks. Popular sites include Flickr and Instagram. Pinterest uses images to link to content.

Platform: A framework or content management system that runs software and presents content. WordPress, for example, serves as a platform for a community of blogs and other content. In a larger context, the Internet is becoming a platform for applications and capabilities through the availability of cloud computing.

Rating System: A feature within online platforms that allows people to uprate or downrate postings or content, sharing their likes or dislikes. Some networks use stars for rating. Others use Like buttons. Reddit is one social network that makes the up and down ratings central to their engagement.

Search Engine Optimization (SEO): Elevating certain words in a website so that search engines rank them higher than similar sites. It seeks to affect unpaid or "organic" search results.

Sentiment Analysis: A metric that identifies and measures the tone of a conversation across a social network, usually by categorizing it as positive, negative, or neutral.

Social Business: Connecting people to people, information, and insights within an organization.

Social Capital: The good will and positive reputation that flows to a person through his or her relationships with others in social networks.

Social Graph: A data structure that represents the interconnection of relationships in an online social network between people, places, and the things those people interact with online.

Social Learning: Participating with other people to make sense of new ideas, learning with them and from them online or side by side. Social learning naturally occurs at conferences, in groups, and among old friends in a cafe as easily as it does in a meeting or among colleagues online who have never met in person. We experience it when we go down the hall to ask a question and when we post that same question on Twitter or Facebook, anticipating that someone will respond.

Social Media: A set of Internet-based social technologies designed to engage two, three, or more people. What makes this special is that most interaction supported by technology is either narrowcast (one to one), often with a telephone call or an email message; niche cast (one to small groups), for instance using email distribution lists or small-circulation newsletters; or broadcast (one to many), as in large online magazines or a radio show. In more general terms, social media refers to any online technology that enables people to publish, connect, converse, and share content online.

Social Media Optimization (SMO): A set of practices for generating publicity through social media, online communities, and social networks. The focus is on driving traffic from sources other than search engines, such as from the referrals by friends and colleagues. In marketing, generally referred to as earned media.

Social Network: Online space to connect with people, similar to an online community (the terms are often interchanged). Technically, a social network consists of people who personally know one another but may also include people with whom you have loose ties that closer friends can strengthen through your mutual connections. Popular social networks are Facebook, LinkedIn, Instagram.

Social Network Analysis (SNA): Mapping and measuring relationships and information flow among people, groups, organizations, computers, and websites, referred to as nodes, and their relationships or connectedness, referred to as ties.

Social Profile: A personal page within a social network that displays information about that person such as interests, expertise, location, connections, updates, and links to authored content.

Social Technology: The broader set of automated solutions that enable social media and social interaction, including the Internet itself; also referred to as social tools.

Social Tools: Software or platforms that enable participatory culture. Examples include social networks, blogs, podcasts, forums, wikis, shared videos, and shared presentations. Social tools leave a digital audit trail, documenting an online journey and leaving a path for others to follow and share.

Trackback: A link used to facilitate communication across blogs. When one blogger refers to another blog in his or her post, the trackback will notify the owner of the original post that the blogger has referred to and linked to his or her post. Each blog post has a permanent link address (a permalink), which directs the reader to a specific entry within a blog.

Trending Topics: Typically defined by an algorithm designed to identify topics that are currently being talked about online more than they had been previously.

Troll: Internet slang for someone who posts irrelevant, inflammatory, or off-topic messages in an online forum to provoke others into an emotional response or to generally disrupt on-topic conversation.

Tweet: A 140-character update shared across Twitter. RT stands for Retweet, whereby you share what someone else has tweeted. DM stands for Direct Message. A TweetChat is an organized gathering of people using a specified #hashtag to consolidate group tweets, creating a virtual chat room that's visible to any twitter user following that tag. A Tweetup is a gathering of people using an agreed-upon hashtag while they meet in person.

User-Generated Content (UGC): Refers to all forms of materials such as blog posts, reviews, podcasts, videos, comments, and more designed by the users of the content (such as employees or customers).

Videosharing: Embedded capabilities or dedicated social networks designed for people to upload, manage, and share recorded digital videos or streaming video publicly or with their personal networks; popular platforms: YouTube, Vimeo, and Vine (for looping videos no longer than six seconds).

Virtual Event: A live event, such as a trade show or job fair, that takes place across the web in real time, often using a virtual environment designed to emulate a face-to-face event of the same kind.

Web 2.0 (and Enterprise 2.0): Easy-to-use, socially focused, and commercially available software that moves services, assets, smarts, and guidance closer to where they are needed—to people seeking answers, solving problems, overcoming uncertainty, and improving how they work. It is software that facilitates collaboration and informs choices on a wide stage, fostering learning from a vast, intellectually diverse set of people.

Wiki: A web page or collection of documents designed to be edited by multiple people and requiring little, if any, knowledge of markup language, thereby facilitating collaboration on page content. Wikipedia is an example.

Work Out Loud (WOL): Sharing ideas, learning, and what you are working on in an open, generous, and connected way.

About the Authors

Tony Bingham is the president and CEO of the Association for Talent Development, formerly ASTD, the world's largest professional association dedicated to those who develop talent in organizations. Tony works with a staff of 130, a Board of Directors, and a worldwide network of volunteers to empower professionals to develop talent in the workplace.

Tony believes in creating a culture of engaged, high-performing teams that deliver extraordinary results. Deeply passionate about change, technology, and the impact of talent development, he focuses on adding value to ATD members and the global community of talent development professionals. He believes that aligning talent development efforts to business strategy, while utilizing the power of social and mobile technology for learning, is a key differentiator in business today.

Marcia Conner is a former corporate executive who now dedicates her time to reinventing a vibrant and healthy global ecosystem. Described as a "blank page systems architect," she works closely with risk-taking leaders, impact entrepreneurs, and unreasonable thinkers, ready to use their superpowers for good.

Marcia is a SupporTED Mentor, contributes to *Fast Company* and *Wired*, is an activist with Change Agents Worldwide, and a fellow at the Darden School of Business. She is advisor to the Way to Wellville and MMinddLabs. She is also the author of *Learn More Now*; coauthor of *Creating a Learning Culture: Strategy, Technology, and Practice*; contributor to *Changing The World of Work: One Human at a Time*, and speaks across the globe on outcompeting current structures through system innovation and ingenuity.

Index

HOW TO PURCHASE ATD PRESS PUBLICATIONS

ATD Press publications are available worldwide in print and electronic format.

To place an order, please visit our online store: www.td.org/books.

Our publications are also available at select online and brick-and-mortar retailers.

Outside the United States, English-language ATD Press titles may be purchased through the following distributors:

United Kingdom, Continental Europe, the Middle East, North Africa, Central Asia, Australia, New Zealand, and Latin America
Eurospan Group
Phone: 44.1767.604.972
Fax: 44.1767.601.640
Email: eurospan@turpin-distribution.com
Website: www.eurospanbookstore.com

Asia
Cengage Learning Asia Pte. Ltd.
Phone: (65)6410-1200
Email: asia.info@cengage.com
Website: www.cengageasia.com

Nigeria
Paradise Bookshops
Phone: 08033075133
Email: paradisebookshops@gmail.com
Website: www.paradisebookshops.com

South Africa
Knowledge Resources
Phone: +27 (11) 706.6009
Fax: +27 (11) 706.1127
Email: sharon@knowres.co.za
Web: www.kr.co.za

For all other territories, customers may place their orders at the ATD online store: **www.td.org/books**.

0215145.62220